湖北省博物館
HUBEI PROVINCIAL MUSEUM

四萬萬人民

The 400 Million People

中国抗日战争暨世界反法西斯战争胜利七十周年特展

An Exhibition Dedicated to 70th Anniversary of Victory of War of Resistance against Japanese Aggression and World Anti-fascist War

湖北省博物馆　编
Edited by Hubei Provincial Museum

文物出版社
Cultural Relics Press

展览主办 Organizers	湖北省博物馆 Hubei Provincial Museum
	中华世纪坛世界艺术馆 Beijing World Art Museum, China Millennium Monument
	昆明市博物馆 Kunming Museum
	云南滇西抗战纪念馆 Dianxi Anti-Japanese War Memorial Hall, Yunnan
	台湾美术馆 Chang Foundation（Taiwan）
	香港翰墨轩（香江博物馆） Han Mo Xuan (Xiangjiang Museum, Hong Kong)
	北京华协国际文化有限公司 Beijing Huaxie Cultural Development CO.,LTD.
展出时间 Date	2015年5月30日至9月6日 May30 – September 6, 2015
展览委员会 Exhibition Committee	
展览总策划 Exhibition Planner	方勤（湖北省博物馆馆长） Fang Qin (Dierctor of Hubei Provincial Museum) 冯光生（中华世纪坛世界艺术中心副主任） Feng Guangsheng (Deputy Director of China Millennium Monument & the World Art Center) 田建（昆明市博物馆馆长） Tian Jian (Director of the Kunming Museum) 杨素红（滇西抗战纪念馆馆长） Yang Suhong (Director of Dianxi Anti-Japanese War Memorial Hall, Yunnan) 廖桂英（财团法人鸿禧文教艺术基金会董事长） Liao Guiying (Director of Chang Foundation) 许礼平（香港翰墨轩主人） Hui Laiping (The Host of Hong Kong Han Mo Xuan) 汤毅嵩（华协北京文化公司董事长） Tang Yisong (Chairman of Beijing Huaxie Cultural Development CO.,LTD.)
展览制作 Exhibition Production	万全文（湖北省博物馆常务副馆长） Wan Quanwen
策展和文本 Curator & Text	王纪潮 Wang Jichao

项目负责 Project Leader	黄建 Huang Jian
展览协调 Coordinators	湖北省博物馆：曾攀、余文扬、伍莹、姚嫄、张翔、程陶、黄翀宇、王圆圆、许倩、魏冕、胡微 Hubei Provincial Museum: Zeng Pan, Yu Wenyang, Wu Ying, Yao Yuan, Zhang Xiang, Cheng Tao, Huang Chongyu, Wang Yuanyuan, Xu Qian, Wei Mian and Hu Wei 中华世纪坛世界艺术馆 Beijing World Art Museum, China Millennium Monument 昆明市博物馆：李晓帆、高静铮、梁钰珠 Kunming Museum: Li Xiaofan, Gao Jingzheng and Liang Yu Chu 滇西抗战纪念馆：伯绍海、马娟、邵维波 Dianxi Anti-Japanese War Memorial Hall: Bo Shaohai, Ma Juan and Shao Weibo 北京华协文化发展有限公司：段志鹏、路平、杜希来 Beijing Huaxie Cultural Development CO.,LTD.: Duan Zhipeng, Lu Ping and Du Xilai 财团法人鸿禧文教艺术基金会：李立恒、王顺成、杨敦尧、周海圣、王水衷、吉民立、董良彦、潘安仪（康奈尔大学）、白若缤（康奈尔大学） Chang Foundation: Li Liheng, Wang Shuncheng, Yang Dunyao, Zhou Haisheng, Wang Shuizhong, Ji Minli, Dong Liangyan, Pan Anyi (Cornell University) and Bai Ruobin(Cornell University)
图录编辑 Catalogue Editor	湖北省博物馆 Hubei Provincial Museum
主编 Editors-in-chief	方勤 Fang Qin
副主编 Deputy Editor-in-chief	万全文 Wan Quanwen
编辑 Editor	王纪潮 Wang Jichao
英文翻译 English Translation	中国对外翻译出版公司 China Translation & Publishing Corporation

目　录
CONTENTS

总　序
PREFACE

近代中国贫弱，饱受外强欺凌。辛亥革命后建立的中华民国，加快了中国现代化的进程，而日本军国主义鲸吞中国之心也日渐显露。因《辛丑条约》和日俄战争，日本在中国的平、津和东北一带驻军，埋下了九一八和七七事变的导火索。第一次世界大战结束后，日本已将中国东北、内蒙、山东纳入势力范围，并企图强迫国民政府签署丧权辱国的"二十一条"。此事影响至远，中国遂陷入军阀割据，现代化进程完全中断。

1931年9月18日，日本关东军趁中国军阀内战发动九一八事变，占领东北，后又染指华北。1937年7月7日晚，日本中国驻屯军寻衅制造卢沟桥事变，北平、天津等地先后失守，抗日战争遂全面爆发。日军妄称三个月灭亡中国。在这最后关头，国共两党再度携手。7月17日，国民政府军事委员会委员长蒋介石发表庐山谈话，号召全中国四万万同胞，"地无分南北，年无分老幼，无论何人，皆有守土抗战之责任"，表明了中国政府和军民"牺牲到底，抗战到底"的决心。7月22日，中共也毅然发表《共赴国难宣言》，宣布把红军改编为国民革命军，"受国民政府军事委员会之统辖，并待命出动，担任抗日前线之职责。"

从1937年到1945年，中国军民团结一致，国共两党捐弃前嫌，共赴国难，在海外华侨、国际友人和英美苏同盟国的支持和援助下，四万万同胞开始了艰苦卓绝的八年抗战。国民革命军在正面战场先后进行了淞沪、南京、太原、徐州、兰封、武汉、随枣、第一、二、三次长沙、桂南、枣宜、豫南、上高、晋南、浙赣、鄂西、常德、豫中、长衡、桂柳、湘西等22场会战，重要战斗1117次，小型战役38931次，国军死伤365.465万人。在敌后战场，由中共领导的国民革命军第八路军、国民革命军陆军新编第四军成为敌后战场的中流砥柱，举行了百团大战等作战125165次，毙伤俘日军数以十万计。中国军民共毙伤俘日军155万余人，占日军二战伤亡总数的75%以上。

日本的侵略战争给中国造成了巨大损失，日军占领我城市930座，强掳劳工900余万人（含115万台湾人），掠走3350万吨钢铁、5.86亿吨煤炭，1亿立方米木材；日军还公然违背国际公约使用生化武器2000余战例，在南京悍然屠杀30万人。整个抗战期间，我军民约伤亡3587.9万人，财产损失6500亿美元以上。

中国抗战也是中华民族复兴的重要起点。中国共产党在抗战中起到了中流砥柱作用并逐渐壮大，成为中华民族复兴的旗帜；中国坚持抗战并成为世

中国抗日战争暨世界反法西斯战争胜利七十周年特展
An Exhibition Dedicated to 70th Anniversary of Victory of War of Resistance against
Japanese Aggression and World Anti-fascist War

界反法西斯同盟国后，帝国主义在近代强加于中国的各种不平等条约在1943年基本被废除；从1943年开罗会议后，中国正式位列世界大国之席，1945年联合国成立，中国因抗战的巨大牺牲和贡献而成为联合国常任理事国，并与联合国其他国家奠定和规划了战后的现代国际秩序。它标志着中华民族已摆脱受屈辱受压迫的历史地位而重新立于世界民族之林。

中国抗战是世界反法西斯战争的重要组成部分，也是中华民族历史上首次取得了反抗帝国主义侵略的彻底胜利的战争。其胜利原因约可归为五点：一、英勇不屈的四万万人民；二、国共合作、团结御侮，中国共产党领导的抗日民族统一战线；三、百战不挠、勇于牺牲的中国军队；四、得道多助的国际友人和海外华人的援助；五、中国抗战后期，世界反法西斯同盟国的有力支持。中国抗战尽管惨胜，中华民族不屈的伟大的精神、为捍卫世界和平的巨大牺牲却永远彪炳于世界史册。

抗战期间，湖北和云南分别是中国抗战的前沿和胜利反攻起点。武汉会战、随枣会战、枣宜会战、石牌保卫战、鄂西会战、苏联援华志愿航空队、美国飞虎队、跨越驼峰飞行、滇缅印战役等重大战役不仅在中国的抗战史，在世界反法西斯战争史上都堪称绝唱。湖北省博物馆、中华世纪坛世界艺术博物馆、昆明市博物馆、台湾鸿禧美术馆、香港翰墨轩等文博单位在抗战胜利七十周年之际，联合举办《四万万人民——中国抗日战争暨世界反法西斯战争胜利七十周年特展》。我们相信，本次展览将为警示后人、维护世界反法西斯战争胜利成果和世界永久和平作出贡献。

展览委员会
2015年7月

In modern times, China was a weak country which had suffered from foreign powers' bullying. The Republic of China founded after the Xinhai Revolution accelerated the process of modernization of China, and the Japanese militarists gradually showed their intention of annexing China. Because of the Boxer Protocol and the Russo-Japanese War, Japanese troops were stationed in Beijing, Tianjin and northeast China, making preparations for the September 18 Incident and Lugou Bridge Incident. After the World War I, Japan had brought northeast China, Inner Mongolia and Shandong into its sphere of influence, and forced the government of the Republic of China to sign the humiliating Twenty-one Demands, which had had profound influence. China was torn by warlordism, and the modernization process was totally interrupted.

On September 18, 1931, the Japanese Kwantung Army, taking advantage of the Chinese warlords' civil war, launched the September 18 Incident. They occupied northeast China and began to expand forces in north China. On the night of July 7, 1937, the imperial Japanese army in China provoked the Lugou Bridge Incident, and successively occupied Beiping and Tianjin, marking that Chinese People's War of Resistance against Japanese Aggression broke out. The Japanese side claimed that they would annex China in three months. At this critical moment, the Kuomintang and the Communist Party of China （CPC） joined hands for another time. On July 17, Chiang Kai-shek, the then Chairman of the National Military Council of the government of the Republic of China, issued the Lushan Statement, saying that "once war breaks out, every person, young or old, in the north or in the south, must take up the responsibility of resisting Japan and defending our homeland", which showed the Chinese government and people's resolution to "fight to the end". On July 22, the CPC issued the Declaration of the Communist Party of China on the Announcement of KMT-CPC Cooperation, and announced to recognize the Red Army into the National Revolutionary Army under the National Military Council, follow its orders

and shoulder the responsibility of fighting against the Japanese aggression at the battlefront.

From 1937 to 1945, Chinese army and people united, and both the Kuomintang and the CPC put their differences aside and joined hands to rescue the country. With the support and help from overseas Chinese, international friends and the Allied Powers （UK, US and Russia）, the 400 million Chinese people began the extremely arduous anti-Japanese war which lasted for eight years. The National Revolutionary Army had participated in 22 mass campaigns in the frontline battlefields in Songhu, Nanjing, Taiyuan, Xuzhou, Lanfeng, Wuhan, Suizao, southern Guilin, Changsha （the 1st, 2nd and 3rd battles）, southern Guilin, Zaoyang-Yichang, southern Henan, Shanggao, southern Shanxi, Zhejiang-Ganzhou, western Hubei, Changde, central Henan, Changsha-Hengyang, Guilin-Liuzhou and western Hunan, involved in 1,117 major battles, and 38,931 small-scaled fights, with 3.65465 million casualties. In battlefields behind enemy lines, the Eighth Route Army and New Fourth Army of the National Revolutionary Army, both were under the leadership of the CPC, became the mainstay. They participated in 125,165 battles including the Hundred Regiments Offensive, killed, wounded and captured hundreds of thousands of Japanese soldiers. In total, Chinese army and people killed, wounded and captured more than 1.55 million Japanese troops, taking up over 15% of the Japanese casualties during the World War II.

The Japanese aggression caused tremendous loss to China. The Japanese troops occupied 930 Chinese cities, captured over 9 million labors （including 1.15 million from Taiwan）, plundered 33.50 million tons of iron, 586 million tons of coal and 100 million cubic meters of wood. Moreover, they flagrantly violated the international conventions by using biochemical weapons in more than 2,000 battles, and massacred 300,000 people in Nanjing. During the whole anti-Japanese war, Chinese army and people suffered about 35.879 million casualties and a property loss of more than USD 650

中国抗日战争暨世界反法西斯战争胜利七十周年特展
An Exhibition Dedicated to 70th Anniversary of Victory of War of Resistance against
Japanese Aggression and World Anti-fascist War

billion.

The Chinese People's War of Resistance against Japanese Aggression was also an important turning point for the rejuvenation of the Chinese nation. During the war, the CPC played a mainstay role and gradually expanded its forces, becoming a banner leading the rejuvenation of the Chinese nation. Because of China's persistence and after its joining into the anti-fascist Allied Powers in the war, the unequal treaties that the imperialist powers forced China to sign in modern times had been basically abolished by 1943. After the Cairo Conference in 1943, China officially ranked among major powers of the world. In 1945 when the United Nations was founded, China became a permanent member state of the UN Security Council for its enormous sacrifice and contributions, and helped to lay the cornerstone of and to construct the post-war international order with other members of the United Nations. This indicates that the Chinese nation had seen a shift of historical status from being humiliated and repressed to standing among powerful countries in the world.

The Chinese People's War of Resistance against Japanese Aggression was a major part of the World Anti-fascist War, and also the first time that the Chinese people won a complete victory against imperialist aggression in history. This could be attributed to five reasons: 1. unyielding 400 million people; 2. cooperation between Kuomintang and the CPC and the Anti-Japanese National United Front under the leadership of the CPC; 3. unswerving and self-sacrificing Chinese army; 4. assistance from international friends and overseas Chinese; 5. generous support from the anti-fascist Allied Powers. Though China won a Pyrrhic victory against the Japanese aggression, the Chinese people's indomitable spirit and enormous contributions to safeguarding the world peace will always be remembered in history.

During the anti-Japanese war, Hubei and Yunnan were respectively the forefront and starting point for counter-offensives in China. Such major campaigns conducted in Wuhan, Suizao, Zaoyang-Yichang, Shipai, western Hubei, and Yunnan-Burma-India battlefields, those launched by Soviet Air Force Volunteer Group and the American Flying Tigers, as well as task of flying over the Hump, were unprecedented in both Chinese history of anti-Japanese war and even the world history of anti-fascist war. On the occasion of the 70th anniversary of the Chinese People's War of Resistance against Japanese Aggression, several museums and cultural heritage institutions including Hubei Provincial Museum, the China Millennium Monument World Art Museum, Kunming Museum, Chang Foundation Museum of Taiwan, and Hong Kong Han Mo Xuan jointly held "The 400 Million People: An Exhibition Dedicated to 70th Anniversary of Victory of War of Resistance against Japanese Aggression and World Anti-fascist War". We will present a truthful picture of Chinese anti-Japanese war and demonstrate its significance to the public from all-around, fair and objective perspectives, so that we can make contributions to warning later generations and safeguarding the victory of the World Anti-fascist War and the permanent peace of the world.

Exhibition Committee
July 2015

四万万人同誓死

王纪潮

"民国三十四年八月十日为苏夫人生辰，时余居战时首都重庆之国府路。余夫妇及一女两儿在家。晚间邀约友人赵文喆女士同来便饭。八时晚饭方毕，忽闻国府路人声鼎沸，方拟探寻何事，则有奔而入者谓：'日本已表示投降，事已证实。'余等欣喜之下即入厨觅得酒一瓶，六人欢饮立尽。越四日，日本正式宣布无条件投降。是日，重庆各报皆出号外。事隔十余年，赵女士忽在其行箧中觅得当日重庆号外四纸见遗，因即装裱以留纪念并志当年欢祝双庆之盛云。"

今年5月，我们意外得到著名学者、第一届中央研究院院士、铁道专家凌鸿勋先生（1894-1981）生前所收藏的一批抗日战争胜利后的重庆各大报纸的号外。在其中一件号外上发现了他的题跋，记述了1945年8月10日重庆民众获知日寇投降时的情景。

抗日战争是近代以来中华民族反抗帝国主义侵略首次赢得完全胜利的战争。八年抗战中国军民伤亡3500万以上，按照1937年比价，中国官方财产损失和战争消耗达1000多亿美元，间接经济损失达5000亿美元。这场以中华民族巨大牺牲为代价赢得的胜利，在教科书、学术论著、民间传播乃至影视作品中都有大量的描述或艺术表现，民众并不陌生。我们在策划组织这次展览时意外收集到几件不同寻常的文物，它们从不同侧面真实地反映出了四万万人民的力量。

文化人的抗战

1937年7月7日卢沟桥事变爆发后，国民党接受中共第二次国共合作主张，蒋介石7月17日在庐山发表"最后关头"重要谈话，号召"地无分南北，人无分老幼，无论何人，皆有守土抗战之

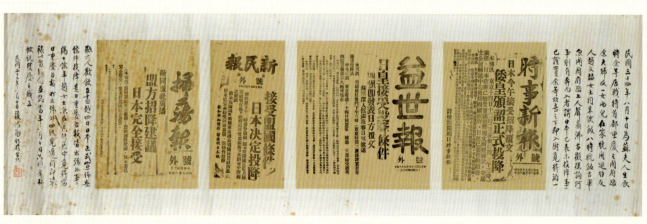

日本投降重庆报纸号外

中国抗日战争暨世界反法西斯战争胜利七十周年特展
An Exhibition Dedicated to 70th Anniversary of Victory of War of Resistance against
Japanese Aggression and World Anti-fascist War

中华全国文艺界抗敌协会原照

责。"中国开始全民抗战。

沪宁沦陷后，武汉一时成为全国抗战的文化中心，各地文人不分党派、政见都汇聚于此，为建立中国文化界的统一战线，动员全民抗战，中国共产党倡导成立了"中华全国文艺界抗敌协会"。

"文协"成立之初会员97人，除周恩来、陈立夫、邵力子、冯玉祥、陈铭枢等军政要员外，中国各党派和无党派文化名人差不多都在其中，如左联作家阳翰笙、夏衍、张天翼、姚蓬子，"南国社"的田汉，"七月社"的胡风，右翼"中国文艺社"的张道藩、王平陵，被左派批评为"第三种人"的施蛰存，和鲁迅打过笔仗的陈西滢、梁实秋、胡秋原等。

"文协"是中国抗战最广泛、最有效的统一战线机构之一，从1938年3月27日成立到1945年8月15日更名为"中华全国文艺协会"，会员发展到300余人。

长期以来，有关"文协"成立时的照片只有局部与会人员的照片，像会议组织者之一的老舍就不在其中，老舍之子舒乙都感到纳闷。2006年，舒乙终于从藏家手中发现了全体合影原照，其狂喜之情见于他为《新文学史料》所撰的《沉寂六十七年半的珍贵老照片》一文。舒乙从那张原照片中认

出了邵力子、冯玉祥、陈铭枢、周恩来、张道藩、老舍、胡风、田汉、马彦祥、盛成、姚蓬子、鹿地亘、爱泼斯坦等13人。

筹办本次展览时，我们在香港著名文化人许礼平先生处又见到一幅"文协"成立大会的合影照原件。在胡风之女张晓风的帮助下我们辨认出更多的人，包括周恩来左前的荒芜，合众社记者爱泼斯坦之后的塔斯社记者罗果夫和爱泼斯坦右边戴眼镜的茅盾。

七七事变后的中国文化界不分左右，同仇敌忾共赴国难。老舍曾撰文说，"文人在平日似乎有点吊儿郎当，赶到遇到要事正事，他们会干得很起劲，很紧张。"筹备文协的有胡风、老舍、阳翰笙、冯乃超、王平陵等人。会后选周恩来、孙科、陈立夫等为名誉理事，选出理事郭沫若、茅盾、胡风、老舍、张道藩、姚蓬子、陈西滢、王平陵等45人，左中右人士均在其列。这张合影就是非常生动的证明。

艰难的抗战

在滇西抗战纪念馆，我们注意到有许多士兵的培训教材。这是以前所没有见到的。比如国民革命军第三军军官学校的教材，包括《劈刺术教范》《陆军礼节》《步兵工作教范》《陆军惩罚令》

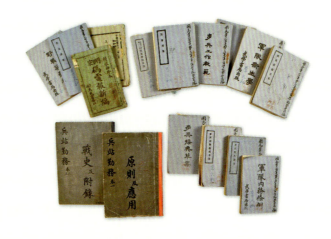

士兵教材

《军队卫生学》《体操教范草案》《简易测绘》《中国革命史》《步兵射击教范草案》《军队内务条例》等等。这些简单的教材反映了一个令人痛苦的事实：我们的士兵不仅武器不如敌人，教育更不如人。台湾学者根据国民政府军训部1944年的材料做过研究，抗战初期技术兵种炮兵中下级军官的教育程度最高，"已受养成教育者"也没有超过50%，而士兵80%是农民，90%近于文盲，受过初中教育的只有5%，受过高中教育的是0%！在太平洋战争爆发后，经过相关的培训，士兵的素质才得到了较大的提升。

美军参谋长马歇尔说过，中国军人吃苦耐劳守纪律，如果能吃饱、训练、装备和适当的领导，不输于任何国家的普通士兵。抗战中的中国军人大多数不过就是四万万人民中的普通农民，他们在武器落后、匮乏无援的条件下，以坚韧、吃苦、服从、英勇和牺牲的精神，筑起了捍卫民族生存的血肉长城，赢得了世界的尊敬。

中国抗战是世界反法西斯战场上时间最漫长、牺牲最巨大，最为艰苦卓绝之战，其原因之一在于这是一场不对称的战争。仅以钢铁论，1937年中国的钢铁产量为约18万吨，日本为约750万吨。在兵力上，一个中央军的满员师1万人，步枪2000支，子弹每人才20发，轻重机枪60挺，山炮5门，汽车20辆。而一个日军甲种师团约2.2万人，步枪9000支，轻重机枪600挺，汽车1000辆，山炮200门，装甲车20辆，子弹每人月耗300发。以军需论，日本战争期间生产了5.5万架飞机、4800辆坦克和244艘舰船。而我们差不多是靠血肉长城苦撑了14年。

盟国的抗战

在此次展览中，还有一架当年美军飞虎队P51野马战机的残骸。

事情的经过是这样的：1944年5月6日，美军飞虎队P51野马战机的飞行员格林·本尼达，驾驶飞机攻击日军在武汉的目标返航时，被监利白螺机场起飞的日机

等待起飞

击落于监利的周老嘴村。本尼达跳伞后被村民围住，略懂英语的罗毓垓连比带划才弄清了他是美军飞行员，但本尼达一直害怕村民，直到新四军抗日游击队派懂英语的方云霞告诉本尼达这是新四军第五师李先念的部队时，他才安心。本尼达后来被送到江陵赵家垴的新四军第五师第三军分区襄南指挥部，在李先念的安排下，他返回了重庆。2005年，中国对外友协帮助本尼达重返监利，并见证了当年被击落飞机的打捞。

得道多助。苏联援华航空志愿队、陈纳德飞虎队在中国的抗日战争中曾与中国人民并肩作战，留下了许多传奇故事。

中国抗日战争暨世界反法西斯战争的胜利为建立今天的国际秩序打下基础，其中奠定中国大国地位的《开罗宣言》是第一份要求日本无条件投降，必须归还所侵略的包括台湾、澎湖列岛在内之中国领土的国际文件。正由于关系重大，日本少数人否认《开罗宣言》的存在。但现藏于台北故宫博物院的《开罗宣言》英文原稿曾在2013年公开展出，上面有罗斯福、丘吉尔的修改痕迹，文件的真实性毋庸置疑。令人惊喜的是，香港著名文化人许礼平先生为本次展览提供了另一份《开罗宣言》钞

中国抗日战争暨世界反法西斯战争胜利七十周年特展
An Exhibition Dedicated to 70th Anniversary of Victory of War of Resistance against
Japanese Aggression and World Anti-fascist War

本。蒋氏夫妇参加开罗会议带有20余人，负责新闻工作的是郭斌佳、董显光，负责行政工作的是王宠惠。钞本或出自王宠惠的班子。王宠惠为著名法学家，曾任国民政府外长，在开罗会议上他为日本"放弃"还是"归还"主权的字眼与丘吉尔大吵，彰显了民族气节。钞本有立法院图书馆章，表明该钞本曾作为官方文件收藏于立法院图书馆备案，应该是1949年后流失海外的。

幸运的是，今天我们不但能够在海内外的众多档案馆、博物馆中看到那场战争的文物，而且能够从摄影前辈、众多烈士的家属、众多参与者的遗物中拾取过去难得一见的大量资料，它们虽然只是历史的碎片，但连缀在一起却能勾画出抗战的方方面面。它们的存在就是一种昭示，提醒着我们永远铭记曾经的苦难，珍惜来之不易的和平。

补记

70年前，积弱之中国赢得了抗日战争的胜利。这场以中华民族巨大牺牲赢得的惨胜在教科书、在学术论著、在民间口碑乃至影视作品中都有大量描写，民众并不陌生。但是全面客观展现这段历史的展览却少见，这一方面是由于海峡两岸分治的历史，我们很难获得对方保存的抗战材料，另一方面是长期极左思潮占主导的现实，即使有材料，展览主办方也不愿意找麻烦。直到2005年，国共两党恢复联系之后，人们对抗战历史的认识逐渐开始较为客观理性。随着抗战暨世界反法西斯战争胜利70周年的临近，对博物馆而言，举办一个真实客观反映抗战历史的展览就是"铭记历史、缅怀先烈，珍爱和平、开创未来"的体现。为此，举办方特别邀请台湾鸿禧美术馆、香港翰墨轩等单位参加展览并提供展品。由于有两岸三地的文物机构合作，《四万万人民——中国抗日战争暨世界反法西斯战争胜利七十周年特展》无论是策展理念和表现手法、还是展览形式和展览内容，在大陆博物馆所举办的抗战展中都有新意，广受好评。展览于5月底开幕后，《人民日报》约我们就展览撰写专文，遂有上文。原稿字数较多，经压缩调整后更为精炼，以"四万万人民同誓死"为题刊发在2015年07月16日的《人民日报》，并加编者按如下：

"湖北是中国抗日战争的重要战场之一。武汉、随枣、枣宜等正面战场的重大会战发生在这里，二战中牺牲的盟军最高级将领张自忠上将在湖北宜城殉国；中共领导的国民革命军新编第四军五师的敌后抗战在这里；苏联援华志愿航空队、美国飞虎队也在这里与日军作战……湖北省博物馆收藏有大量的抗战文物，近日他们与重庆中国三峡博物馆、滇西抗战纪念馆、台湾鸿禧美术馆等众多文博单位合作，举办了《四万万人民》这样一个恢宏的展览，用文物讲述了一个民族同仇敌忾的故事。展览的策展人从数千件展品中挑选了几件有意义的文物为读者进行解读。——编者"

本来我为展览图录写了题为"真实的力量——介绍抗战展《四万万人民》中的若干文物"的文章，《人民日报》选用了部分，而且把题目改得富有激情，挺好的，于是就原样照录了。

《开罗宣言》钞本

The Four Hundred Million People Ready to Lay Down for the Country (Abstract)

Wang Jichao

Resistance of Intellectuals

After the fall of Shanghai and Nanjing, Wuhan became the cultural center of national resistance. Artists and writers were gathered here, regardless of their party affiliation and political opinion. And the Communist Party of China established the All-China Association of Artists and Writers against Japanese Aggression.

For a long time, we have only found photos of the inaugural ceremony showing some of the attendees of the association. Yet in 2006, Shu Yi discovered an original group photo of all the attendees, and we found another group photo of all attendees in the collection of Xu Liping, a well-known intellectual in Hong Kong.

Chinese intellectuals fought side by side against foreign invasion, regardless of their political preferences, in the wake of the July 7 Incident. Hu Feng, Lao She, Yang Hansheng, Feng Naichao and Wang Pingling prepared the establishment of the association. Zhou Enlai, Sun Ke and Chen Lifu were elected as honorary council members, while Guo Moruo, Mao Dun, Hu Feng, Lao She, Zhang Daofan, Yao Pengzi, Chen Xiying, and Wang Pingling as council members. Intellectuals of all political leanings were included, as seen in the group photo.

Tough Resistance

When visiting the Dianxi Anti-Japanese Memorial Hall, we found some literacy-teaching books for the soldiers. They are a reminder of a painful fact: China lagged considerably behind Japan in weapons, and, education. Research reveals that at the early days of national resistance, middle-and-low ranks of military officials in the artillery were most educated, yet still 50 percent of them were illiterate, compared to 90 percent of soldiers. After the outbreak of the Pacific War, the capacity of Chinese soldiers was significantly increased due to adequate training courses.

George Catlett Marshall, Chief of Staff of the United States Army during World War II, said that Chinese soldiers were hard-working and disciplined, and that they would be no weaker than soldiers of other countries if they had enough food, training and equipment under proper leadership. A majority of Chinese soldiers during the war were farmers chosen from the 400 million Chinese people. Although they lacked advanced weapons and enough international support, they were resilient, devoted, brave and ready to lay down for the country in the war for national salvation, which won the respect of the entire world.

Resistance of the Allies

The Chinese victory and the global victory over fascism paved the way for the establishment of the international order as it is. In particular, the Cairo Declaration, which proclaimed China's status as a great power, is the first international document demanding Japan to surrender unconditionally, and stipulates that all the territories Japan had stolen from the Chinese, such as Taiwan and the Pescadores, shall be restored to China. And for the exhibition, the renowned Hong Kong-based intellectual Xu Liping provides a handwritten copy of the Declaration.

Fortunately, today we can see artifacts and other objects of the war in archives and museums both at home and abroad, and discover rare documents among the legacy of senior photographers, family members of martyrs and those witnesses of history. These materials are just pieces of history, and remind us of the sufferings of the war and the hard-won peace.

Supplement

We invited Taiwan Chang Foundation Museum, Hong Kong Han Mo Xuan and other organizations to participate in the exhibition with their own items to celebrate the 70th anniversary of the victory of the war. The exhibition was widely acclaimed, and People's Daily hoped that we could write an article about it. And on July 16, 2015, *The 400 Million People Ready to Lay down for the Country* was published, and the title is used in the catalogue.

中国抗日战争暨世界反法西斯战争胜利七十周年特展
An Exhibition Dedicated to 70th Anniversary of Victory of War of Resistance against
Japanese Aggression and World Anti-fascist War

幸存的"抗战墙报"及与事者

许礼平

这张"墙报",题为"大家看报"。这是民国廿七年（1938）十月五日的第二十七期,由"第八集团军——战地服务队"所编制的。先要说明这"第八集团军——战地服务队"是何种团体。

"第八集团军"全称"国民革命军第八集团军",建于1937年8月中,首任总司令为张发奎。1938年初该集团军转为军事委员会直辖兵团,而该集团军的"战地服务队",则是国共合作产物。那是张发奎驻浦东时,请郭沫若帮忙筹建的政工队伍。郭受张委托,并得周恩来指示,遂会同上海中共党组刘晓、潘汉年、钱亦石、夏衍等,动员组织一批文化界人士和热血青年,到第八集团军总司令部建立"战地服务队",首任队长是周恩来推荐的钱亦石。时维1937年9月25日。"战地服务队"的宗旨是"动员战区民众,实行军民联合抗战",而任务在于"宣传调查,沟通军民意志"（见杜国庠《忆钱队长亦石》）。

这钱亦石是早年共产党员（湖北咸宁人,1924年4月由董必武、陈潭秋介绍入党）,其所率之文化人包括了杜国庠、何家槐、林默涵、左洪涛、柳倩、刘田夫、孙慎、唐瑜、沈振黄、杨应彬、郑黎亚、沈丹风、郭弼昌、杨冶明等等。整队人大都是共产党,更有不少是刚从国民党监狱中释放的。1937年10月12日,据周恩来指示,中共在"战地服务队"建立特别支部,特支书记是左洪涛,直属长江局领导。在"同仇御侮"的大时代中,这是国民党部队中唯一由共产党领导的宣传队。这"战地服务队"随第八集团军沿浙、赣、粤、桂进发,从事抗日宣传。

更须一提,张发奎并不是黄埔出身,不是老蒋嫡系。他明知"战地服务队"的班底是共产党。他在回忆录中说,钱亦石曾"坦诚告诉我,他是共产党员"。而且钱亦石向张声明:"在战地服务队我将主要聘用共产党员"。钱还问张"是否害怕使用中共党员"。张"清楚地告诉他,我不怕。"更说:"我不在乎,我们现在共赴国难。"

而现存的这张"墙报"就是由"战地服务队"三位队员在湖北阳新编制。其内容由郭弼昌与杨治明合力手写,插画则为队中美术股的沈振黄所作。也就是说:在这文盲居多的穷乡僻壤,以粗劣的白报纸,没有机器印刷,只是手写笔划,居然做出一份"墙报",而与事者只三人,都是共产党人。

我珍视这一文物。

首先,在意义上它是国共之间同仇御侮的时代见证。我常闲中静对,想象那战火纷披杀伐有声的年代。我爱那"墙报"之纸败色颓,是那物质匮乏艰难时代的见证。更何况,"墙报"背后牵系的人和事,都足以令人为之感喟、唏嘘!

"墙报"不是寻常物,因为能在数十年的战火纷飞中幸存下来,是件大大难事。试问,普天之下，有多少能经过战火洗礼而岿然幸存的"政治墙报"？更何况是"文化名人"所手写的！别看那纸败色颓，这当中会感受到一股"时穷节乃见"的凛然之气。

说一个例，往日在上海有个钱化佛，他也是无独有偶的"墙报"藏家，郑逸梅在《艺林散叶》第1109则曾说到他：

"抗战时，上海沦为孤岛，凡敌伪所出告示，钱化佛都一一揭取，揭取必于昏夜，防人发觉也。先以水湿润，然后以轻捷之手法为之，尤以雨夜为宜。直至抗战胜利，先后具有系统，共一百数十幅，悉归公家保存。当时其冒险行径，并家人不之知，盖知则必加阻拦，不能达其目的矣。"

引上述，是在于说明揭存"墙报"之难。但我这"墙报"却是很"阳光"和"正面"的，和钱氏无二致。

该墙报的主编杨冶明先生就这样回忆：

"新墙报张贴时，我们便把旧墙报揭下，珍惜得很。本文刊出的一张，就是难得的战地珍品！"

上引杨先生既说了"珍惜得很"，又说"难得的战地珍品"，事隔四十多年后又将珍藏的墙报图像刊诸书上，由此可见其对"墙报"之欷歔深情。可惜，笔者和杨冶明先生虽然稔熟，也曾在他指导下共过事，但却从未直接问过杨先生，他对"珍品"的"珍惜"，是到了何种的程度？

直到十多年前，杨冶明先生在九龙商务印书馆作个人书画展，当时全场瞩目的是这杨公编制的"墙报"，但这展品是非卖品，观众都欲购无途。只有我仗着是杨公的"旧部"，大胆相求，而且是作几度相求，才承蒙杨公割爱。佛家言有"爱别离苦"，我从杨先生的表情上看到了！

从此，这"墙报"进驻寒斋。闲中开箧，检读神往。是神往于那段"国共相携，共御外敌"的庄严历史，那"墙报"是能令后生为之鼓舞的

岁月见证。至于纸败色颓，那更是抗战时匮乏艰难的见证。

前面说过，"新墙报张贴时，我们便把旧墙报揭下"，但这"揭下"之后，却并不是由杨先生作第一手搜藏，杨在其所著《杂志·画报编辑与设计》（南粤出版社1986年版）上回忆说："本书珍贵史料'大家看报'承北京沈丹风、郭以实见寄，重见四十多年前的战地墙报，得见郭弼昌的字迹、沈振黄兄的战地漫画，他们都已牺牲在战争年代，空留遗作感后人了！"

提及的郭弼昌，其人的生平资料极少，在《特支十年》末章有"中共特支成员简况表"当中有谓："郭弼昌：男，1938年6月参加战地服务队，后任张发奎长官部的连指导员、附员，1940年夏撤出。1939年在战地服务队入党，1945年病故。"而关于沈丹风此人且容后再说。

但杨冶明那番说话，可以作说明的是"墙报"的第一手搜藏，该是在沈丹风的手上。至于沈丹风的转赠杨冶明，那是后话。

"墙报"在沈丹风手上再转赠给杨冶明，这在1986年杨著的《杂志·画报编辑与设计》中首作披露，开始让人知道有"大家看报"墙报的存在。以后，杨先生再作展览，令"墙报"为全场之瞩目点，而墙报当中插画"抗日军人休息站"又是瞩目点中之最。后来，嘉兴党史办公室编《沈振黄》一书，复将该《抗日军人休息站》图放大转载。到近年，寒斋又将原件远借武汉参展，这后续的一切，都是滥觞于此。

且回说到插图者沈振黄烈士。

在"大家看报"墙报上的插图名"抗日军人休息站"。画的是两位受伤军人受老百姓的热爱，其作者是沈振黄，题中所称"抗日军人"，是有意笼统地、涵盖地指称国共双方的抗日军人。该作者沈振黄在其流星一耀的人生中留下的遗墨就只有这

中国抗日战争暨世界反法西斯战争胜利七十周年特展
An Exhibition Dedicated to 70th Anniversary of Victory of War of Resistance against
Japanese Aggression and World Anti-fascist War

"抗日军人休息站"的漫画。此所以在20世纪80年代末中共嘉兴市委党史办公室编集《沈振黄》一书时，曾作慨叹："遗憾的是，由于三、四十年代的历史环境所致，沈振黄大批宣传抗日的漫画及一些著作等没有能很好保存下来，无法征集编辑进这一本小册子。"

从画风而言，沈振黄很受丰子恺的影响，沈振黄死后，在重庆的追悼会上丰子恺是副主祭，似乎两人的关系不止于是私淑，可能亦师亦友吧？惜这推想暂无证明。

以下概其生平大略：

沈振黄（1912-1944），原名沈耀中，乳名粹官（他的画作有署一"粹"字），浙江嘉兴人。

其父沈辛嘉，曾赴日本习军事，入同盟会，后参加辛亥革命。抗战间拒当汉奸被打至残。生三女三男，沈振黄为长子。二子沈耀华，1938年赴延安抗日军政大学学习，后为新四军四师彭雪枫之司令部作战参谋，1944年牺牲，时二十七岁。（据2005年9月14日沈丹风致杨治明函）

沈振黄原在上海中法工学院专攻机械专业，九一八事变后即离校参加抗日救国宣传工作。曾为开明书店《中学生》杂志画封面得奖，因探索木刻版画之道而与鲁迅通信结缘。（见《鲁迅书信》1934年10月24日）鲁迅逝世时，沈振黄赶去上海万国殡仪馆哀悼，并拍摄鲁迅遗容和出殡照片，刊诸上海报刊。

1937年12月，经夏衍介绍，参加了第八集团军战地服务队，任美术股股长。次年开赴武汉，继往广东惠阳，1940年抵广西柳州。所到之处沈振黄爬梯在墙壁上画抗日漫画。1939年秋，在广东曲江入党，属南方局领导的特支成员。1944年6月，田汉、邵荃麟在桂林成立文抗队，沈振黄亦是其中一员。

1944年11月，负责护送文化界人士疏散转移。11月25日，日军逼近柳州，沈振黄和两位战友护送妻儿等人员最后撤离。当时车已满员，半路有老妇要求上车，沈让出座位，自己爬上车顶。但当汽车急驰拐弯时，沈从车顶摔下殒命。时年三十有二。其遗体由演剧队田汉等好友运到独山薄葬在公路边。夫人朱曼琪哀恸而致早产。

1945年4月1日九时，重庆文化界人士在夫子池忠义堂举办追悼会，柳亚子、沈钧儒、茅盾、郭沫若、夏衍、金仲华、范寿康、丰子恺等二百余人参加。沈钧儒主祭，复题挽联："小己生命轻一掷，服务精神足千秋。"郭沫若在开追悼会前题挽联："民主前途欲明还暗，我兄高义虽死犹生。"其后《新华日报》刊登宋云彬、夏衍、王亚平、徐迟、马蹄疾、孙源等人的悼念文章。

1950年，中共中央华东局追认沈振黄为革命烈士。

好友对他的记忆都是正面的。只是时人描述英雄，总是有太多相同的词语和一样的脸谱，我可喜欢一些人性化的评说。以下选两则评语。

夏衍在《悼振黄》说：

"他的死，在旁人看来是壮烈，是太可惨。可是在他，也许并不觉得这样吧。因为，从他参加社会活动以来，在人生的旅途中，他也是一直地'把自己的座位让给别人'，而甘心情愿地自己爬在既不舒服而又危险的车顶上的。"夏衍又说："在许许多多激昂慷慨的人群中，他没有给我不平常的印象。抗战开始，他要我把他介绍给钱亦石先生领导的战地服务队，他的态度是平静到一点点'慷慨从军'的痕迹都没有的。"

徐迟的回忆是：

"我记得他满面阴云，说话声音也低沉：'我还是回香港去，他们在香港过得好舒服，我不说物质生活，我说精神生活上，让我回香港去吧？'这时我听到他妹妹数了他一顿，'你这是逃兵的行为！'""他的妹妹却猛烈地打击他，辛辣地奚落他，无情地批判他，'你不要我们X战区政工队了吗？还有你看，他，你好意思离开他，一个人逃向香港去。'这样相持了很久，我们上路了，他跟着，忽然他的动摇了的心情又坚定了。"（徐迟《为纪念沈振黄而写》1944年12月）

徐迟回忆中的"他的妹妹"，就该是上文所说的沈丹风，亦即是以"墙报"寄赠杨冶明的人。她当时也参加了战地服务队（后来改称"第四战区政工队"），她活到八十八岁，本文的一些资料就是得自她和杨冶明的通信。

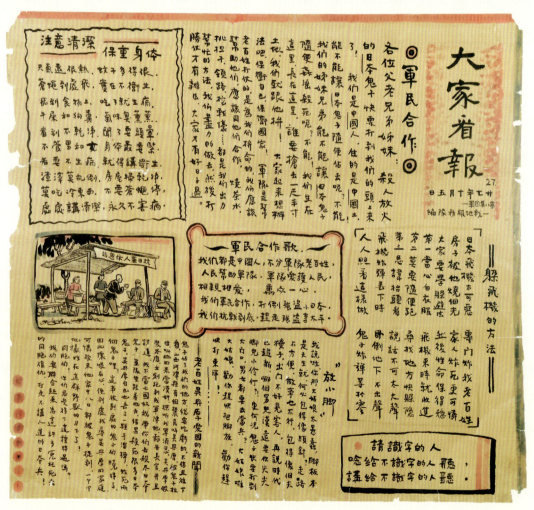

抗战墙报《大家看报》

中国抗日战争暨世界反法西斯战争胜利七十周年特展
An Exhibition Dedicated to 70th Anniversary of Victory of War of Resistance against
Japanese Aggression and World Anti-fascist War

The Wall Newspaper and Its Creators (Abstract)

Hui Laiping

The wall newspaper, titled Let Us Read, is the 27th issue written on October 5, 1938, by the Battlefield Service of the Eighth Army Group.

The Battlefield Service was an outcome of cooperation between the Communist Party of China (CPC) and the Kuomintang. It was a team of political work initiated by the Kuomintang military official Zhang Fakui in Pudong, who asked the writer Guo Moruo to prepare the establishment. Instructed by Zhou Enlai, Guo worked together with CPC members in Shanghai, including Liu Xiao, Pan Hannian, Qian Yishi and Xia Yan, and a wide array of intellectuals and young activists. At the Eighth Army Group headquarters they set up the Battlefield Service with Qian Yishi as the leader, and this was the only CPC-led publicity team in the Kuomintang army.

Qian Yishi, born in Xianning, Hubei, joined the CPC in April 1924, with recommendation of Dong Biwu and Chen Tanqiu. In the Battlefield Service, he worked together with many intellectuals, most of who were CPC members, such as Du Guoxiang, He Jiahuai, Lin Mohan, Zuo Hongtao, Liu Qian, Liu Tianfu, Sun Shen, Tang Yu, Shen Zhenhuang, Yang Yingbin, Zheng Liya, Shen Danfeng, Guo Bichang, and Yang Yeming. They travelled with the Eighth Army Group in Zhejiang, Jiangxi, Guangdong and Guangxi, spreading anti-Japanese ideas along the way.

This wall newspaper was created by three members of the Battlefield Service in Yangxin, Hubei. The content was written by Guo Bichang and Yang Zhiming, and the illustrations were created by Shen Zhenhuang from the fine art group of the team. They were all CPC members.

Shen Zhenhuang (1912-1944), formerly known as Shen Yaozhong, was born in Jiaxing, Zhejiang. He became a friend of the writer Lu Xun as they worked on woodcut prints together (see Lu Xun's Letters, October 24, 1934). When Lu Yun passed away, he mourned over the death in the Shanghai International Mortuary and took photos of Lu Xun and the funeral, which were published in major newspapers in Shanghai.

In December 1937, Shen acted as the director of fine art group in the Battlefield Service, with the recommendation of Xia Yan. In the autumn of 1939, he joined the CPC in Qujiang, Guangdong, and was a significant member under the CPC Southern Bureau. Shen was a member of the Team of Writers and Artists against Japan, which was founded by Tian Han and Shao Quanlin in Guilin in June 1944.

As Japanese army approached Liuzhou in November 1944, Shen and his two colleagues were evacuated with their family members, but he fell off the hood of a car and died, at the age of 32. At 9:00 on April 1, 1945, intellectuals organized a memorial service at Zhongyi Hall in Fuzichi of Chongqing. About 200 writers and artists attended the funeral, including Liu Yazi, Shen Junru, Mao Dun, Guo Moruo, Xia Yan, Jin Zhonghua, Fan Shoukang, and Feng Zikai. The host Shen Junru commented in his elegy that "though Shen Zhenhuang passed away, his spirit of commitment continues", and Guo Moruo commented that "although the prospect of democracy is bright at one time and dark at another, my brother (Shen Zhenhuang) has noble morality and his spirit lives on". The Xinhua Daily also published articles by Song Yunbin, Xia Yan, Wang Yaping, Xu Chi, Ma Tiji and Sun Yuan, mourning for Shen Zhenhuang.

In 1950, the CPC Eastern Bureau awarded a posthumous title of revolutionary martyr to Shen Zhenhuang.

《乐群社题辞册》补跋

许礼平

值抗战胜利七十周年，由湖北省博物馆联合云南滇西抗战纪念馆领衔举办抗战文物展览会，筹办期间，当事不耻下问，向小轩征借有关文物。以事关大义而义不容辞，乃恭检数十所藏，用以应命。而诸品当中，有八开墨迹纪念册，题辞者大都为抗战时期中流砥柱。而所关系之时、地、人，又皆有足纪述者。惜展览限于篇幅，未能详载。今翻阅展览图档，忽兴补跋之念，谨掇短文，用申微慕兼飨读者。

题册者计有：周恩来、蔡廷锴、陈铭枢、黄琪翔、萨空了、李济深、张文元、黎寄吾。而受题者为文尧先生。

册首即为周恩来行书题辞："模范的广西，现在已成西南抗战的重心，今后必为西南抗战的模范根据地无疑。文尧先生，周恩来。廿七，十二，九，于桂林乐群社。"

周题辞只一句，计卅二字，即使连题款也只是五十字。当中分逗作三个分句，亦说出了三层意思——就是说桂林的过去、现在和将来。

首句的"模范的广西"，句意指广西过去十年的锐意建设。其时广西正有"模范省"的称誉。该"模范"词始见于1936年美国《纽约时报》远东特约记者考察报导，是作为广西的尊称。其时广西是政简刑清，苞苴不行，广受称赞。

胡适在《广西的印象》文中也说："广西给我的第二个印象是俭朴的风气。一进了广西境内，到处都是所谓'灰布化'。"又云："上至省主席总司令，下至中学生和普通士兵，一律都穿灰布制服"、"提倡俭朴，提倡土货，都是积极救国的大事。"

按，胡适说的"灰布化"的土布，是指当时广西大小官员以至庶民，都自奉俭素，是当时广西的风气时尚，也即是和谐建设的精神所在。所以，周恩来题辞首冠"模范"二字，是对广西建设的肯定。其实，周是从延安过来的人，类此艰苦奋斗的现象，该是知之稔矣的。然周仍袭用国统区流行称呼来作推崇。这正是周恩来儒雅、亲和、虚心、谦恭的本性所在，在周恩来身上就是找不出列宁、鲁迅那种峥嵘和挖苦的词锋。

接着，周氏题辞的第二分句是："现在已成为西南抗战的重心"。这是高瞻远瞩胸罗全局的说法，也说出整个中国形势。

其时桂林是少数能连通西南、华南的重要枢纽城市。那时海外战略物资也只能由越南海防入口广西或由香港进入广西，于是桂林成了抗战生命线的中接点。

桂林成了"西南抗战的重心"，除了地理因素之外，当然也有政治因素、人文因素。这些下文会谈到。

至于题辞的第三分句，是"今后必为西南抗

中国抗日战争暨世界反法西斯战争胜利七十周年特展
An Exhibition Dedicated to 70th Anniversary of Victory of War of Resistance against
Japanese Aggression and World Anti-fascist War

战的模范根据地无疑"。在这里又再提"模范"二字，意思是鼓励模范精神能长此下去。那是善颂善祷。但考诸日后广西在抗战中的表现，也确不负周恩来的期望。

以上，是说周恩来题辞的三层意思。

题辞之后总有题款，周恩来题辞之后的题款是"文尧先生，周恩来。廿七，十二，九，于桂林乐群社"。

据知，这位受题人文尧先生就是乐群社的经理。但乐群社又是怎样的地方？

据程思远回忆，周恩来到桂林曾下榻于乐群社。程思远说：

> "我是桂林乐群社的理事长，乐群社主楼三层是接待部。周恩来在1938年冬第一次到桂林时，也曾住过乐群社，他就是在那里接见陈逖冬的。主楼左侧有中西餐厅，右侧是一小礼堂，原来专演话剧，后改为放陕西片的场所。特别是晚上的'草地会'，是桂林文化人会友品茗的好去处"（见程思远《我的回忆》页142-143）。

然而，现时的一些记载，都说周恩来三到桂林（解放前），是三次均住在桂林市的桂北路138号的八路军办事处（该处二楼即为处长李克农的办公室兼卧室）。事实上周恩来一行人等要有秘书、有机要室、有电台、有警卫，试问"乐群社"又怎么能方便这一切？后人们的争论，颇有怀疑程思远所云，"周恩来曾住过乐群社"？

但这册页却解答了纷争。要是周恩来不住乐群社，那乐群社的文尧经理何以夤缘得到题辞？此题辞册该能为程思远所说作一佐证。

按：桂林的乐群社建于1935年，是大型饭店。是广西政府高级招待所。内中有住房、电影院、茶座、球场。抗战间接待过许多军政要人、文化名人，如陈嘉庚、郭沫若、徐悲鸿、陈纳德等

等。周恩来是次到桂林的第三天（12月6日），是应蒋介石约见会谈。第五天出席国际反侵略运动大会中国分会桂林支会筹备会议并致词。第六天，为乐群社经理题此纪念册。题写地点就在乐群社。

在周恩来题辞之后，有李济深楷书题诗："别来国事不堪闻，逝去流光忍细陈。无限江山无限恨，重游羞作避秦人"。这里是要申明他所持的并不是遁世观念。如果揆诸数月后的"桂南会战"，李济深与陈诚合力襄赞白崇禧，帷幄运筹，功在史册，当然不是什么"避秦人"，而只是藉此典故反衬桂林山水如桃花源之美丽而已。

论李济深的历史，他曾任黄埔军校副校长，而正校长是蒋介石。但两人并不投契。在1929年他被蒋介石囚于汤山。1933年发动闽变（即福建事变）当中李的角色很重要，他是"中华共和国人民政府主席兼军事委员会主席"。闽变失败，逮至抗战，再任党政委员会副主任、军委会西南办公厅主任、军事参议院院长。观其简历，当知其一直以反蒋为职志。

而1938年底的"桂南会战"虽然没有共产党的参与，却让人看出中共统战的内涵。

桂南会战是发生在1939年11月8日，距周恩来的题辞未及一年，当时是日军集结十万兵力，在钦州登陆，攻防城、钦县，再越过十万大山攻陷南宁、昆仑关。我方桂林行营主任白崇禧指挥反攻，而李济深、陈诚为之协助督战。使蔡廷锴任东路军总司令，夏威为西路军总司令，徐庭瑶为北路军总司令，三路围敌于邕江北部。12月18日拂晓开始三路夹击，经四昼夜苦战告捷，毙敌四千余人，收复昆仑关。由于我方是仰攻，伤亡多达万四千人，此役可谓壮烈，也可谓惨胜。

是役也，诚如周恩来题词谓（桂林）必成为"西南抗战的模范根据地"的预言。

李济深不单是军事上运筹帷幄，在文化上也曾

为桂林博得"文化城"的美名。

因在广州失守之后，桂林已隐然为大后方之枢纽。从前人口仅七万，1938年底（即题册之时）已激增至十二万，外来人口的激增，使该城的救亡文化空前兴盛（香港沦陷，又有大批文化人士撤到桂林，人口达三十万，那是后话）。

因之，桂林被称"文化城"，这当中，必要有有力人士为之造就庇荫施为，而这"有力人士"当中就要数李济深。

当时，文化界有疑难总是找李济深帮忙解决。像周恩来之初到桂林，李济深就为周举行了欢迎会。他还与周同场出席"国际反侵略运动大会"并在会上讲话。各方筹集经费，也找李济深协助。李济深甚至和何香凝一起领衔为左派"文协"发起国庆筹金游行，期间李济深和柳亚子、田汉等走在队前。谁说李济深是"避秦"？他是"狙秦"！他在运筹帷幄之余，还与老百姓同呼吸。

"桂南会战"，蔡廷锴是独当一面的总司令。

而这位总司令曾在题辞册中题上"军民一致共同杀敌"。只一句话便足见爱国之忱和军人的本色。其款署"廿八年元月十五日"。缅想戎马倥偬，尚挥毫矢言杀敌，这是羊叔子般的裘带雍容，就很有横刀草檄、倚剑题诗的意味。

另外一个题辞者是黄琪翔，作行书题辞"我爱桂林"。那只四个字，比蔡廷锴的八个字还要简省。蔡廷锴题旨是"同杀敌"，而黄琪翔的题旨是"爱桂林"，一杀一爱，两者同为题册，但两者的出发点都是爱国。而两者都是百战将军。

黄琪翔将军，广东梅县人。北伐任第四军（铁军）军长，年仅29岁。追随邓演达，后与李济深等发动"闽变"，也曾参加八一三抗战。1943年，中国远征军建立，黄琪翔任副司令长官。1944年5月发动滇西缅北战役，苦战六个多月，歼日寇精兵五万余，收复失地两万四千平方公里。震惊中外。由于抗战功高，荣获"抗日战争胜利勋章"、"青天白日勋章"以及美国"自由勋章"。而战争结束，黄琪翔公开声明："从此退役，绝不参加内战。"可是这位得世界荣誉的将军，晚年躬逢文革，遭多般凌辱，天天罚洗厕所，要检讨请罪。谁会可怜这位获得最高自由勋章的英雄！

说回来，在周恩来、李济深、蔡廷锴、黄琪翔题辞之后，还有陈铭枢行书诗："岁岁南朝祀岳神，石顽依旧寺容新。风云络绎移居者，莫道桃源可避秦。游南岳绝句之一。'认'误写'道'。文尧先生。陈铭枢"。

有署一"元"字之画："驾长车踏破富士山缺"。疑系漫画家张文元。

题辞册尚有萨空了行书题辞："贡献力量于抗战就是自救"等等。在此不一一详述了。

中国抗日战争暨世界反法西斯战争胜利七十周年特展
An Exhibition Dedicated to 70th Anniversary of Victory of War of Resistance against
Japanese Aggression and World Anti-fascist War

Postscript to Inscriptions Album of Lequn Society (Abstract)

Hui Laiping

Inscribers include: Zhou Enlai, Cai Tingkai, Chen Mingshu, Huang Qixiang, Sa Kongliao, Li Jishen, Zhang Wenyuan, and Li Jiwu. All the inscriptions were made for Mr. Wen Yao.

Zhou's inscription contains three sentences, showing the past, present and future of Guilin. "Guangxi as a model" in the first sentence hails the unswerving efforts and achievements of Guangxi in the previous decade. The second sentence demonstrates the overall situation in China. The third calls for passing on such model spirit. Mr. Wen Yao, for whom the inscription was made, was then manager of Lequn Society. Cheng Siyuan recalled Zhou Enlai once lived in the building of Lequn Society when he was in Guilin, while existing records say that Zhou Enlai lived in the office of the Eighth Route Army. This inscription proves Cheng's words.

Li Jishen wrote a poem in regular script. He was not only an outstanding military leader, but also a scholar whose great fame in the cultural scene helped Guilin secure the title of "cultural city".

Another inscriber, Huang Qixiang, used to be the vice commander of China Expeditionary Force. Due to his military exploits during the Anti-Japanese War, he was awarded "Order of Anti-Japanese War Victory", "Order of Blue Sky and White Sun" and US "Medal of Freedom". After the war, he declared that "I will leave the army and would never fight in any civil war." However, the Cultural Revolution decades later brought him great humiliation and injuries in his twilight years. Who had pity for him when this great hero and winner of Medal of Freedom was forced to clean toilets and "repent his wrongdoings" every day?

前　言

　　中国抗日战争是近代以来中华民族反抗帝国主义侵略首次赢得完全胜利的战争。战争始于1931年九一八事变，止于1945年9月9日日本向国民政府宣告投降，分为局部抗战（1931-1937）和全国抗战（1937-1945）两个时期。第二次世界大战尤其是太平洋战争爆发后，中国抗日战争成为世界反法西斯战争的重要组成部分。

　　第二次世界大战（1939-1945）是以德国、意大利、日本法西斯等轴心国为一方，以世界反法西斯同盟国家为另一方的世界战争，涉及到61个国家和地区、20亿以上的人口。战争造成军民共伤亡约9000余万人，4万多亿美元的损失，仅中国在1937-1945年就伤亡约4000万人，直接财产损失超过1000亿美元。

　　中国抗日战争暨世界反法西斯战争的胜利使中国和世界都发生了深刻变化，它促进了中国的民族觉醒和新中国的建立；二战期间，同盟国所发表和签署的《开罗宣言》、《雅尔塔协定》、《波茨坦公告》等文献奠定了现代的国际秩序。为使后人牢记中国抗日战争暨世界反法西斯战争这段艰苦卓绝的伟大历史，特举办本展览予以纪念。

中国抗日战争暨世界反法西斯战争胜利七十周年特展
An Exhibition Dedicated to 70th Anniversary of Victory of War of Resistance against
Japanese Aggression and World Anti-fascist War

INTRODUCTION

The War of Resistance against Japanese Aggression is a war in which China claimed the first total victory over imperialist invasion. It started from the September 18 Incident in 1931, and ended with the surrender of Japan to the government of the Republic of China on September 9, 1945. The war can be divided into two stages: localized engagements (1931-1937) and nationwide resistance (1937-1945). And with the outbreak of World War II, especially of the Pacific War, the war in China turned into a significant part of the global campaign against fascism.

World War II is a global war that lasted from 1939 to 1945 between the Axis formed by Germany, Italy and Japan, and the Allies of countries that opposed fascism. It involved more than two billion people from 61 countries and regions, and resulted in an estimated 90 million fatalities of military personnel and civilians and more than four trillion dollars in economic losses. The war in China, in particular, caused 4 million causalities and more than 100 billion dollars of property damage, from 1937 to 1945.

The victory of the Chinese people's anti-Japanese war has brought profound changes to China and beyond. It led to national awakening in China and the establishment of the People's Republic of China. The Cairo Declaration, Yalta Agreement and Potsdam Proclamation and a host of documents published and signed by the Allies during World War II created the foundation for a modern international order. The exhibition is organized to help us remember the history of the arduous war in China, in which the Chinese devoted themselves, with heroic and tireless efforts, to the conflict against fascism.

甲午战争后，日本军国主义为达到吞并中国的野心，在中国先后发动了九一八、一·二八、华北和卢沟桥等事变。从卢沟桥事变始，中华民族的生存到了最危险的时候。

在民族危亡之际，中国共产党秉持民族大义，以抗日救亡为己任，努力建立以国共合作为基础的抗日民族统一战线。全国各民族、各阶级、各党派、各社会团体、各界爱国人士、港澳台同胞和海外侨胞团结一心，义无反顾地投身到这场事关民族存亡的战争中，用鲜血和生命书写了中华民族历史抗击侵略的伟大篇章。

Since the Sino-Japanese War of 1894-1895, Japanese militarists engineered a series of incidents in China in a move to occupy the entire country, including the September 18 Incident in 1931, the January 28 Incident in 1932, the North China Incident in 1935 and the Lugou Bridge Incident in 1937, after which China came to a point where its existence was at stake.

In response, the Communist Party of China (CPC) took it as its own duty to save the nation and strived to build the Anti-Japanese National United Front based on its cooperation with the Kuomintang (KMT). All the Chinese, including those in the Chinese mainland, Hong Kong, Maocao, Taiwan or overseas countries, were united in the war that would make a life-or-death difference for the nation, regardless of ethnic group, social status, party affiliation and location. And their commitment, support, and sacrifice constituted a great chapter of Chinese history of struggle against foreign invasion.

中国抗日战争暨世界反法西斯战争胜利七十周年特展
An Exhibition Dedicated to 70th Anniversary of Victory of War of Resistance against
Japanese Aggression and World Anti-fascist War

一 第二次国共合作的形成

I THE SECOND KMT- CPC COOPERATION

　　1931年九一八事变后，中共即为建立抗日民族统一战线进行努力。1935年8月1日，中共发表《为抗日救国告全体同胞书》，再次呼吁各党派和军队停止内战，共同抗日救国。1936年12月12日，张学良、杨虎城在西安发动兵谏，扣留了国民政府军事委员会委员长蒋介石。在中共的主导下，蒋介石接受了停止内战，联共抗日的主张。

　　1937年卢沟桥事变爆发，7月15日，中共在《为公布国共合作宣言》中，宣布红军改编为国民革命军，担任抗日之责。8月22日，红军主力正式改编为国民革命军第八路军（南方红军游击队年底改编为陆军新编第四军）。9月23日，蒋介石发表《对中国共产党宣言的谈话》承认共产党的合法地位，第二次国共合作正式形成。

　　The CPC begun to work on building the Anti-Japanese National United Front in the wake of the September 18 Incident in 1931. It published A Letter to the Fellowmen about the Anti-Japanese War and National Salvation¬ on August 1, 1935, calling for all the parties and military forces to end the civil war and to jointly fight against Japan. On December 12, 1936, Chang Hsueh-liang and Yang Hucheng arrested Chiang Kai-shek, the then Chairman of the National Military Council of Kuomintang government in what came to be known as the Xi'an Incident. At last, with mediation of the CPC, Chiang agreed to ending the civil war and making a united front with the CPC against Japan.

　　Following the Lugou Bridge Incident, the CPC declared the incorporation of the Red Army into the National Revolutionary Army (NRA) in an official paper Declaration of Cooperation between KMT and CPC on July 15, 1937. On August 22, CPC's main force was reorganized into the Eighth Route Army of the NRA, and guerrilla forces in southern China into the New Fourth Army by the end of the year. On September 23, Chiang Kai-shek recognized CPC's status in A Talk on the CPC's Declaration, marking the formation of the second cooperation between the two parties.

1 九一八事变
September 18 Incident

1931年9月18日夜，日本关东军炸毁沈阳柳条湖附近的南满铁路，并以此为借口，炮轰沈阳北大营。次日，日军侵占沈阳，后又陆续侵占了东北三省。九一八事变标志着中国抗日战争的开始，同时也揭开了第二次世界大战东方战场的序幕。

On the night of September 18, 1931, Japanese troops stationed in northeastern China blew up a section of a railway line owned by Japan's South Manchuria Railway near Shenyang. They accused the Chinese of the act, and bombed the Chinese garrison of Beidaying. The next day Japanese troops occupied Shenyang and the three provinces in northeast China later on. The incident is recognized as the beginning of the War of Resistance against Japanese Aggression and as the prelude for of the Eastern theater of World War II.

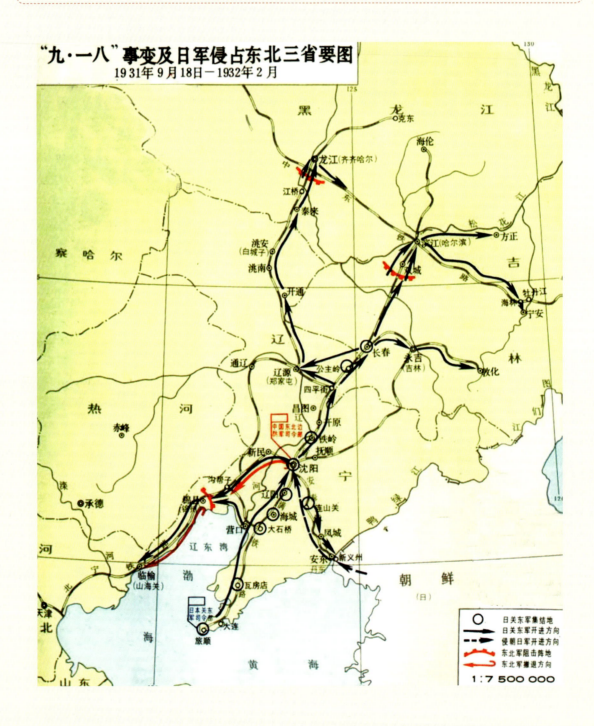

中国抗日战争暨世界反法西斯战争胜利七十周年特展
An Exhibition Dedicated to 70th Anniversary of Victory of War of Resistance against
Japanese Aggression and World Anti-fascist War

攻上沈阳城头的日军

Japanese soldiers who seized hold of the portal of Shenyang

向东北各地进军的日军

Japanese soldiers who marched towards northeast China

田中义一
Tanaka Giichi

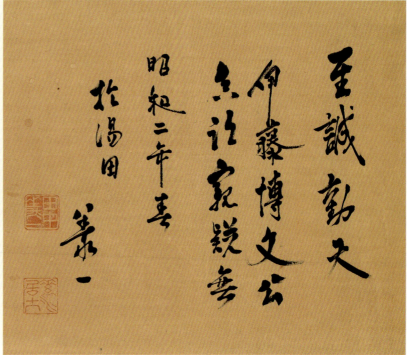

田中义一 行书 "至诚动天"
Tanaka Giichi running script, "Great Sincerity Moving the Heaven"

1920年代
纵36.5、横32.4厘米
台湾董良彦先生提供

田中义一(1864-1929)，日本陆军大将，日本第26任首相（1927-1929）。"欲征服世界，必先征服支那；欲征服支那，必先征服满蒙"即出自他在20世纪20年代向昭和天皇提出的《田中奏折》（今考证是另一甲级战犯铃木贞一之作），日本后来的侵略行径完全以此进行。

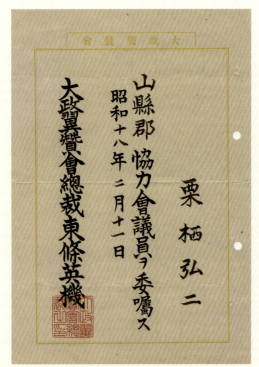

东条英机署 "大政翼赞会协力会议员委嘱状"
昭和18年（1943）
Hideki Tojo signed a document for the assisting committee for Imperial Rule Assistance Association

纵25.8、横18.2厘米
台湾董良彦先生提供

东条英机（1884-1948），日本头号甲级战犯。1937年任关东军参谋长。1940年任陆军大臣，1941年10月任日本首相。1948年11月12日被远东国际军事法庭判处死刑。大政翼赞会是日本1940年成立的极右组织，1945年6月13日解散。

中国抗日战争暨世界反法西斯战争胜利七十周年特展
An Exhibition Dedicated to 70th Anniversary of Victory of War of Resistance against
Japanese Aggression and World Anti-fascist War

白川义则致大里常弘信札
Letter written by Shirakawayoshinori to Ohsatotunehiro

纸本手卷
长逾 4米
台湾董良彦先生提供

白川义则（1869-1932），日本大正时代的陆军大
将，一二八事变后率日军攻击上海。1932年4月29日
在上海虹口公园被王亚樵派遣的朝鲜爱国志士尹奉
吉刺杀。

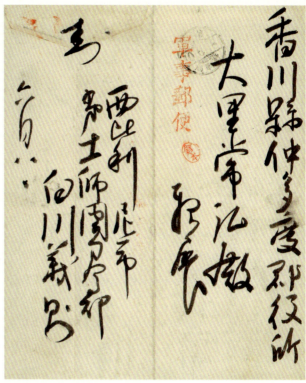

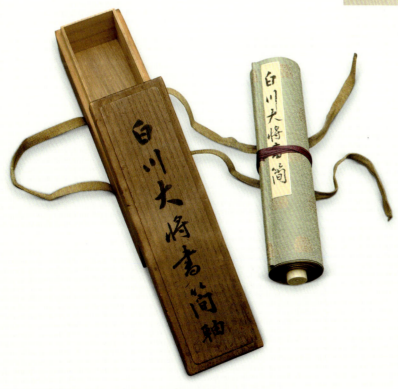

日本高级将领随身携带的中国战区地图（战利品）

Map of the China Theater carried by Japanese senior generals (trophy)

1930年代
边长37厘米
吉星文将军之子吉明立提供

国民革命军第三十三集团军总司令冯治安赠吉星文将军之纪念物。

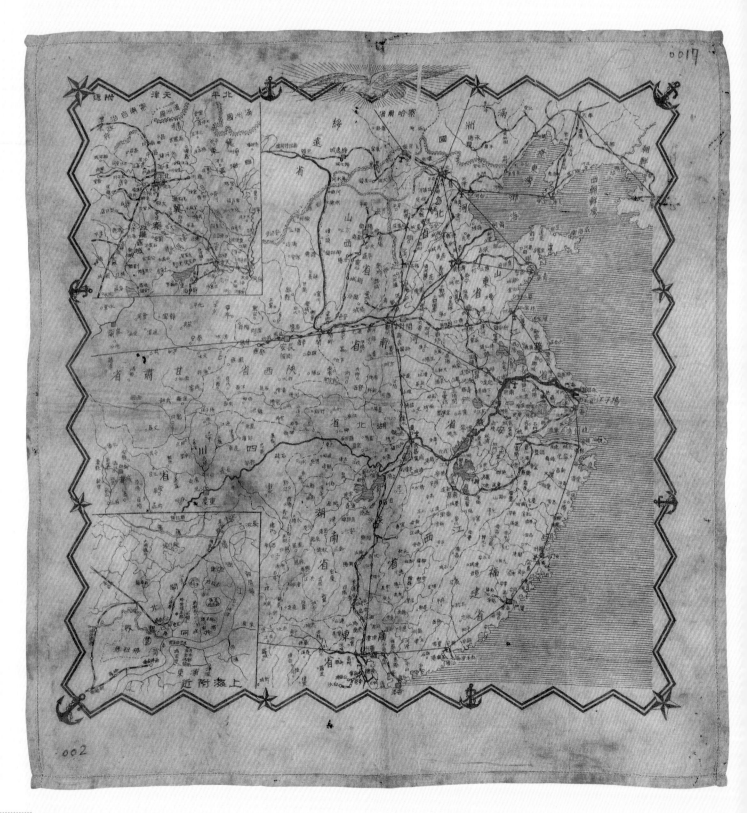

中国抗日战争暨世界反法西斯战争胜利七十周年特展
An Exhibition Dedicated to 70th Anniversary of Victory of War of Resistance against
Japanese Aggression and World Anti-fascist War

2 东北抗联
Northeast Anti-Japanese United Army

　　日本侵占中国东北以后，部分原东北军、抗日游击队、东北抗日义勇军在中共领导下组成东北抗日联军，同日本侵略者进行了长达14年的艰苦斗争，牵制76万日军，消灭日本关东军18万，表现了中华民族英勇不屈的精神，有力地支援了全国的抗日战争和世界反法西斯战争。

　　After the fall of Manchuria the CPC formed the Northeast Anti-Japanese United Army which included some troops of the Northeast Army, guerrilla units and the Northeast People's Anti-Japanese Volunteer Army. In the following 14 years, the army tied down an estimated 760,000 Japanese soldiers and killed 180,000 stationed in the northeast. They were persistent and unfailingly gallant, providing an excellent example of the spirit of the Chinese nation and contributing a lot to the war of resistance against Japan in China and the global campaign against fascism.

马占山将军
General Ma Zhanshan

马占山（1885-1950），河北丰润人。九一八事变后，马占山在齐齐哈尔就任黑龙江省政府代理主席兼军事总指挥，率领爱国官兵奋起抵抗日本侵略军，打响了抗日第一枪。

杨靖宇将军
General Yang Jingyu

杨靖宇（1905-1940），原名马尚德，河南确山人。1932年，他受中共中央委派到东北组织抗日联军，任抗日联军总指挥、政委等职。他率领东北抗日联军抗击日寇，最后壮烈牺牲。

赵一曼烈士
Martyr Zhao Yiman

赵一曼（1905-1936），原名李坤泰，四川宜宾人。曾就读于莫斯科中山大学，毕业于黄埔军校六期。1935年担任东北抗日联军第三军二团政委，在与日寇的斗争中于1936年8月被捕就义。

东北义勇军以迫击炮攻击日军
The Army of Volunteers in northeast China used mortars to attack Japanese armies

东北抗日联军第一路军第二方面军之一部
The First Group of the Second Area Army under the First Route Army of the Northeast Anti-Japanese United Army

中国抗日战争暨世界反法西斯战争胜利七十周年特展
An Exhibition Dedicated to 70th Anniversary of Victory of War of Resistance against
Japanese Aggression and World Anti-fascist War

3 长城抗战
Defense of the Great Wall

　　长城抗战是中国抗日军民在长城沿线抗击日本侵略者的斗争，是中国人民早期抗日斗争的重要组成部分。1933年3月至5月，中国国民政府指挥下的国民革命军（东北军、西北军、中央军等），在长城的义院口、冷口、喜峰口、古北口等地抗击侵华日军进攻。

　　The Defense of the Great Wall was a campaign between Chinese troops and civilians and Japanese troops along the Great Wall, and it was critical to the early days of the war. From March to May in 1933, troops of the NRA, including the Northeastern Army, the Northwestern Army and the Central Army, fought against the Japanese in strategic passes of the Great Wall, including Yiyuankou, Lengkou, Xifengkou and Gubeikou, under the command of the KMT government.

在长城前线作战的大刀队
Glaives fighting in the frontal line of Great Wall

我军戍守长城要隘
Chinese soldiers who guarded the strategic pass of the Great Wall

1933年长城战役期间，我军于长城隘口罗文峪附近组织战线

Chinese troops in Luowenyu, a Great Wall pass, during the Defense of the Great Wall, 1933

中国抗日战争暨世界反法西斯战争胜利七十周年特展
An Exhibition Dedicated to 70th Anniversary of Victory of War of Resistance against
Japanese Aggression and World Anti-fascist War

喜峰口、罗文峪抗日战役纪念奖章

Medal in memory of the 80th anniversary of the victory in
Xifengkou-Luowenyu battle against Japanese aggression

径6.5、厚0.4厘米
宋哲元将军孙女制作，吉星文将军之子吉民立提供

1933年初，长城抗战爆发后，二十九军奉命在长城要塞喜
峰口至罗文峪一线抗战。军长宋哲元派大刀队突袭日军，
大胜，也由此诞生了《大刀进行曲》。在随后的罗文峪战
役中同样夜袭获胜。宋哲元特制该纪念奖章。

黄少强居庸关长城图

A Map of Juyong Pass of the Great Wall, by Huang Shaoqiang

1930年代
纵65、横380 厘米
香港翰墨轩（香江博物馆）藏

黄少强（1901–1942），广东佛山人，著名岭南画派画家。

吉鸿昌将军
General Ji Hongchang

吉鸿昌隶书七言联

A poem in clerical script and seven-syllable form, by Ji Hongchang

1930年代
纵166、横26厘米
香港翰墨轩（香江博物馆）

吉鸿昌（1895-1934），河南扶沟人。1913年入冯玉祥部，从士兵升至军长。1932年加入中共，1933年同冯玉祥、方振武等将领在张家口宣布成立"察哈尔民众抗日同盟军"。1934年11月9日，在天津法租界遭特务杀伤，被引渡关押在北平陆军监狱。11月24日，被蒋介石下令杀害。

中国抗日战争暨世界反法西斯战争胜利七十周年特展
An Exhibition Dedicated to 70th Anniversary of Victory of War of Resistance against
Japanese Aggression and World Anti-fascist War

4 一·二八事变
January 28 Incident

九一八事变后，日本为迫使国民政府屈服，于1932年1月28日在上海发动侵略战争。驻守上海的十九路军在军长蔡廷锴、总指挥蒋光鼐的率领下，奋起抵抗。2月14日，蒋介石命张治中率第五军参战。3月20日，中日在英、美、法、意各国调停之下停战。

After the September 18 Incident, Japan began to attack Shanghai on January 28, 1932, to force the KMT government to surrender. But the attacks met with dogged resistance of the 19th Route Army, of which Cai Tingkai was the general and Jiang Guangnai was the commander in chief. On February 14, Chiang Kai-shek ordered the 5th Army led by Zhang Zizhong to join the battlefield. The battle ended on March 20 with the mediation of western powers, including the UK, the United States, France and Italy.

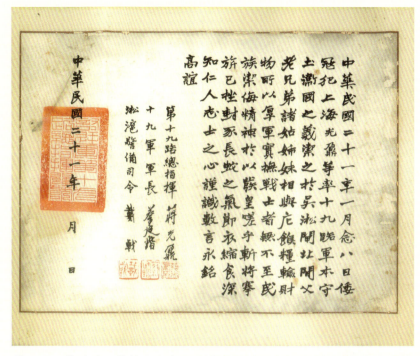

蒋光鼐、蔡廷锴、戴戟致上海民众感谢函
A Thank-you Letter by Jiang Guangnai, Cai Tingkai and Dai Ji

1932年
纵25.2、横35.5 厘米
香港翰墨轩（香江博物馆）藏

十九路军在一·二八事变中的抗日行动受到上海市民的大量支持，本件系事后蒋光鼐、蔡廷锴、戴戟致上海民众感谢函。

蔡廷锴行书"军民一致 共同杀敌"
Running script by Cai Tingkai. It reads "the military and civilians need to be united in eliminating the enemy".

1939年
纵11、横17厘米
香港翰墨轩（香江博物馆）藏

蔡廷锴（1892-1968），广东罗定广府人。一·二八事变爆发，率领十九路军奋起抗日。新中国成立后，任中国人民政治协商会议副主席。

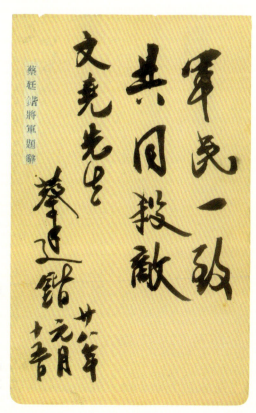

麗洋房錯雜居費死盡心裁圖享樂復興民族意何如
雄知否錙銖都取盡國防未固競虛榮陵園住宅兩名區華
忘報國輸將敵愾向誰論中山路上盡王宮衙署輝煌各逞
明月照台城十年王氣付輕塵幾萬雄師委敵人不是六軍
龍蟠虎踞話金陵十載繁華夢未醒金粉六朝成往事孤懸

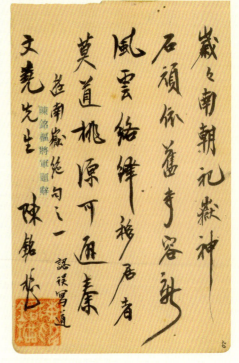

陈铭枢行书七言诗

A poem in running script and seven-syllable form, by Cheng Mingshu

1940年代
纵17、横11厘米
香港翰墨轩（香江博物馆）藏

陈铭枢（1889-1965），广东合浦曲樟（今属广西）人，十九路军为其所创。一·二八事变中，令蒋光鼐、蔡廷锴、戴戟抗日。新中国成立后任全国人大常委会委员。文尧系抗战期间桂林乐群社经理。诗云："岁岁南朝礼岳神，石顽依旧寺容新。风云络绎移居者，莫道桃源可避秦。"

李济深楷书七言诗

A poem in regular script and seven-syllable form by Li Jishen

1938年（？）
纵122、横 32厘米
香港翰墨轩（香江博物馆）藏

李济深（1885-1959），广西梧州苍梧人。十九路军原系李济深任军长的第四军（即北伐铁军）之第十师。新中国成立后任中央人民政府副主席、全国人大副委员长、全国政协副主席等。诗云："龙蟠虎踞话金陵，十载繁华梦未醒。金粉六朝成往事，孤悬明月照台城。十年王气付轻尘，几万雄师委敌人。不是六军忘报国，输将敌忾向谁论？中山路上尽王宫，衙署辉煌各逞雄。知否锱铢都取尽，国防未固竞虚荣。陵园住宅两名区，华丽洋房错杂居，费死(点去)尽心裁图享乐，复兴民族意何如。"

中国抗日战争暨世界反法西斯战争胜利七十周年特展
An Exhibition Dedicated to 70th Anniversary of Victory of War of Resistance against
Japanese Aggression and World Anti-fascist War

马相伯、章炳麟长城战役行书成扇

Running-script handwriting about the Defense of the
Great Wall (fan), by Ma Xiangbo and Zhang Binglin

1933年
纵17.6、横 48.8厘米
香港翰墨轩（香江博物馆）

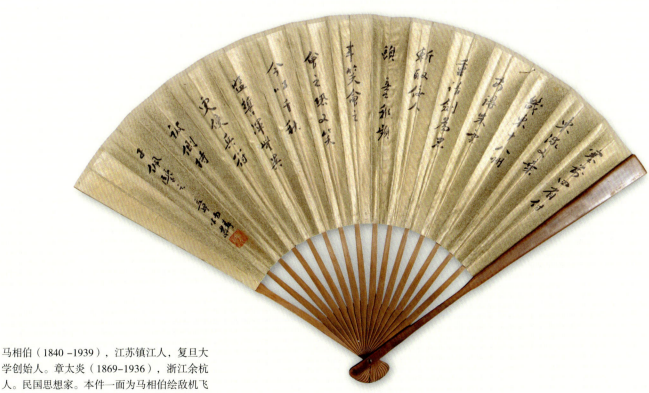

马相伯（1840 –1939），江苏镇江人，复旦大
学创始人。章太炎（1869–1936），浙江余杭
人。民国思想家。本件一面为马相伯绘敌机飞
临长城，一面为章太炎手书七绝，诗云："塞
前四省付东流，又弃畿东十八州。安得朱云重
请剑，为君斩得倭人头"。

一·二八淞沪战役，十九路军与日军进行巷战
Our 19th Route Army resisted the enemy without fear.

蔡廷锴将军（1892－1968）
General Tsai Tingkai

纵10、横7.7厘米
香港翰墨轩（香江博物馆）藏

蒋光鼐将军
General Jiang Guangnai

淞沪前线我宪兵在虬江路口守卫
Our military policemen guarding at the cross of Qiujiang Road during the Songhu Battles

中国抗日战争暨世界反法西斯战争胜利七十周年特展
An Exhibition Dedicated to 70th Anniversary of Victory of War of Resistance against
Japanese Aggression and World Anti-fascist War

5-1 华北事变
North China Incident

九一八事变东北沦陷之后，1935年驻华日军策动华北各省脱离国民政府的一系列事件，以蚕食和侵犯华北。

After the capture of the northeast, Japanese troops in 1935 engineered a series of events to instigate provinces in northern China to break away from the KMT government and to encroach on northern China.

5-2 瓦窑堡会议
Wayaobu Meeting

1935年12月17日，中共中央在陕北子长县瓦窑堡召开政治局扩大会议。会议在毛泽东的主持下，分析了华北事变后国内阶级关系的新变化，批判了党内的左倾关门主义，制定了抗日民族统一战线的策略方针。

On December 17, 1935, CPC Central Committee held an enlarged meeting of the Political Bureau in Wayaobu of Zichang, a county in northern Shaanxi. Participants of the meeting, which was hosted by Mao Zedong, made an analysis of the changes in domestic class relations after the North China Incident, criticized the left-leaning sectarianism, and made plans to form the Anti-Japanese National United Front.

毛泽东在瓦窑堡会议上做报告
Mao Zedong speaking in the Wayaobu Meeting

6 西安事变
Xi'an Incident

1936年12月12日，东北军领袖张学良、西北军领袖杨虎城为劝谏时任国民政府军事委员会委员长的蒋介石停止内战、一致抗日，在西安发动兵谏。在中共的主导下，蒋介石接受了"停止内战，联共抗日"的主张。西安事变的和平解决标志着第二次国共合作开始、抗日民主统一战线初步形成。

Chang Hsueh-Liang, commander of the Northeastern Army, and Yang Hucheng, commander of the Northwestern Army, arrested Chiang Kai-shek, the then Chairman of the National Military Council, on December 12, 1936, in Xi'an, after failing to persuade him to stop the civil war. With the mediation of the CPC, the incident ended with Chiang agreeing to stop the civil war and form a united front with the CPC. The peaceful resolution of the incident marked the emergence of the second KMT-CPC cooperation and of the Anti-Japanese National United Front.

西安事变后的张学良将军
General Zhang Xueliang

1936年12月14日
纵17.8、横12.8厘米
香港翰墨轩（香江博物馆）供图

张学良（1901-2001），辽宁盘锦人，西安事变时任西北剿总副司令并代行总司令职权。西安事变后被长期软禁，1990年始恢复人身自由。

西安数万人集会，一致拥护张、杨的八项救国主张
Thousands of people assembled in the Revolutionary Park of Xi'an, advocating the 8 proposals of Mr. Zhang and Mr. Yang to save the nation.

中国抗日战争暨世界反法西斯战争胜利七十周年特展
An Exhibition Dedicated to 70th Anniversary of Victory of War of Resistance against
Japanese Aggression and World Anti-fascist War

西安事变和平解决后，1937年5月，国民党中央考察团到达延安，受到中共中央和群众欢迎

May of 1937, Central Delegation of NPC arrived in Yan'an

西安事变发生后，中共派出以周恩来、博古、叶剑英为首的代表团赴西安，以促成事变和平解决，国共共同抗日

A delegacy of CPC led by Zhou Enlai, Bo Gu and Ye Jianying got to Xi'an to facilitate solving Xi'an Incident peacefully so as to join CPC and NPC together to resist Japanese invaders

宋子文 行书格言
Motto in running script by Soong Tse-ven

1938年
纵25、横31厘米
香港翰墨轩（香江博物馆）

宋子文（1894–1971），海南文昌人。西安事变爆发后，宋赞成和平解决，与其姊宋美龄前往西安同张学良、杨虎城及中共代表等进行谈判，为西安事变的和平解决和国共联合抗日作出贡献。
书云："以不忍人之心，行不忍人之政"。

7-1 七七事变
Lushan Speech by Chiang Kai-shek

1937年7月7日晚，驻北平丰台日军在卢沟桥附近举行"军事演习"，诡称一名士兵失踪，要求进宛平县城搜查，在遭到拒绝后，炮轰宛平县城，并向卢沟桥一带的中国驻军发动攻击。七七事变是日本发动全面侵华战争的标志，也是中国全国抗战的起点。

On the night of July 7, 1937, Japanese troops stationed in Fengtai, Beijing was carrying out a military exercise, and they demanded a permission to enter Wanping County to search for a missing soldier. The Chinese refused, and Japanese troops began to bomb Wanping and attacked Chinese troops near the Lugou Bridge. The incident was the start of Japan's full-scale aggression, and led directly to the war of resistance against Japan in China.

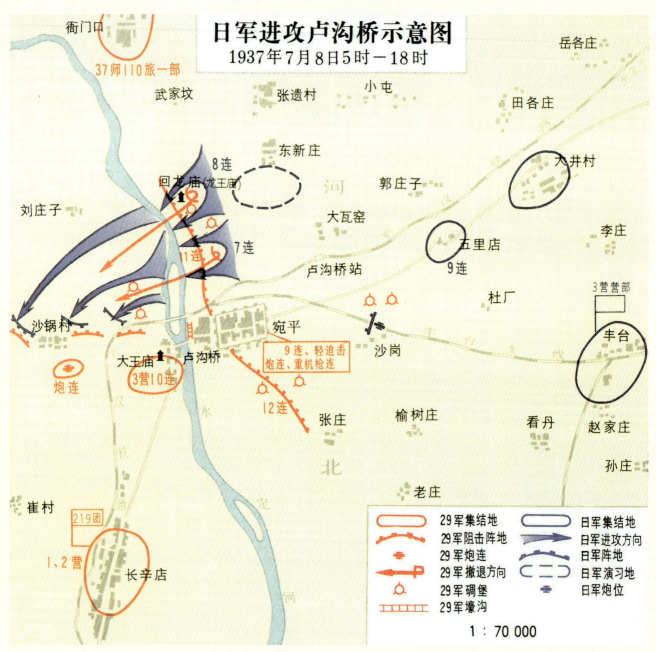

引自武月星主编：《中国现代史地图集（1919–1949）》，中国地图出版社，2000年。

中国抗日战争暨世界反法西斯战争胜利七十周年特展
An Exhibition Dedicated to 70th Anniversary of Victory of War of Resistance against
Japanese Aggression and World Anti-fascist War

戍守卢沟桥的国民革命军第二十九军

The 29th Corps of the National Revolutionary Army
guarding the Lugou Bridge

宛平城守军闻日军侵犯，紧急出城参战

By hearing of Japanese invasion, the guarding army of
Wanping rushed out of the city emergently to fight the
enemies

**第二十九军在北平城内的十字路口修筑工事，
防范日军进攻**

Soldiers of the 29th Corps built fortified works at
crosses in Beijing to resist Japanese armies

二十九军士兵出击敌人前，在北平城高呼口号宣誓
Soldiers of our 29th Corps were shouting an oath in Beiping before going out of the city to fight the enemies

冯治安将军像
General Feng Zhian
纵18.8、横13.7厘米
吉星文将军之子吉民立提供

冯治安（1896–1954），河北故城人。1937年他任国民革命军二十九军三十七师师长、兼河北省政府主席。七七事变爆发他毅然率部抗敌。历任国民革命军七十七军军长、国民革命军三十三集团军总司令等职。1954年因病在台北逝世。

中国抗日战争暨世界反法西斯战争胜利七十周年特展
An Exhibition Dedicated to 70th Anniversary of Victory of War of Resistance against
Japanese Aggression and World Anti-fascist War

吉星文将军任上校团长时像
Photo of General Ji Xingwen acting as Regimental Commander (Colonel)

1937年
纵12.5、横9.7厘米
吉星文将军之子吉民立提供

吉星文（1908–1958），河南扶沟人。1922年随族叔吉鸿昌参加西北军。1933年在长城抗战中升为团长。七七事变爆发，他率二十九军二一九团在卢沟桥奋勇抗击日军，揭开中国全面抗战的序幕，成为名扬中外的抗战英雄。

吉星文将军手书卢沟桥事变经过纪要（复印件）
Brief report of the Lugou Bridge Incident written by General Ji Xingwen (copy)

1950年代
吉星文将军之子吉民立提供

吉星文将军七七事变中于宛平城外合影
Photo of General Ji Xingwen taken outside Wanping City during the Lugou Bridge Incident

1937年
纵15、横11厘米
吉星文将军之子吉民立提供

第一、第二幅中穿白衣柱拐杖为吉星文。照片上为吉星文将军亲笔注记。第一幅："'七七'抗战在芦沟桥首先与日军殊死战，余在此处受伤，同各官长留影纪念。星文书"。第二幅："'七七'在芦沟桥首先与日军作殊死战时同各官长留影卢沟桥畔"。第三幅："'七七'在芦沟桥抗战时，我忠勇干部杀敌归来，在'芦沟晓月'留影"。

中国抗日战争暨世界反法西斯战争胜利七十周年特展
An Exhibition Dedicated to 70th Anniversary of Victory of War of Resistance against
Japanese Aggression and World Anti-fascist War

吉星文中央军校毕业证
Ji Xingwen's graduate diploma granted by the Central Military Academy

1937年6月10日
纵9.9、横7.2厘米
吉星文将军之子吉民立提供

国民政府军委会任职令
（任命吉星文为陆军第三十七师少将师长）

Commission of the National Military Council of Kuomintang government
to appoint Ji Xingwen as Division Commander (Major General) of the 37th
Division of the Army

1941年
纵33.5、横28.4厘米
吉星文将军之子吉民立提供

吉星文将军第五战区作战人员
研究训练班毕业证书

General Ji Xingwen's graduate diploma on taking the research and
training course granted for personnel who would participate in battles at
the 5th War Area

1941年
纵37.2、横32.5厘米
吉星文将军之子吉民立提供

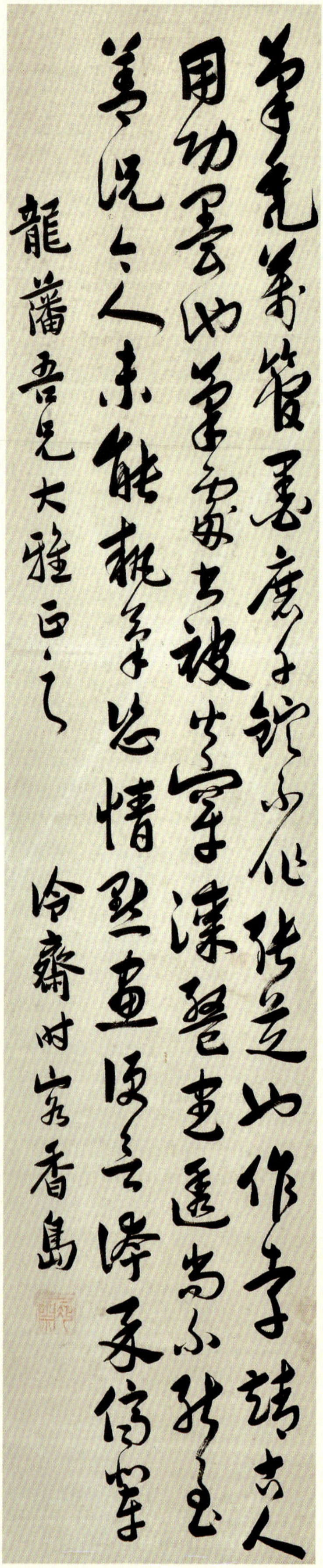

王冷斋行书

Running script by Wang Lengzhai

1940年（？）
纵115、横 24厘米
香港翰墨轩（香江博物馆）藏

王冷斋（1891-1960），七七事变时任河北省第三区行政督察专员兼宛平县县长。事变当晚，王冷斋与日军谈判，坚决回绝了日方的威胁利诱和进城的要求。1939年客居香港，1941年流亡贵阳。新中国成立后，任北京文史馆馆长。书云："笔秃万管，墨磨千锭，不作张芝，也作索靖。古人用功，墨池笔冢，书被皆穿，漆盘尽透，尚不能至善，况今人未能执笔，恣情点画，便言夸示侪辈。龙藩吾兄大雅正之。冷斋时客香岛。"

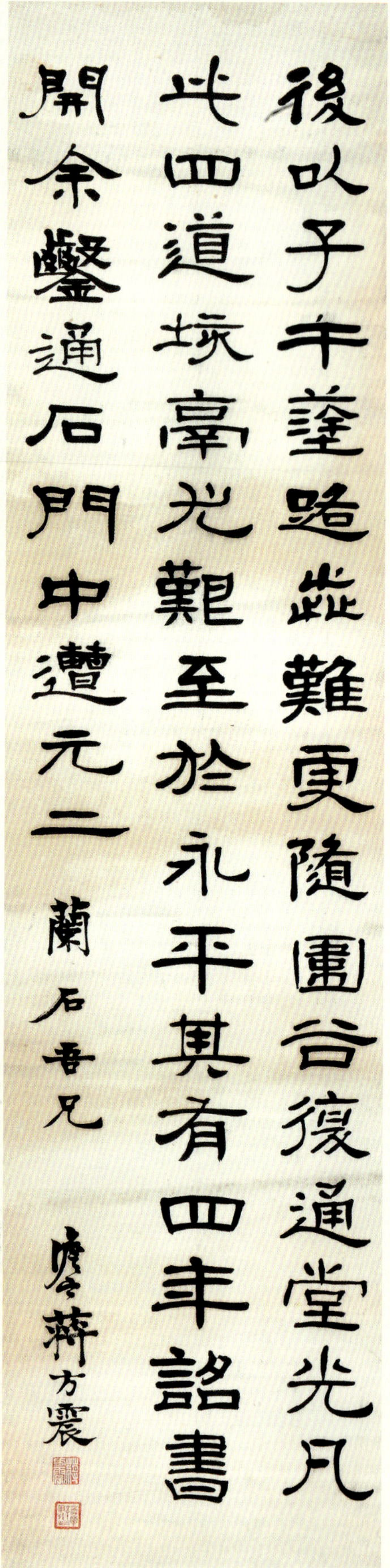

蒋百里隶书

Clerical script by Jiang Baili

1930年代
纵129、横32厘米
香港翰墨轩（香江博物馆）藏

蒋百里（1882-1938）名方震，以字行，浙江海宁人。1912年任保定陆军军官学校校长。1937年在《国防论》中提出了抗日持久战的战略。书《石门颂》云："后以子午，塗路崾难。更随围谷，复通堂光。凡此四道，埃崾尤艰。至于永平，其有四年。诏书开余，凿通石门。中遭元二"。

中国抗日战争暨世界反法西斯战争胜利七十周年特展
An Exhibition Dedicated to 70th Anniversary of Victory of War of Resistance against
Japanese Aggression and World Anti-fascist War

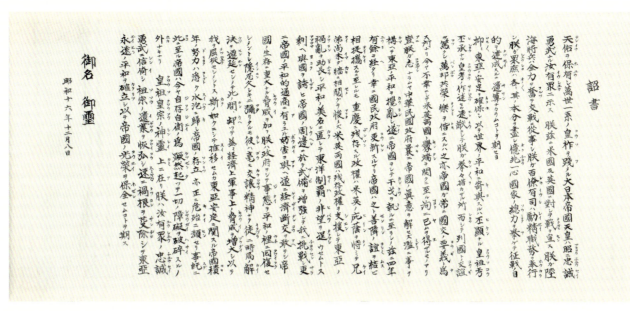

日本天皇宣战诏书卷

The Declaration of War by the Empire of Japan

昭和十六年（1941）十二月八日
纵38、横120厘米
香港翰墨轩（香江博物馆）藏

1941年12月7日，太平洋战争爆发后第二
天，日本天皇即向同盟国宣战。本件为当
时日本宣战印刷品。

支那事变纪念章

Medal for the Shina Incident (Japan)

1937年
长15、宽10.5厘米
滇西抗战纪念馆藏

本章系日本造币局制作，有银、铜、锡三类，日本投降
后大规模销毁，仍有少量存世，是日本侵华罪证。

日本北支那部队纪念烟盒

Commemorative cigarette case of the Japanese Northern
China Area Army

昭和十二年7月7日（1937年7月7日）
长7.7、宽9.5 、高1.8厘米
吉星文将军之子吉民立提供

7-1 蒋介石庐山讲话
Lushan Speech by Chiang Kai-shek

1937年7月17日，蒋介石在庐山发表讲话，宣布卢沟桥事变是我国绝续存亡之最后关头，要求全国人民奋起进行全面抵抗。庐山讲话是抗日战争全面开战的象征。

Chiang Kai-shek delivered a speech on Lushan on July 17, 1937. He said that the Lugou Bridge Incident reduced China to the "final point" of its survival, and that people across the country should rise to resist Japanese aggression. The declaration marks the beginning of a full-scale war between China and Japan.

中国抗日战争暨世界反法西斯战争胜利七十周年特展

An Exhibition Dedicated to 70th Anniversary of Victory of War of Resistance against
Japanese Aggression and World Anti-fascist War

**蒋介石批示陈果夫呈萧栋材报告补训机关虐杀壮
丁影响抗战事**

An instruction of Chiang Kai-shek to Chen Guofu

1941年
纵33.5、横26.5 厘米
香港翰墨轩（香江博物馆）藏

陈果夫（1892–1951），浙江吴兴东林镇人。陈果夫、陈立夫
兄弟与蒋介石关系密切，曾负责国民党内组织及党务。抗战爆
发后，陈果夫坚决主张抗战与国共合作。

**蒋介石批示陈果夫呈雷殷报告维持市内区镇保甲
之编组事**

An instruction of Chiang Kai-shek to Chen Guofu

1942年
纵33.5、横26.5 厘米
香港翰墨轩（香江博物馆）藏

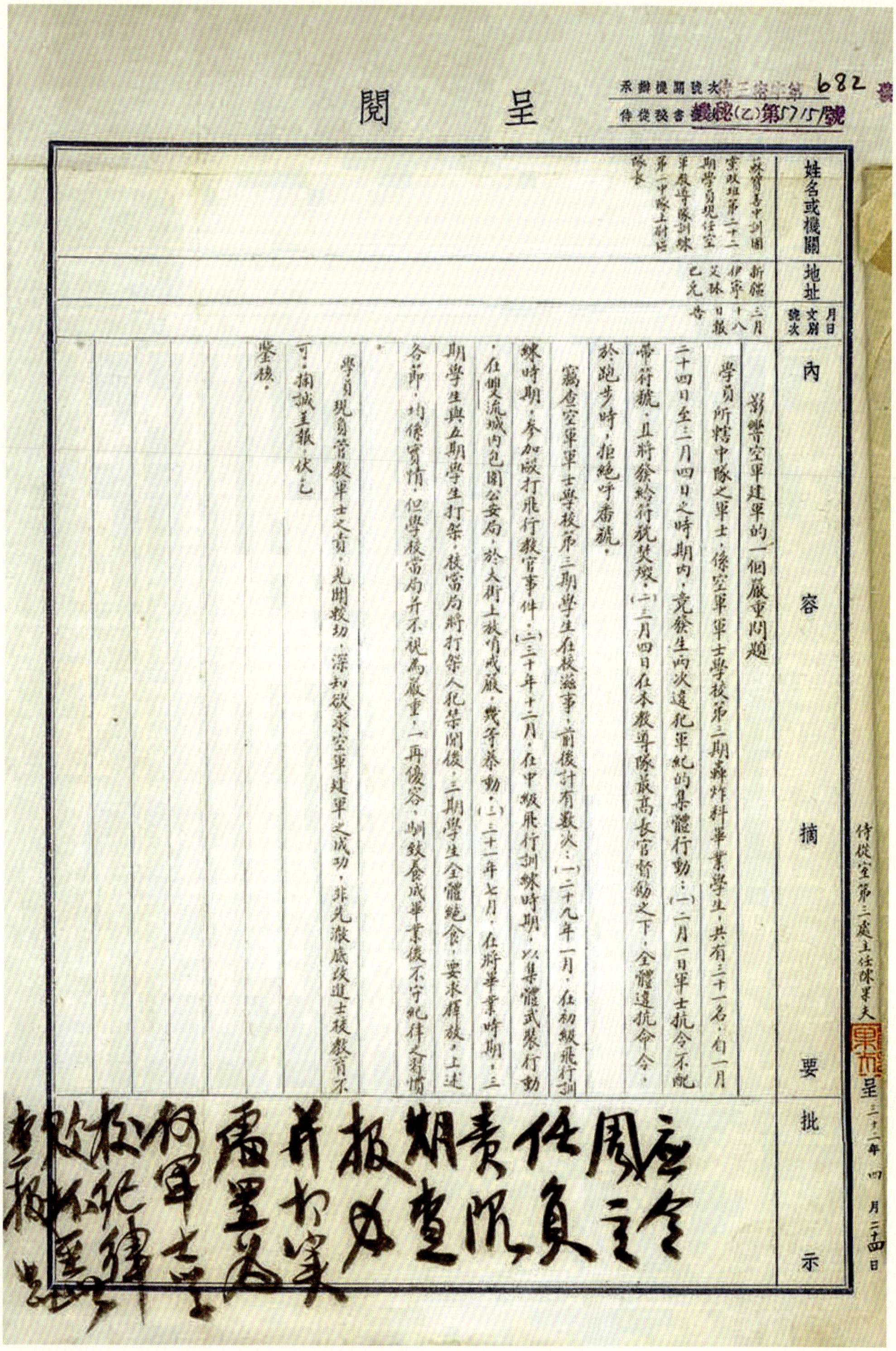

呈閱

承辦機關號次 682
侍從秘書發 機秘(乙)第5715號

姓名或機關	地址	月日 文別 號次
蘇寶善中訓團黨政班第二十三期學員現任空軍教導隊訓練第一中隊上尉區隊長	新疆伊寧艾林巴克	三月十八日 報

內容摘要

影響空軍建軍的一個嚴重問題

學員所轄中隊之軍士，係空軍軍士學校第三期爆炸科畢業學生，共有二十一名，自一月二十四日至三月四日之時期內，竟發生兩次違犯軍紀的集體行動：(一)二月一日軍士抗令不配帶符號，且將發給符號焚燬。(二)三月四日在本教導隊最高長官督飭之下，全體違抗命令，於跑步時，拒絕呼番號。

竊查空軍軍士學校第三期學生在校滋事，前後計有數次：(一)二十九年一月，在初級飛行訓練時期，參加毆打飛行教官事件。(二)三十年十二月，在中級飛行訓練時期，以集體武裝行動，在雙流城內包圍公安局，於大街上放哨戒嚴，幾等暴動。(三)三十一年七月，在將畢業時期，三期學生與五期學生打架，校當局將打架人犯禁閉後，三期學生全體絕食，要求釋放。上述各節，均係實情，但學校當局並不視為嚴重，一再優容，馴致養成畢業後不守紀律之習慣。

學員現負當教軍士之責，凡期教功，深知欲求空軍建軍之成功，非先澈底改進士校教育不可。謹據誠呈報，伏乞鑒核。

批示

侍從室第三處主任陳果夫 呈 三十二年四月二十四日

蒋介石批示陈果夫呈苏宝善报告影响空军建军严重问题

An instruction of Chiang Kai-shek to Chen Guofu

1943年
纵34、横26.5 厘米
香港翰墨轩（香江博物馆）藏

蒋介石和宋美龄非常重视空军，本件为陈果夫呈报中央航空学校第五期学员苏宝善反映军校问题，蒋介石批示要严肃军纪。

中国抗日战争暨世界反法西斯战争胜利七十周年特展
An Exhibition Dedicated to 70th Anniversary of Victory of War of Resistance against
Japanese Aggression and World Anti-fascist War

林语堂上蒋委员长外交方策意见书(稿)

A position paper submitted by Lin Yutang to Chairman Chiang Kai-shek

1943年

纵28、横21.6厘米

台湾中华海峡两岸文化资产交流促进会名誉理事长王水衷藏，台湾美术馆提供

林语堂（1895–1976），福建漳州人，著名文学家。抗战期间，林语堂、胡适
等文人学者都积极投身抗战。

林語堂敬上

民國卅一年度十二節

滿此其一也

十九、統視大勢我方手中好牌有三。一以親俄手段連聯美國的
、和平會議蘇俄為英美對象我方亦為英美對象合作。

二遠東如由我國支撐抗日局面支撐手必有相當代價權衡
在手筆以美一封鎖抗日有力與額達之手段救濟無氣
油無輪胎何以抗日第三我必推中國與英美合作了
此當西方之救援視中國之備之理由特我不自
覺身人之自俗如以人倫之外國大阪國中貿解皆不足以言
外交盖人理中毒甚深也

二十以上各点計劃先必擇行過有局部解決使吾國說話自如
有力名別手中無牌惟有作人台異意國外形勢甚惡不得不
好擇手段与目標須認明耳語無次又不成章惟

要望諒之

民國卅一年夏十節
提前
林語堂敬上口

8-1 《中共中央为公布国共合作宣言》
CPC Central Committee's Declaration of Cooperation between KMT and CPC

　　七七事变后，为促成第二次国共合作，中共中央于1937年7月15日将《中共中央为公布国共合作宣言》（即《共赴国难宣言》）送交国民党，提出抗战奋斗总目标（发动民族革命抗战、实现民权政治、实现中国人民的幸福生活）和国共合作的四项保证（实现三民主义、取消推翻国民党政权政策、取消苏维埃政府、改编红军为国民革命军）。9月22日，中央通讯社发表此宣言，抗日民族统一战线遂正式形成。

　　After the July 7 Incident, the CPC Central Committee presented the Declaration of Cooperation between KMT and CPC to the KMT on July 15, 1937. In the paper the CPC defined the general goals of the war against Japan: to defeat Japan with a national revolution, to build a political system guaranteeing civil rights, and to deliver a happy life for the Chinese people. To make the cooperation possible, the CPC also stated that it would follow the Three Principles of the People, abolish policies that aimed at overthrowing the KMT government, dismiss the CPC government, and reorganize the Red Army into the National Revolutionary Army. On September 22, the Central News Agency published the declaration, marking the ultimate formation of the Anti-Japanese National United Front.

中国抗日战争暨世界反法西斯战争胜利七十周年特展
An Exhibition Dedicated to 70th Anniversary of Victory of War of Resistance against
Japanese Aggression and World Anti-fascist War

1937年7月13日，毛泽东在延安号召"共产党员和抗日的革命者应随时出动到抗日的最前线"

Mao Zedong in Yan'an says that "the CPC members and revolutionaries who are opposed to Japan should be ready to march towards the anti-Japanese frontlines", July 13, 1937

1937年7月17日，中共代表与国民党代表蒋介石就两党合作在庐山谈判

Representatives of the Kuomintang and Communist Party negotiated in Lushan, on July 17, 1937

8－2 红军改编
Reorganization of the Red Army

中共中央为团结抗战，在《为公布国共合作宣言》中决定将红军改编为国民革命军第八路军（简称八路军），将南方红军游击队改编为国民革命军新编第四军（简称新四军）。图为在延安召开的红军改编誓师大会。

A morale-building meeting in Yan'an before the reorganization of the Red Army. According to the Declaration of Declaration of Cooperation between KMT and CPC, the CPC Central Committee reorganized its Red Army into the Eighth Route Army of the National Revolutionary Army, and its guerrilla forces in the south into the New Fourth Army.

1937年8月，国民政府军事委员会在南京召开国防会议，中共代表朱德、周恩来、叶剑英与张群、黄琪翔、郭秀仪会上合影

CPC representatives Zhu De, Zhou Enlai, Ye Jianying, and representatives of other parties including Zhang Qun, Huang Qixiang and Guo Xiuyi at a meeting of national defense organized by the National Military Council of the KMT government in Nanjing, August 1937

八路军总司令朱德（1886—1976）
Eight Route Army commander Zhu De

八路军副总司令彭德怀（1898—1974）
Eight Route Army deputy commander Peng Dehuai

新四军军长叶挺（1896—1946）
New 4th Army commander Ye Ting

新四军代军长陈毅（1901—1972）
New 4th Army deputy commander Chen Yi

中国抗日战争暨世界反法西斯战争胜利七十周年特展
An Exhibition Dedicated to 70th Anniversary of Victory of War of Resistance against
Japanese Aggression and World Anti-fascist War

1939年春，周恩来在皖南新四军军部与军长叶挺（右）、政委兼副军长项英（左）合影

The spring of 1939, Zhou Enlai, Ye Ting (right) as New 4th Army commander, Xiang Ying (left) as political commissar and deputy commander in southern Anhui

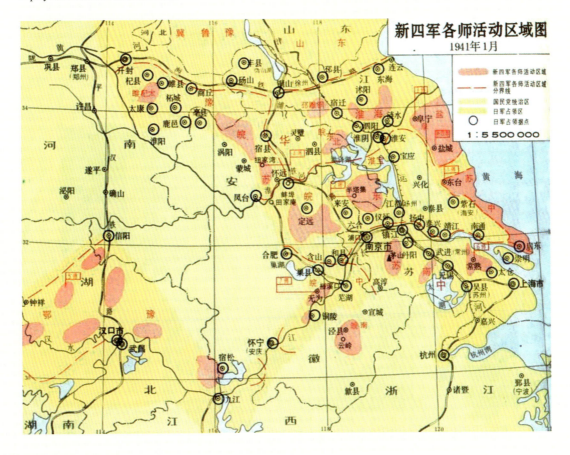

叶挺将军用过的宜兴方陶壶
A pottery pot used by Ye Ting

抗战时期
恩施城关公社征集
湖北省博物馆藏

叶挺（1896-1946），广东惠州人，
中国人民解放军创始人之一。南方
红军游击队改编为国民革命军新
编第四军后，任新四军军长。1941
年，叶挺在皖南事变中被俘，先后
被囚禁于湖北恩施、桂林等地。

新四军八大队标语
A banner of the 8th Group of the New Fourth Army

抗战时期
纵63.2、横15.8厘米
湖北省博物馆藏

中国抗日战争暨世界反法西斯战争胜利七十周年特展
An Exhibition Dedicated to 70th Anniversary of Victory of War of Resistance against
Japanese Aggression and World Anti-fascist War

兵之最要關鍵也 遜于吾兄雅屬 民國三十一年仲春書應 余漢謀

確實則準備周妥 則誤調度 此治

軍旅之事 勝敗無常 總貴確實 而戒虛惶

余汉谋 行书治军论
On Military Management in running script, by Yu Hanmou

1942年
纵136、横 32厘米
香港翰墨轩（香江博物馆）藏

余汉谋（1896—1981），广东高要人。抗战中率部参加淞沪、武汉会战等，历任第十二集团军总司令、第四战区副司令、第七战区总司令。书云："军旅之事，胜败无常，总贵确实，而戒虚惶。确实则准备周妥，虚饰则误调度，此治兵最要关键也。"

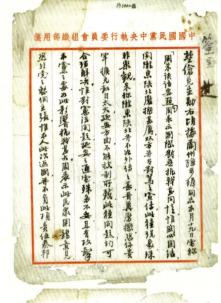

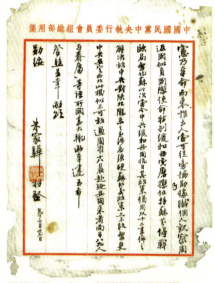

朱家骅致叶楚伧行书手札、叶楚伧行书呈报孙步墀报告周恩来与朱绍良谈话要点
A letter in running script by Zhu Jiahua to Ye Chucang

1940年
纵33、横26厘米
香港翰墨轩（香江博物馆）藏

朱家骅（1893–1963），浙江湖州人，著名教育家、科学家，政治家。抗战中代行中央研究院院长。1944年任教育部长。叶楚伧（1887–1946），江苏周庄人，南社诗人、政治活动家。抗战期间，任国防最高会议秘书长、国民党六届中央执行委员会常委，与周恩来、董必武交往。朱绍良（189–1963），江苏武进人，抗战中任第八战区司令长官兼陕甘宁边区总司令。本件为朱家骅为叶楚伧呈报孙步墀报告周恩来与朱绍良谈话要点事致叶楚伧行书手札，反映抗战中国共双方虽有摩擦，但共同抗战仍是主流。

二 全民抗战

II RESISTANCE OF THE NATION

七七事变揭开了中国全民抗战的序幕。中共中央7月8日发出《中国共产党为日军进攻卢沟桥通电》，呼吁"只有全民族实行抗战，才是我们的出路"。7月17日，蒋介石在庐山发表"最后关头"的讲话，指出"再没有妥协的机会，如果放弃尺寸土地与主权，便是中华民族的千古罪人。""战争一旦发生，地无分南北，人无分老幼，皆有卫国守土之责任"。至此，全国的工农兵学商及海外华人华侨都投入到这场中华民族抗日救亡的洪流中。

As the whole nation was mobilized to resist Japanese aggression after the July 7 Incident, the CPC Central Committee published an open telegram across the country, insisting that "the only way out is a war of total resistance by the whole nation". On July 17 on Lushan Mountain, Chiang Kai-shek said that "there is no room for compromise any more. If we abandon an inch of land and sovereignty, we will be criminals of the nation, and the infamy lives after us", and that "once the war breaks out, every person has the responsibility of protecting the country and the land, be them living in the north or south, old and young." After Chiang's talk all the Chinese people began to dedicate themselves to the battle against Japan, regardless of their social status and location.

9 《全民抗战》
Resistance of the Nation

抗战时期在国统区出版的进步报刊。1938年7月7日在武汉创刊。由沈钧儒的《全民周刊》和邹韬奋的《抗战》三日刊合并出版。初仍为三日刊。以邹韬奋、沈钧儒、艾寒松、张仲实、胡绳、柳湜等6人组成编委会，邹韬奋任主编，柳湜任副主编。

The Resistance of the Nation was a newspaper published in KMT-controlled areas during the war. Founded on July 7, 1938, it was the result of the merging of Shen Junru's National Weekly and Zou Taofen's Anti-Japanese War. Initially it was published every three days. The editorial committee included Zou Taofen, Shen Junru, Ai Hansong, Zhang Zhongshi, Hu Sheng and Liu Shi. Zou Taofen was the editor-in-chief, and Liu Shi was the associate editor-in-chief.

中国抗日战争暨世界反法西斯战争胜利七十周年特展
An Exhibition Dedicated to 70th Anniversary of Victory of War of Resistance against
Japanese Aggression and World Anti-fascist War

10 国民参政会
National Political Council

　　1938年春，中共建议成立民意机关，国民政府接受这一建议，决定成立国民参政会，由各党、各界派代表参加。7月6日至15日，国民参政会第一次会议在汉口举行。国民参政会的成功召开，对于团结全国人民，发扬抗日民主，推动全面抗战产生了积极的作用。

　　In the spring of 1938, CPC suggested that a political consultative council be set up and the National Government accepted it. The National Political Council was set up and joined by the representatives of various parties and from walks of life. From July 6 to 15, the first council meeting was held in Hankou. The successful opening of the council played an active role in unifying the people, promoting democracy and advancing full-scale anti-Japanese effort.

1938年7月6日至15日，接受中共建议成立的民意机构国民参政会第一次会议议员在武汉合影
The political consultants of the first National Political Council meeting

1940年4月，《新华日报》总经理熊瑾玎（右一）、国民党代表周至柔（左一）等人到机场迎接出席第五次国民参政会的中共参政员秦邦宪（左二）、邓颖超（左三）、林伯渠（左四）
General Manager of Xinhua Daily Xiong Jinding (first from right) and KMT representative Zhou Zhirou (first from left) receiving Qin Bangxian (second from left), Deng Yingchao (third from left) and Lin Boqu (fourth from left), CPC representatives participating in the Fifth National Political Assembly, April 1940

11 全国各界救国联合会
Chinese Association of National Salvation

1936年5月31日在上海成立，沈钧儒、章乃器、陶行知、邹韬奋等人发起组织。

The Chinese Association of National Salvation was an organization formed by Shen Junru, Zhang Naiqi, Tao Xingzhi and Zou Taofen, in Shanghai on May 31, 1936, to enlist support for the war against Japan.

抗战时期宋庆龄在重庆
Soong Ching-ling in Chongqing during the war

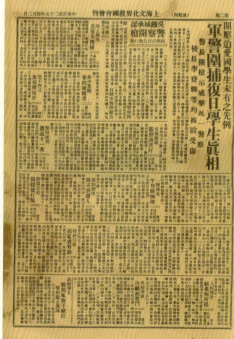

《上海文化界救国会会刊》第二号
The second issue of the official journal of the Shanghai Association of Artists and Writers for National Salvation

1936年4月2号
纵37.5、横25.5厘米
香港翰墨轩（香江博物馆）藏

中国抗日战争暨世界反法西斯战争胜利七十周年特展
An Exhibition Dedicated to 70th Anniversary of Victory of War of Resistance against
Japanese Aggression and World Anti-fascist War

全国各界救国联合会领导人史良在重庆妇女集会上高呼团结口号

Shi Liang, leader of the Association of National Salvation from All Walks of Life, shouting the slogan at a rally of women in Chongqing

周恩来、董必武、邓颖超在红岩13号接待美国华侨领袖、中国致公党创始人司徒美堂（左三）和黄兴夫人徐宗汉（右二）的合影

Zhou Enlai, Dong Biwu and Deng Yingchao receiving Situ Meitang (third from left) and Huang Xing's wife Xu Zonghan (second from right), at No. 13, Hongyan Road

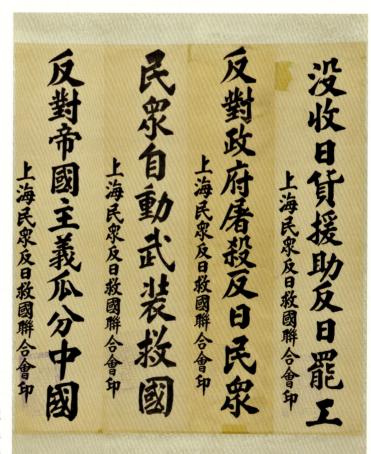

抗日救国标语

Anti-Japanese banners

1930年代
纵53.5、横49 厘米
香港翰墨轩（香江博物馆）藏

抗战标语实物极其罕见，本件系日军侵略上海期间由标语书写者本人保留。

没收日货援助反日罢工
上海民众反日救国联合会印

反對政府屠殺反日民眾
上海民眾反日救國聯合會印

民眾自動武裝救國
上海民眾反日救國聯合會印

反對帝國主義瓜分中國
上海民眾反日救國聯合會印

12 中国工人抗敌总会
Chinese Federation of Anti-Japanese Workers

　　1938年3月，全国工界发起筹备组织中国工人抗敌总会，实现了国统区工会和共产党领导的抗日根据地工会的公开合作，上海总工会负责人朱学范为筹备会主要负责人。

　　The Chinese Federation of Anti-Japanese Workers was formed in March 1938. It facilitated cooperation between the labor unions in KMT- and CPC-controlled areas, and Zhu Xuefan, director of Shanghai Labor Union, was one of the members of the organizing committee.

13 新生活运动妇女指导委员会
The Women's Instruction Committee for New Life Movement

　　1938年7月1日，新生活运动妇女指导委员会在汉成立，促进了各阶层各党派妇女之间的友好合作，宋美龄、沈兹九、史良、刘清扬为主要成员。

　　On July 1, 1938, The Women's Instruction Committee for New Life Movement set up in Wuahn, it promoted the friendly cooperation in various sectors between the political parties for women, Soong May-ling, Shi Liang, Liu Qingyang are a principal member.

中国工人抗敌总会成立的报道
The reports about the organization of anti-aggression group by industrial sector

新生活运动妇女指导委员会成员合影
Members of the Women's Instruction Committee for New Life Movement

中国抗日战争暨世界反法西斯战争胜利七十周年特展
An Exhibition Dedicated to 70th Anniversary of Victory of War of Resistance against
Japanese Aggression and World Anti-fascist War

14 战时儿童保育会
National Association for Refugee Children

1938年3月10日，在武汉圣罗以女子中学（今武汉市第二十中学)正式成立战时儿童保育会。推选出理事56人，宋美龄、李德全为理事长、副理事长。

On March 10, 1938, the association was established in what is known the No. 20 Middle School of Wuhan today. It had 56 council members. Soong May-ling acted as the director-general of the council, and Li Dequan as the assistant director-general.

战时儿童保育会部分发起人合影（左起：李德全、冯弗伐、邓颖超、唐维贞、安娥、刘清扬、郭秀仪、谢兰郁）
Members of Wartime Children's Nurturing Council

1939年，台湾少年团加入抗战在浙江金华进行操练
Taiwan Cadets trained in Jinhua, Zhejiang, 1939

15 献金运动
Donation campaign

　　为纪念抗战一周年，激发全国人民的爱国热情，坚定抗日信心，在国民政府军事委员会政治部的直接指导下，武汉各界抗战周年纪念筹备会决定组织大规模纪念活动，并将募捐献金活动作为主要内容，这一活动得到了各界的广泛支持。

　　To commemorate the first anniversary of the anti-Japanese war, boost patriotism among the Chinese people and build up the confidence in defeating the invaders, the organizing committee of the first anniversary in Wuhan decided to launch massive activities. Directly under the leadership of the Political Department of the Military Committee, the National Government, the organizing committee decided to launch a donation campaign, which was widely supported by various circles of the society.

武汉民众献金盛况
Wuhan residents made their donations

《新华日报》有关中共及八路军战士献金的报道
Xinhua Daily's reports about the donations from CPC and troops
of the Eighth Route Army

中国抗日战争暨世界反法西斯战争胜利七十周年特展
An Exhibition Dedicated to 70th Anniversary of Victory of War of Resistance against
Japanese Aggression and World Anti-fascist War

《新华日报》在重庆中央公园组织的"义卖献金"活动场景
A fund-raising event organized by Xinhua Daily at the Central Park, Chongqing

重庆市民为开展抗日献金活动搭建的"献金台"
A stage set up by Chongqing residents to collect donations for anti-Japanese efforts

16 国民政府军事委员会政治部第三厅
The Third Bureau of the Political Department of the Military Council of the KMT Government

　　1938年4月1日，周恩来领导的主管抗日宣传工作的政治部第三厅在武昌昙华林正式成立，郭沫若任厅长。三厅下设第五、第六、第七三个处，一个漫画宣传队，四个抗敌宣传队，十个抗敌演剧队，一个电影制片厂，三个电影放映队，孩子剧团和新安旅行团。三厅协助文艺界各抗敌协会的工作，促进国统区文艺界的团结和抗战文艺的空前发展，领导开展了轰轰烈烈的全民抗日文化宣传活动。

　　On April 1, 1938, the third bureau of the Political Department under the leadership of Zhou Enlai, mainly responsible for publicity of anti-Japanese ideas, was formed in Tanhualin, Wuchang, Hubei. Guo Moruo acted as the director. The bureau consisted of three departments, one comics team, four publicity teams, ten troupes, one film studio, three film-screening teams, a children troupe and the itinerant Xin'an troupe. It helped artistic organizations to spread anti-Japanese ideas, promote unity and artistic development across the country.

厅　长：郭沫若	副厅长：范　扬	
主任秘书：阳翰笙	秘　书：傅抱石、钱远铎	
第五处：一般宣传	处　长：胡愈之	
第一科：文字编纂	科　长：徐寿轩	刘季平
第二科：民众动员和一般宣传	科　长：张志让	徐　步、陈同生、潘念之
第三科：印刷发行	科　长：尹伯休	钱远铎、罗髯渔
第六处：艺术宣传	处　长：田　汉	
第一科：戏剧音乐	科　长：洪　深	常任侠、辛汉文、石凛鹤、万籁天、张文光、金　山、郑君里、傅心一、龚啸岚、冼星海、张　曙、沙　梅、林　路、任　光、赵启海、李广才
第二科：电影制作发行	科　长：郑用之	应云卫、史东山、程步高、马彦祥
第三科：美术宣传	科　长：徐悲鸿（未到职）吕霞光	叶浅予、张乐平、陆志庠、张　仃、胡　考、宣文杰、梁白波、陶谋基、沈国衡、廖冰兄
第七处：对日宣传和国际宣传	处　长：范寿康	
第一科：对日宣传	科　长：杜国庠	
第二科：国际宣传	科　长：董维健	叶籁士
第三科：辑译资料并研究敌情	科　长：冯乃超	廖体仁
日籍人员	鹿地亘、池田幸子、绿川英子、乔　本	
其　他	全国慰劳总会、战地文化服务处	

国民政府军事委员会政治部第三厅组织结构表
The organization chart of the No. 3 Office of the Political Department of Military and Political Committee under the national government

中国抗日战争暨世界反法西斯战争胜利七十周年特展
An Exhibition Dedicated to 70th Anniversary of Victory of War of Resistance against
Japanese Aggression and World Anti-fascist War

周恩来和三厅部分工作人员在武昌合影

Zhou Enlai was with some staff members of the No. 3
Office inWuchang

1938年夏，周恩来和三厅部分工作人员在武昌
珞珈山合影（前排中一田汉、右二洪深、右三阳
翰笙、右八郭沫若、右九周恩来，后排右一胡愈
之、右四邓颖超、右五于立群、右十四冯乃超、
右十五范寿康）。

**1940年7月27日，三厅成员在赖
家桥永兴场驻地聚会合影**

Staff of the Third Bureau in Yongxing,
Laijiaqiao, Chongqing, On July 27, 1940

**郭沫若夫妇与田汉同三厅、中
国电影制片厂成员在重庆合影**

Mr. and Mrs. Guo Moruo, Tian Han,
staff of the Third Bureau and workers
of the China Film Production Factory in
Chongqing

17 中华全国文艺界抗敌协会
All-China Federation of Anti-Japanese Artists and Writers

中华全国文艺界抗敌协会简称"文协"，是抗日战争时期中国文艺界最广泛的统一战线组织。1938年 3月27日成立于武汉。发起人包括文艺界各方面代表97人。大会选出郭沫若、茅盾、冯乃超、夏衍、胡风、田汉、丁玲、吴组缃、许地山、老舍、巴金、郑振铎、朱自清、郁达夫、朱光潜、张道藩、姚蓬子、陈西滢、王平陵等45人为理事，周恩来、孙科、陈立夫为名誉理事。

The All-China Federation of Anti-Japanese Artists and Writers was the most popular united front in the circle of literature and art during the war. It was founded by ninety-seven social celebrities, many of which were artists and writers, in Wuhan on March 27, 1938. The organization had a 45-member council, which included Guo Moruo, Mao Dun, Feng Naichao, Xia Yan, Hu Feng, Tian Han, Ding Ling, Wu Zuxiang, Xu Dishan, Lao She, Ba Jin, Zheng Zhenduo, Zhu Ziqing, Yu Dafu, Zhu Guangqian, Zhang Daopan, Yao Pengzi, Chen Xiying and Wang Pingling. In addition, Zhou Enlai, Sun Ke and Chen Lifu were honorary members of the council.

中国抗日战争暨世界反法西斯战争胜利七十周年特展
An Exhibition Dedicated to 70th Anniversary of Victory of War of Resistance against
Japanese Aggression and World Anti-fascist War

1938年4月9日在武汉金家花园，胡风与鹿地亘夫妇、艾青夫妇及沙雁

Hu Feng, Mr. and Mrs. Lu Digen, Mr. and Mrs. Ai Qing and Sha Yan at Jin's Garden, Wuhan, April 9, 1938. (provided by Hu Feng's daughter Zhang Xiaofeng)

胡风之女张晓风提供

1939年，"文协"作家战地访问团从重庆出发奔赴山西抗日前线慰问的合影

The delegation of writers in Chongqing preparing to visit Chinese troops in the frontline in Shanxi, 1939

中华全国文艺界抗敌协会原照

The original photo of All-China Artistic Anti-enemy Association

纵27.3、横20.3 厘米
香港翰墨轩（香江博物馆）藏

中华全国文艺界抗敌协会在汉口举行集会，有各地作家300余人参加。日本反战作家鹿地亘也参加该会。该照片是抗战初期全民团结的有力见证，目前传世有两张原件，一件为舒乙征集，藏于中国现代文学馆，周恩来像被遮挡，本件没有。已辨识人物如示：1.邵力子，2.张道藩，3.胡风，4.冯玉祥，5.周恩来，6.陈铭枢，7.鹿地亘，8.盛成，9.姚蓬子，10.爱泼斯坦，11.老舍，12.田汉，13.荒芜，14.茅盾，15.罗果夫。

18 抗战歌咏运动
Singing Movement

　　抗日救亡歌咏运动是中国抗日战争爆发前后遍及全国的群众性爱国歌唱活动。这一运动在1931年九一八事变后开始酝酿，于1935年一二九运动前后形成热潮，至1937年七七事变全面抗战爆发时达到高潮。

　　During the movement the Chinese sang to boost patriotism and promote anti-Japanese ideas. It started after the September 18 Incident of 1931, gained momentum around the December 9 Incident of 1935, and peaked with the outbreak of the July 7 Incident of 1937.

1937年12月25日，全国歌咏协会筹备会成立纪念留影
On December 25, 1937, members of National Singing Association had a group picture

1938年8月9日，武汉举行"漫画歌咏火炬大游行"，在音乐家洗星海的指挥下，游行群众高唱《保卫大武汉》
On August 9, 1938, Wuhan residents launched a massive "art-singing-torch" demonstration. Conducted by famous musician Xian Xinghai, they sang "Defending Great Wuhan"

中国抗日战争暨世界反法西斯战争胜利七十周年特展
An Exhibition Dedicated to 70th Anniversary of Victory of War of Resistance against
Japanese Aggression and World Anti-fascist War

抗日歌曲响彻祖国大地
People sang Anti-Japanese songs everywhere

1938年冼星海在湖北大冶钢厂指挥歌咏队为工人演唱救亡歌曲
In 1938, Xian Xinghai conducted the singing at Hubei Daye Steel Mill in Hubei Province

19 抗战戏剧
Anti-war dramas

抗战戏剧运动，产生于全民抗战的高潮中，其作品丰盛，形式多样，声势浩大，影响深广，在中国现代戏剧史上有独特的重要性。

The Theatric Movement started as the Chinese launched a national war of resistance against Japanese aggression. It witnessed a great variety of plays and had a far-reaching impact on modern Chinese dramatic production.

《放下你的鞭子》剧本(街头剧第一集)

The script of "Put down Your Whip" (Act 1)

1938年
沈西苓等著
湖北省博物馆藏

《三江好》剧本

The script of "Sanjianghao"

1938年
舒强等著
湖北省博物馆藏

该剧描写东北义勇军抗日英雄三江好的传奇故事。

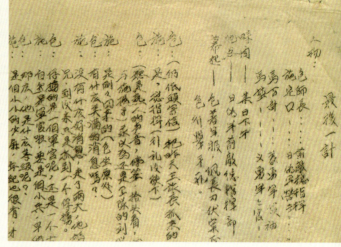

《最后一计》剧本

The script of "Last Trick"

张平群改编
湖北省博物馆藏

该剧改编《凡尔赛俘房》，又名《马百计》。描写敌军围城无法攻破。但是有守军领袖马百计设计的隧道可入城，马被俘后拒不吐实。其弟也被俘，他用最后一计令胞弟饮毒酒而亡。该剧与《放下你的鞭子》、《三江好》合称"好一记鞭子"，抗战时风靡中国。

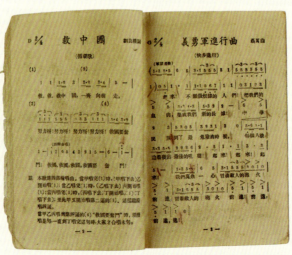

"大家唱"歌本第一集

Volume 1 of Let's Sing, a collection of anti-Japanese songs

抗战时期
16.7、横12.3厘米

中国抗日战争暨世界反法西斯战争胜利七十周年特展
An Exhibition Dedicated to 70th Anniversary of Victory of War of Resistance against
Japanese Aggression and World Anti-fascist War

"芦沟桥"四幕剧本

Script of the four-act play Lugou Bridge

抗战时期
16、横12.5厘米
湖北省博物馆藏

"青救"团员在街头演出"放下你的鞭子"

The members of the Youth Nation-saving Group performed the play "Put down Your Whip"

抗战初期的广场演出"人民战争胜利万岁"

A performance in the early period of the war: "Long Live the Victory of the People's War"

1938年7月，中国电影制片厂拍摄了阳翰笙编剧、应云卫导演的《八百壮士》，主演陈波儿、袁牧之

The film "Eight Hundred Heroes" was shot by China Film Studio in July 1938, written by Yang Hansheng and directed by Ying Yunwei. The cast included Chen Boer and Yuan Muzhi

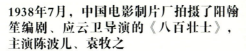

20 抗战美术（一）
Anti-war art

抗战美术是中国美术史辉煌的一页，各种美术类型空前繁荣，抗战美术的最显着特点是美术走向人民，走向现实。

Artworks featuring anti-Japanese themes have a significant role to play in Chinese art history. The art grew and thrived in the war, and the most important characteristic is that they are close to the people and life.

张乐平1938年在武汉街头绘制巨幅壁画《抗战到底》

Zhang Leping painted a huge fresco "Fighting Till the End" on the street of Wuhan (1938)

张善子1937年于武汉创作《怒吼吧，中国！》，并在画旁留影

"Roar, China", by Zhang Shanzi (with his painting) in Wuhan (1937)

叶浅予1938年在武汉创作《为仇恨而生》

"Born to Hate", by Ye Qianyu

中国抗日战争暨世界反法西斯战争胜利七十周年特展
An Exhibition Dedicated to 70th Anniversary of Victory of War of Resistance against
Japanese Aggression and World Anti-fascist War

廖冰兄1938年在武汉创作《筑起我们钢铁的长城》
"Building Our Iron and Steel Great Wall", by Liao Bingxiong

张仃1938年在武汉创作《兽行》
"Beasts' Brutism", by Zhang Ding

李桦1938年在武汉创作《被枷锁着的
中国怒吼了》
"Chained China Roars", by Li Hua

1938年4月10日，在武汉组织抗战美术歌咏火炬游行大会
On April 10, 1938, an "art-singing-torch" demonstration was held at Wuhan
国民党党史馆提供

87

杨立光1938年在武汉创作《保卫大武汉》宣传画

"Defending Great Wuhan" (Poster), by Yang Liguang

1938年春，文艺工作者在湖北航业局团风码头书写"保卫大武汉"

The slogan "Defending Wuhan" on the wall of Tuanfeng Harbor of River Transport Bureau of Hubei Province

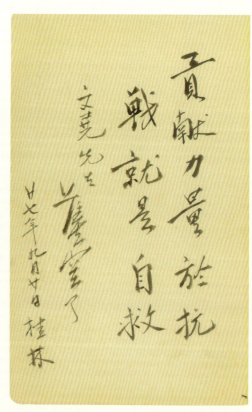

梁寒操行书"待从头收拾旧山河"

Running script by Liang Hancao

1940年代
纵60、横32厘米
香港翰墨轩（香江博物馆）

梁寒操（1898-1975），广东高要人。抗战期间，曾任军事委员会总政治部中将副部长（部长周恩来）兼任中国远征军政治部主任、国民党五届中央宣传部长等。

萨空了行书"贡献力量于抗战就是自救"

Running script by Sha Kongliao

1938年
纵11、横17厘米
香港翰墨轩（香江博物馆）藏

萨空了（1907-1988），内蒙古昭乌达盟翁牛特旗人。抗战中在后方办报纸。新中国成立后协办《光明日报》。

中国抗日战争暨世界反法西斯战争胜利七十周年特展
An Exhibition Dedicated to 70th Anniversary of Victory of War of Resistance against
Japanese Aggression and World Anti-fascist War

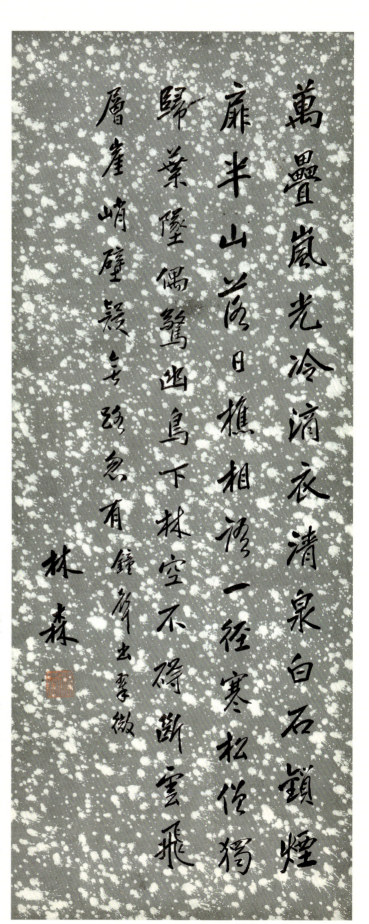

林森行书七言诗

A poem in running script and seven-syllable form, by Lin Sen

1940年代
纵85、横 33.5厘米
香港翰墨轩（香江博物馆）

林森（186-1943），福建闽侯人，民国开国任参议院议长。1931年任国民政府主席。抗战爆发后，林森率国民政府迁都重庆，1941年12月9日，代表国民政府对日宣战。1943年8月1日因车祸在重庆逝世。诗云："万叠岚光冷滴衣，清泉白石锁烟扉。半山落日樵相语，一径寒松僧独归。叶坠偶惊幽鸟下，林空不碍断云飞。层崖峭壁疑无路，忽有钟声出紫微。"

但燾行书诗"慰蒋碧微爱子伯阳参军救国不别而行"

A poem in running script, by Dan Tao

1944 年
纵166、横26 厘米
香港翰墨轩（香江博物馆）

但燾（1881-1970），湖北赤壁人。民国时期著名诗人，抗战中任国民党政府秘书。1946后主持国史馆馆务。蒋碧微（1899-1978），徐悲鸿前妻，其子徐伯阳。诗云："层闱方弃养，子舍远从戎。不负三迁教，安期百战雄。凌云偿壮志，灭虏仁深功。何日收京邑，宁亲笑语同。"

吴佩孚行书七言联

A couplet in running script and seven-syllable form, by Wu Peifu

1930年代
纵168、横 43厘米
香港翰墨轩（香江博物馆）

吴佩孚（1874-1939），山东蓬莱人。抗战爆发后，日本采取拉拢、威逼各种手段都未能让吴佩孚放弃民族气节。董必武评论吴佩孚有两点可贵：一、崇拜关羽、岳飞，不失气节；二、清廉，无私蓄田产。联云："红日半窗临翠榻，绿荫满苑听黄鹂。"

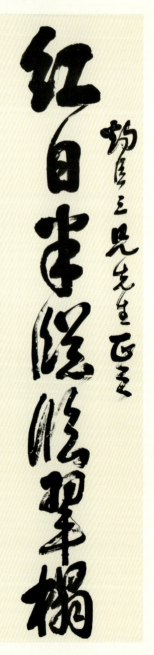

中国抗日战争暨世界反法西斯战争胜利七十周年特展
An Exhibition Dedicated to 70th Anniversary of Victory of War of Resistance against
Japanese Aggression and World Anti-fascist War

張文白先生五十壽頌

天眷有漢若時中興犖犖元帥惟干惟城張君篤生焦湖之瀕翼我元戎

竭厥忠貞黃埔受命小試利器北伐者初策勳飲至江漢洋洋成育多士

闢甕倉卒去官明志浮槎海外偕鏡聞其邦洽聞博見益其閎通遽佐武教

門墻彌崇手裁狂簡千罷萬熊倭夷猾夏四海鼎沸提師抗禦于滬之濱

壬申丁丑兩建旌衔誓過寇虐獻功敲憤管我邦族積弱縈世天挺元戎

攬轡郅治君於其閒命奔馳宛宛周道乃驕乃誹出撫衡湘入贊戎機

忠憂寅恭百賽是儀余始識君戴氏之坐謂君宿將抑何謙下十載還往

以唱以和風雨巴山時溲相適君度休休歃勇韜力鈍不色荏利不自德

古稱有道兩忘得失其薀其淵伊誰䏡測饋國以庸醓爾以臺五十日艾

於君何有春秋既富勳業方盛載筆實賓詩來日之慶

二十八年十月弟陳布雷謹誤

陈布雷楷书张文白先生
五十寿颂

For the 50th Birthday of Zhang
Wenbai, regular script, by
Chen Bulei

1939年
纵115.6、横51.5 厘米
香港翰墨轩（香江博物馆）

陈布雷（1890–1948），浙江慈溪人。抗战中任国民党中央政治会议副秘书长、蒋介石侍从室第二处主任。蒋介石抗战文件多经其手。本件系1939年书与张治中（1890–1969）将军。

周恩来行书

Running script by Zhou Enlai

1938年

纵11、横17 厘米

香港翰墨轩（香江博物馆）藏

抗战期间，桂林作为后方重要基地支援全国抗战。桂林乐群社旅店经理文尧先生在接待抗战名流、政要时索要留言。书云："模范的广西现在已成西南抗战的重心，今后必为西南抗战的模范根据地无疑。"

李济深楷书七言诗

A poem in regular script and seven-syllable form, by Li Jishen

1938年

纵82、横36厘米

香港翰墨轩藏

诗云："别来国事不堪闻，逝去流光忍细陈。无限江山无限恨，重游羞作避秦人。"

黄琪翔行书"我爱桂林"

Running script by Huang Qixiang

1938年

纵11、横17 厘米

香港翰墨轩（香江博物馆）藏

黄琪翔（1898–1970），广东梅县人。抗战时历任第九集团军副总司令、第八集团军总司令、国民政府军委会政治部副部长、第二十六集团军总司令、第五战区副司令长官、第二十二集团军总司令、第六战区副司令长官、中国抗日远征军副司令长官等。新中国成立后任全国政协常委。

中国抗日战争暨世界反法西斯战争胜利七十周年特展
An Exhibition Dedicated to 70th Anniversary of Victory of War of Resistance against
Japanese Aggression and World Anti-fascist War

杜其章令人太息好湖山图

Painting of Beautiful Landscape,
by Du Qizhang

1930年代
纵112.5、横 34厘米
香港翰墨轩（香江博物馆）

杜其章（1897-1942），福建泉州人。早年参加反清革命，民国后在香港亦商亦文，为当时书画文艺界领袖。抗战中为救国难，他在港澳等地办画展，宣传抗敌救国。本件作于九一八国难日。

梁鼎铭司徒美堂像

Portrait of Situ Meitang, by Liang
Dingming

1942年
纵112.5、横50厘米
香港翰墨轩（香江博物馆）

梁鼎铭（1898-1959），广东顺德人。著名画家。1926年聘为黄埔军校教官。司徒美堂（1868-1955），旅美侨领，中国致公党创始人。抗战时，他发起成立"纽约华侨抗日救国筹饷总会"。1955年病逝于北京。

20 抗战美术（二）
Anti-war art

　　1937年抗战全面爆发后，武汉一时成为全国抗战的中心，版画艺术家也聚集在此。胡风先生在武汉主编的《七月》是扶持、发表抗战版画作品的重要刊物。1938年胡风先生在武汉主办了"全国抗敌木刻画展览会"，对抗战文艺和现代版画艺术起到了重要的推动作用。

　　Wuhan used to be China's capital when the anti-Japanese war broke out in 1937. Woodcut artists went to the city from all over the country. July magazine edited by Mr. Hu Feng in Wuhan served as an important publication for anti-Japanese woodcuts. Mr. Hu Feng organized in 1938 the Exhibition of Anti-Japanese Woodcuts in Wuhan, substantially promoting the development of the anti-Japanese literature and art and modern woodcut art of China.

马达《抗敌军的防御战》

A Defensive Battle against the Japanese Army by Ma Da

1938年
纵9.8、横14.9厘米
北京鲁迅博物馆暨新文化运动纪念馆藏

此画作曾刊登于《七月》第三集第五期封面（1938年7月1日出版），原名"圣地卢沟桥"。

胡风主编抗战刊物《七月》（半月刊）

The fifth edition of Vol. 3 of July magazine (semi-monthly), published on July 1, 1938, by July Magazine; editor: Hu Feng

1938年
胡风之女张晓风捐赠
湖北省博物馆藏

《七月》1937年9月17日创刊于上海，印行3期后迁武汉，改半月刊，印行18期后再迁重庆。1941年9后停刊。前后4年，共出32期计30册。《七月》的作者主要是"七月派"作家群，尤以诗歌见长。

中国抗日战争暨世界反法西斯战争胜利七十周年特展
An Exhibition Dedicated to 70th Anniversary of Victory of War of Resistance against
Japanese Aggression and World Anti-fascist War

野夫《保卫我们的城池》
Safeguarding Our City by Ye Fu

1937年
纵15.5、横21厘米
北京鲁迅博物馆暨新文化运动纪念馆藏

此画作曾刊登于《七月》旬刊第二期第
20页（1937年9月18日出版）。

野夫《拿起我们自己的武器》
Take on Our Weapons by Ye Fu

1930年代
纵19.1、横16.6厘米
北京鲁迅博物馆暨新文化运动纪念馆藏

画面下方有题字："拿起我们自己的武
器。野夫"。

野夫《廿九军之忿恨》
The Hatred of the Twenty-ninth Army by Ye Fu

1930年代
纵22.9、横17.2厘米
北京鲁迅博物馆暨新文化运动纪念馆藏

画面下方有题字："廿九军之忿恨。野夫"。

野夫《到前线去吧！走上民族解放的战场》
Go Fighting! To Liberate Our Nation by Ye Fu

1930年代
纵19.4、横13.7厘米
北京鲁迅博物馆暨新文化运动纪念馆藏

画面右方有题字："到前线去吧！走上民族解放的战场。野夫"。

张慧《台儿庄》
Tai Er Zhuang by Zhang Hui

1938年
纵24.3、横18.6厘米
北京鲁迅博物馆暨新文化运动纪念馆藏

画面右下有标记"XY"。

张慧《不许敌人越雷池一步》
Keep the Enemy Far Away by Zhang Hui

1938年
纵15.9、横12.2厘米
北京鲁迅博物馆暨新文化运动纪念馆藏

画面右侧有题字："不许敌人越雷池一
步。张慧作"。

中国抗日战争暨世界反法西斯战争胜利七十周年特展
An Exhibition Dedicated to 70th Anniversary of Victory of War of Resistance against
Japanese Aggression and World Anti-fascist War

许生《最后关头》

The last minute by Xu Sheng

1937年
纵16、横11厘米
北京鲁迅博物馆暨新文化运动纪念馆藏

此画曾刊登于《七月》第一期第8页
（1937年10月16日出版）。

沃渣《全民一致的力量》

The Power of Unit by Wo Zha

1937年
纵13、横10.2厘米
北京鲁迅博物馆暨新文化运动纪念馆藏

画面左下角有"XXX"符号签名，曾刊
登于《七月》第一期第1页（1937年10
月16日出版）。

**沃渣《敌人同野兽一样的横暴，我们
必须发动全国的力量消灭它》**

We Must Rally Around to Eliminate the Ferocious
Enemies by Wo Zha

1937年
纵15.5、横15.4厘米
北京鲁迅博物馆暨新文化运动纪念馆藏

右下角有"XXX"字样签名。

张在民《骑兵冲锋》

Charging Cavalrymen

1930年代
纵18.1、横6.4厘米
北京鲁迅博物馆暨新文化运动纪念馆藏

左下角有标记"在民"。

卢鸿基《"儿呀，为了祖国，勇敢些！"》

"Be brave, my son! For our homeland!" by Lu Hongji

1930年代
纵27.1、横20.1厘米
北京鲁迅博物馆暨新文化运动纪念馆藏

下方有题字："儿呀，为了祖国，勇敢些！"

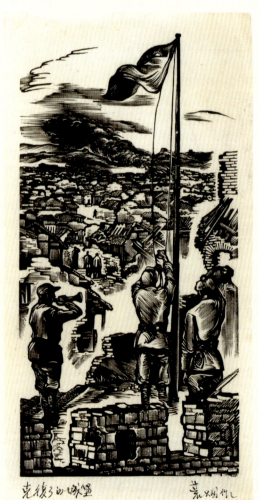

荒烟《克复了的城堡》

A Fort Recovered by Huang Yan

1930年代
纵19.8、横10.4厘米
北京鲁迅博物馆暨新文化运动纪念馆藏

下方有签字："克复了的城堡，荒烟作"。

中国抗日战争暨世界反法西斯战争胜利七十周年特展
An Exhibition Dedicated to 70th Anniversary of Victory of War of Resistance against
Japanese Aggression and World Anti-fascist War

21 卢作孚和民生轮船公司
Lu Zuofu and Minsheng Shipping Company

　　卢作孚（1893-1952），重庆合川人。1938年10月武汉沦陷前，30万吨抗战物资和3万多难民滞留宜昌。卢作孚民生公司在40天内，完成了大部分的积压物资和全部人员的内迁工作。这一壮举，被赞誉为"中国实业界的敦刻尔克"。

　　Lu Zuofu (1893-1952) was born in Hechuan, Chongqing. Within 40 days, his Minsheng Shipping Company succeeded in transferring about 300,000 tons of supplies and more than 30,000 refugees that were trapped in Yichang to the southwest before the fall of Wuhan in October 1938. The mission was acclaimed as the "Dunkirk Evacuation of Chinese Business".

卢作孚像
Lu Zhuofu

1938年，民生轮船公司在川江上搬运抗战物资
Minsheng Shipping Company handling supplieses on the Yangtze River in 1938

三　敌后战场

III BATTLEFIELDS BEHIND ENEMY LINES

日本侵略者占领我东北、华北、华中、华东、华南全部及大部地区后，抗日战场形成了敌后与正面两个战场。敌后战场主要由中共领导的八路军、新四军、华南抗日纵队和东北抗日联军抗击日寇，共作战125165次，毙伤日军52万余人、伪军49万余人，成为中国抗战的中流砥柱。另外，正面战场的9个战区和冀察、鲁苏战区的配属的游击队约80余万人也在敌后作战共17681次。敌后战场钳制和歼灭日军大量兵力，歼灭大部分伪军，在战争后期逐渐成为抗日战争的主战场。

As Japan occupied large territories that spanned northeastern, northern, central, eastern and southern China, there emerged two forms of battlefields: the frontline battlefield and the battlefield behind enemy lines. The latter involved the Eighth Route Army, the New Fourth Army, the Southern China Anti-Japanese Column, and the Northeast Anti-Japanese United Army, all of which were led by the CPC. These troops caused 520,000 Japanese casualties and 490,000 casualties on the part of puppet troops in 125,165 battles, thus making the battlefield behind enemy lines a mainstay of the final victory. In addition, the battlefield saw KMT-led troops in nine war theaters of the frontline battlefields and about 800,000 guerrilla forces in Hebei, Chahar, Shandong and Jiangsu engaged in 17,681 battles behind enemy lines. The battlefield behind enemy lines became the main front in the late period of the war, because they tied down and eliminated a large number of Japanese soldiers and puppet troops.

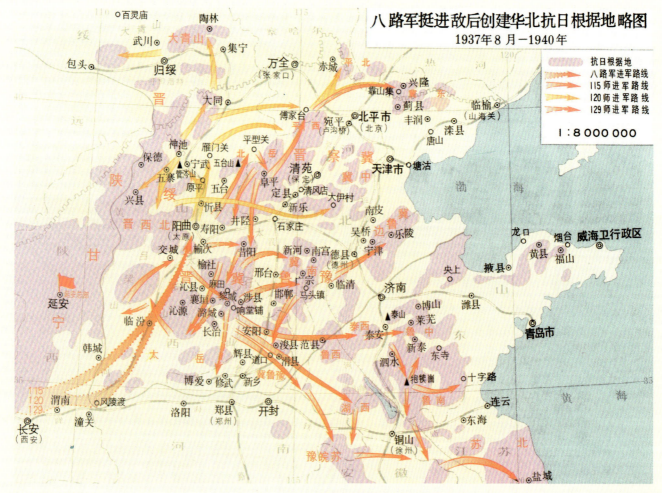

引自武月星主编：《中国现代史地图集（1919-1949）》，中国地图出版社，2000年。

中国抗日战争暨世界反法西斯战争胜利七十周年特展
An Exhibition Dedicated to 70th Anniversary of Victory of War of Resistance against
Japanese Aggression and World Anti-fascist War

新四军第五师参谋处制双河镇地图

A map produced by the Staff Section of the Fifth Division of the New
Fourth Army

抗战时期
纵43.5、横54.2厘米
湖北省博物馆藏

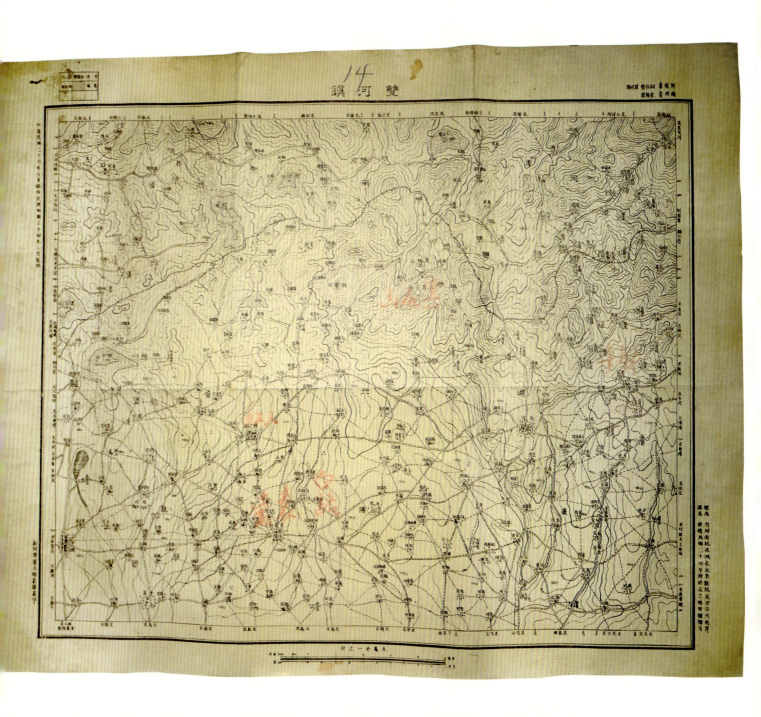

抗日铜牌
A copper medal for anti-Japanese effort

1940年代
长4.3、宽2.3厘米
湖北省博物馆藏

鄂豫边区建设银行印钞票的石板
A stone template used to print banknotes by the Construction Bank of Hubei-Henan Border Area

抗战时期
17.7、横23厘米
湖北省博物馆藏

豫鄂边区根据地为阻止日伪、汪伪货币在根据地的流通，于1940年4月成立建设银行并发行货币的决定。初成立的建设银行发钞。从1941年5月至1942年年底先后组建了印钞厂3个，分别设立于湖北的天汉湖区、大别山地区和湖北黄冈地区。先后共印制五角、壹元、贰元、叁元、伍元、拾元、伍拾元、壹百元、贰百元、伍百元、壹仟元等11种面额、15种版别的纸币。

中国抗日战争暨世界反法西斯战争胜利七十周年特展

An Exhibition Dedicated to 70th Anniversary of Victory of War of Resistance against
Japanese Aggression and World Anti-fascist War

豫鄂边区建设银行伍圆票

Banknotes issued by the Construction Bank
of Hubei-Henan Border Area

抗战时期
纵6.3、横12.1厘米
湖北省博物馆藏

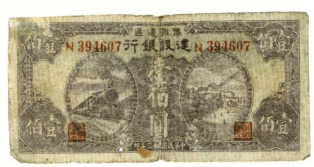

豫鄂边区建设银行壹佰圆票

Banknotes issued by the Construction Bank of Hubei-
Henan Border Area

抗战时期
纵6.4、横13.5厘米
湖北省博物馆藏

豫鄂边区建设银行伍佰圆票

Banknotes issued by the Construction Bank of Hubei-Henan Border
Area

抗战时期
纵6.8、横14.6厘米
湖北省博物馆藏

豫鄂边区建设银行壹仟圆票

Banknotes issued by the Construction Bank of Hubei-Henan
Border Area

抗战时期
纵6.8、横15.4厘米
湖北省博物馆藏

指南针
Compass
抗战时期
直径4.4厘米
钱运铎捐赠
湖北省博物馆藏

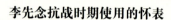

李先念抗战时期使用的怀表
A pocket watch used by Li Xiannian during the war
抗战时期
直径4.8厘米
九江市政府钟华捐赠
湖北省博物馆藏

钱运镜烈士抗日军政大学毕业证书
Martyr Qian Yunjing's graduation certificate, issued by the Anti-Japanese Military and Political College
抗战时期
纵15.5、横19.6厘米
钱运铎捐赠
湖北省博物馆藏

中国抗日战争暨世界反法西斯战争胜利七十周年特展
An Exhibition Dedicated to 70th Anniversary of Victory of War of Resistance against
Japanese Aggression and World Anti-fascist War

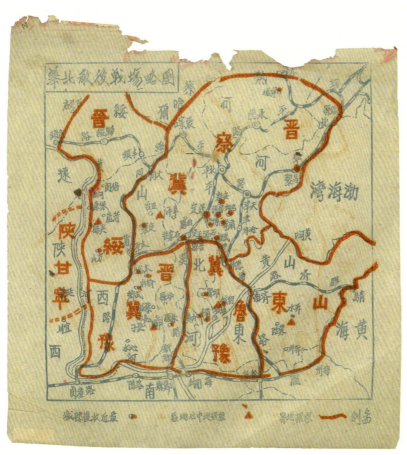

华北敌后战场略图

A map of battlefields behind enemy lines in northern China

抗战时期
纵24.6、横23.1厘米
湖北省博物馆藏

戴笠致显光先生书函

Letters written to Mr. Xianguang by Dai Li

纵30、横21厘米
台湾中华海峡两岸文化资产交流促进会名誉理
事长王水衷藏，台湾美术馆提供

1938年3月13日，戴笠接奉蒋介石电令，收容整
编流散京沪杭沿线国军，以"忠义救国军"名
义进行敌后游击。本件为戴笠答复孙鉴有关开
展敌后抗战事宜。

崇祉

頌

晚 戴笠 歗上 四月廿七日

（八）孫同志與其報務員應於五月二日乘中航班機飛渝實難機票由本局代辦以上八項款請孫同志洽辦為禱專懇專順

（七）工作人員之姓名及履歷等後仍應分別詳報以便轉呈委座否則本局無法報銷也

（六）對為軍策反成功之委任令必要時當呈請 委座准予便宜行事惟須將策反之經過呈報中央時方能照辦

（五）行動工作可不進行破壞工作進展後再議

（四）經臨費國幣壹百萬圓准在渝發給請促來局具領

日来領

（三）家電本准改發小型者並請於出發前二

（二）內勤編審與譯電人員如孫同志能自行物色可准免派抵目的地後依照用人一條例與其他新同志一併報備

（一）電台通報之呼號波長等請即與董益三同志面洽

十四日函弟商討敷事茲分別答復如下

顯光先生賜鑒 孫鑑同志曾於四月二

22 百团大战
Hundred Regiments Offensive

中共领导的八路军从1940年8月15日至1941年1月24日，发动了以破袭正太铁路（石家庄至太原）为重点的战役。作战地区囊括冀察全境、晋绥大部及热南大部，投入兵力105个团。日军110师团、25师团全部，26、35、36、37、41师团部分联队，第1、第2、第3、第4、第5、第7、第9混成旅团全部，第6、第15独立混成旅团一部，还有大量伪军参战。战役歼日伪军5万余人，八路军伤亡一万七千余人。百团大战给日伪军以沉重打击，鼓舞了中国军民的抗战斗志。

The Hundred Regiments Offensive was a major campaign of the CPC's Eighth Route Army from August 15, 1940 to January 24, 1941. One of the strategic goals was to destroy the Shijiazhuang-Taiyuan railway line. A total of 105 regiments were deployed in the campaign that spanned the entire Hebei and Chahar, and large parts of Shanxi, Suiyuan and southern Jehol. Japan responded with the engagement of the entire 110th and 25th divisions, some troops of the 26th, 35th, 36th, 37th and 41st divisions, the 1st, 2nd, 3rd, 4th, 5th, 7th and 9th mixed brigades, and the 1st company from the 6th and 15th independent mixed brigades, as well as puppet troops. The campaign ended with 50,000 Japanese casualties and 17,000 Chinese casualties. It dealt a heavy blow to the Japanese army, while at the same time, boosting the morale of the Chinese army and the general public.

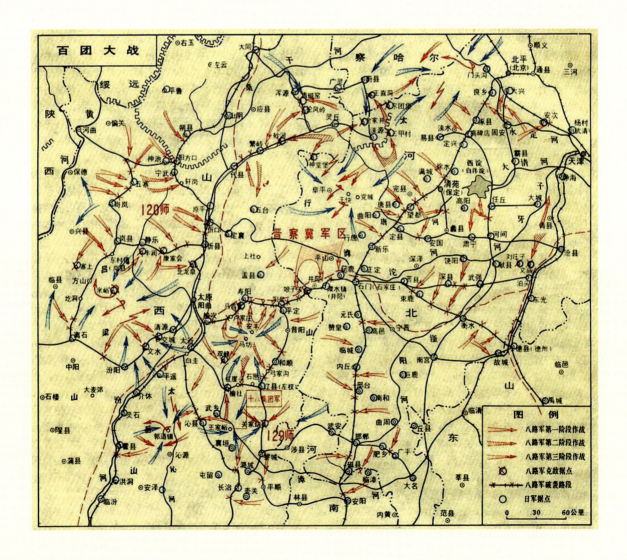

中国抗日战争暨世界反法西斯战争胜利七十周年特展
An Exhibition Dedicated to 70th Anniversary of Victory of War of Resistance against
Japanese Aggression and World Anti-fascist War

指挥百团大战的彭德怀将军
Generals Peng Dehuai is commanding Hundred Regiments Offensive

八路军破坏敌军碉堡
Eighth Route Army destroy enemy bunkers

107

四　日本扶持的主要汉奸政权
IV PUPPET REGIMENTS

甲午战争之后，日本极力在华培植亲日反共势力成为其吞并中国的重要内容。九一八事变之后，日本军国主义在东北扶植溥仪建立伪满洲国，在华北扶植殷汝耕搞"华北自治"，在内蒙扶植德王（即德穆楚克栋鲁普亲王）的伪蒙古联合自治政府。七七事变后，扶植以王克敏为首的华北伪中华民国临时政府和以梁鸿志为首的南京伪中华民国维新政府。1940年，汪精卫投敌后，在维新政府基础上成立伪国民政府。这些汉奸政权在抗战期间助纣为虐，战后都受到历史和正义的审判。

After the Sino-Japanese War of 1894-1895, Japan began to put an emphasis on cultivating pro-Japanese and anti-communist forces in China. Following the September 18 Incident, Japan installed Puyi as the Chief Executive of Manchukuo, a puppet state of the Empire of Japan, instigated Yin Rugeng to launch the so-called "self-governing of North China", and encouraged Prince Demchugdongrub to set up the Mengjiang United Autonomous Government. In the wake of the July 7 Incident, Japan supported the Provisional Government of the Republic of China led by Wang Kemin, and the Reformed Government of the Republic of China led by Liang Hongzhi, which was merged into Wang Jingwei's Nationalist government in Nanjing in 1940. Those puppet regiments, a stooges for the Japanese army, were overthrown and the traitors were brought to justice after the war.

23 伪满洲国
Manchukuo

伪满洲国（1932-1945）是日本占领东三省后扶植的傀儡政权。它以清朝末代皇帝溥仪为执政（后称皇帝），定都新京（长春），先后以"大同"、"康德"为年号。"领土"包括现东三省全境（不含"关东州"，即旅大）及内蒙古东部、河北承德。

Manchukuo (1932-1945) was a puppet state established by Japan after seizing the northeastern region. Puyi, the last Qing emperor, was installed as the head of Manchukuo with the reign title of Kangde. The Changchun-based puppet state controlled the entire northeastern region (excluding Lvda which is called Dalian today), eastern Mongol and Chengde of Hebei province.

24 伪蒙古军政府
Mongol Military Government

1936年至1937年，日本在察哈尔省扶植伪蒙古军政府，由内蒙古民族分裂分子德王（德穆楚克栋普鲁）于1936年策划组建。

The Mongol Military Government was formed in 1936 by Prince Demchugdongrub at the instigation of the Japanese, who had been forming pro-Japanese governments in Chahar in 1936-1937.

德王行书
Running script by Prince Demchugdongrub
纵130、横 38厘米
香港翰墨轩（香江博物馆）藏

德王（1902-1966），即德穆楚克栋普鲁，内蒙古锡林郭勒盟苏尼特右旗人，1908袭爵札萨克多罗杜棱郡王。1913年北洋政府授为札萨克和硕杜棱亲王。抗战时期，日本扶植其出任蒙古联盟自治政府主席。1963年被新中国政府特赦释放。

中国抗日战争暨世界反法西斯战争胜利七十周年特展
An Exhibition Dedicated to 70th Anniversary of Victory of War of Resistance against
Japanese Aggression and World Anti-fascist War

25 南京汪伪政权
Wang Jingwei Collaborationist Regime in Nanjing

　　1938年12月汪精卫逃离重庆，在越南河内发表降敌"艳电"。在日本扶持下于1940年3月30日在南京建立伪国民政府。汪精卫任行政院院长兼代主席，伪阁员有立法院院长陈公博、司法院院长温宗尧、监察院院长梁鸿志、考试院院长王揖唐、财政部长兼中央政治委员会秘书长周佛海等。1945年日本投降后随之覆灭。

　　In December 1938, Wang Jingwei left Chongqing for Hanoi, Vietnam, where he announced his support for a negotiated settlement with the Japanese. On March 30, 1940, he formed the Reorganized National Government of China in Nanjing, serving as the President of the Executive Yuan and Chairman of the government. Chen Gongbo was the President of the Legislative Yuan, Wen Zongyao the President of the Judicial Yuan, Liang Hongzhi the President of the Control Yuan, Wang Yitang the President of the Examination Yuan, and Zhou Fohai the Minister of Finance and Secretary of the Central Political Committee. The regimen collapsed after the surrender of Japan in 1945.

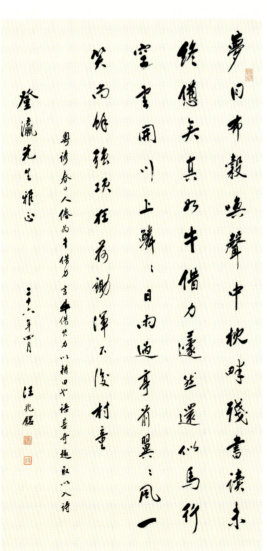

汪兆铭（精卫）行书七言诗

A poem in running script and seven-syllable form, by Wang Jingwei

1937年
纵126.5、横62.5 厘米
香港翰墨轩（香江博物馆）藏

汪精卫（1883–1944），广东三水人，本名汪兆铭，笔名精卫。孙中山遗嘱执笔人。1938年12月29日汪精卫发出"艳电"投敌。本件为投敌前所作，诗云："梦回布谷唤声中，枕畔残书读未终。惫矣真如牛借力，蓬然还似马行空。云开川上鳞鳞日，雨过亭前翼翼风。一笑尚余强项在，荷锄浑不后村童。"

周佛海行书

Running script by Zhou Fohai

1940年代（？）
纵118、横 31.5厘米
香港翰墨轩（香江博物馆）

周佛海（1897–1948），湖南省沅陵人，中共一大代表，后脱党投蒋介石。抗战中叛国投日，战后被处决。
书云："赵吴兴为中锋书全类李北海，其诗亦学韩昌黎。古川宪之先生正之。"

26 伪中华民国临时政府
Collaborationist Provisional Government of the Republic of China

1937年12月14日，日本侵略者扶植汉奸王克敏、王揖唐等在北平成立的汉奸政权。1940年3月30日，汪精卫的伪"中华民国国民政府"在南京成立后，北平伪"临时政府"改称"华北政务委员会"，名义上隶属南京汪伪政权，实际上仍保持相对的独立性。

On December 14, 1937, Wang Kemin and Wang Yitang formed the Provisional Government of the Republic of China in Beijing, with the backing of Japan. After the establishment of Wang Jingwei's Reorganized National Government in Nanjing on March 30, 1940, the puppet government was renamed the North China Political Affairs Commission. It was affiliated to Wang's government only in the nominal sense; it remained virtually independent.

江朝宗行楷诗赠寺内寿一大将
Jiang Chaozong, a poem in running-regular script to General Terauchi Hisaichi

1938
纸本
纵39、横144.5厘米
台湾董良彦先生提供

江朝宗（1861–1943），安徽省旌德人。北洋政府时期曾任国务院代总理。抗战中投日沦为汉奸，任伪北平市长。寺内寿一，日本陆军大将，甲级战犯。七七事变后任北支那派遣军司令，1941年任南方军总司令，占领东南亚全境，晋封元帅。1946年病死南洋。

齐燮元行书五言诗
A poem in running script and five-syllable form, by Qi Xieyuan

1940年代
纵130、横 38厘米
香港翰墨轩（香江博物馆）藏

齐燮元（1879–1946），河北宁河人。曾任江苏军务督办、苏皖赣巡阅副使。与王克敏、王揖唐等成立伪华北临时政府，任华北政务委员会委员兼治安总署督办、伪华北绥靖军总司令，1946年在南京被处决。诗云："生前谁是我，身后我是谁。无我方为我，欺人是自欺。"

中国抗日战争暨世界反法西斯战争胜利七十周年特展
An Exhibition Dedicated to 70th Anniversary of Victory of War of Resistance against
Japanese Aggression and World Anti-fascist War

"中华民国临时政府"成立二周年纪念章
Medal in memory of the 2nd anniversary of the foundation
of the 'provisional government of the Republic of China'

1939年
径2.4厘米
台湾董良彦先生提供

27 维新政府
Reformed Government of the Republic of China

日军占领上海、南京后扶植伪中华民国维新政府，管辖苏、浙、皖三省的日占区和宁、沪两个特别市。梁鸿志、温宗尧、陈群、任援道、傅筱庵等为其要员。1940年并入汪伪政权。

After the capture of Shanghai and Nanjing, Japan authorized the creation of the Reformed Government of the Republic of China. It was assigned control of Jiangsu, Zhejiang and Anhui as well as the two municipalities of Nanjing and Shanghai, all of which were occupied by Japan. The top officials of the puppet regime included Liang Hongzhi, Wen Zongyao, Chen Qun, Ren Yuandao and Fu Xiaoan. In 1940 it was merged into Wang Jingwei collaborationist regime.

梁鸿志行书赠郑孝胥诗
Zheng Xiaoxu's poem written in running script by Liang Hongzhi

1940年代
纵28、横29.7 厘米
香港翰墨轩（香江博物馆）藏

梁鸿志（1882-1946），福建长乐人。为人狂傲，以东坡自许。抗战期间投靠日本，沦为汉奸，出任伪中华民国维新政府行政院长。郑孝胥（1860-1938），福建省闽候人。前清遗老，1932年出任伪满洲国总理大臣兼文教总长，有《海藏楼诗集》。诗云："液池一角未荒残，中有畸人警岁寒。自写幽忧成独往，强标清赏泥朋欢。千桑万海供谈茗，菊后梅前此倚栏。历劫瀛台东去水，等闲休作画图看。"

第二单元 正面战场

七七事变后，中国抗战分为正面（内线）和敌后（外线）两个战场。从1937年到1945年，正面战场的态势又分为战略守势（含淞沪、太原、徐州、武汉会战）、相持（含南昌、随枣、第一次长沙、桂南、枣宜、豫南、上高、晋南、第二、第三次长沙会战）、同盟作战（含滇缅路、浙赣、鄂西、常德、豫中、长衡会战）、反攻（含缅北、桂柳、豫西-鄂北、湘西会战）四个阶段。因中日国力悬殊，国民政府虽坚持抗战，但国军在初期的会战败多胜少，直到太平洋战争后期，同盟国援助加大才扭转劣势。据统计，正面战场22场会战（不计滇缅战场）共毙、伤日军170余万人（日方数字为约45万），为世界反法西斯取得胜利作出了重大贡献。

After the July 7 Incident, the war was fought both in the frontlines and behind enemy lines. It can be divided into four stages between 1937 and 1945. In the first stage Chinese troops were on the defensive in Shanghai, Taiyuan, Xuzhou and Wuhan; and then Chinese and Japanese troops reached a stalemate in Nanchang, Suixian-Zaoyang, southern Guilin, Zaoyang-Yichang, southern Henan, Shanggao, southern Shanxi and three major battles in Changsha; afterwards Chinese troops fought alongside the Allies along the Yunnan-Burma Road and Zhejiang, Ganzhou, western Hubei, Changde, central Henan and Changsha and Hengyang; and in the fourth stage Chinese troops launched counterattacks in northern Burma, Guilin and Liuzhou, western Henan and southern Hubei, and western Hunan. Despite the persistent resistance of the Kuomintang government, the NRA suffered more defeats than victories, due to a huge gap of national strength. The situation was reversed at the end of the Pacific War with more support from the Allies. Chinese troops killed and injured 1.7 million (about 450,000 according to Japanese statistics) Japanese troops in 22 major battles in the frontlines (Yunnan-Burma Theater excluded), making great contributions to the success of the global war against fascism.

一　重要会战
I MAJOR BATTLES

抗战期间，敌我双方在指挥、装备、战术、士兵素质方面差别巨大，但我军与日军在正面战场仍进行了多次重大会战。何应钦在《抗战八年之经过》中列举了22场。事实上，抗战期间大型战役不止这22场。像百团大战，规模是战役级别。而有些会战，如兰封会战、南昌会战也是徐州会战和武汉会战的延续。缅北和滇西战役是太平洋战争的组成部分，也不在22次会战中。我军正面战场的会战伤亡惨重，但也粉碎了日军灭亡中国的野心。

During the war Chinese troops engaged in many serious frontal battles against Japan, despite the huge gap in military leadership, equipment, tactics, and soldiers' performance. In his Eight Years of War against Japanese Aggression, He Yingqin enumerated 22 major battles, though the actual number is much larger. For example, the Hundred Regiments Offensive is of a campaign scale, and the Battle of Lanfeng and the Battle of Nanchang are part of larger campaigns in Xuzhou and Wuhan, respectively. Battles in northern Burma and western Yunnan are not included into the 22 engagements, though they are critical to the Pacific War. China suffered great casualties in frontal battles, but it frustrated Japanese ambition of subjugating China.

1-1　淞沪会战（1937. 8.13-11.11）
Battle of Songhu (1937. 8.13-11.11)

淞沪会战是中日在不宣战的情况下之首场会战，也是中国抗战规模最大的战役。七七事变后，中方意图将日军南侵方向变为由东向西，以利于长期作战，在上海主动反击日军而引发。战役持续三个月，中方兵力约80万，伤亡33万，日方兵力20余万，伤亡约10万。淞沪会战中方损失惨重，但也彻底粉碎了日本"三个月灭亡中国"的狂妄计划。

The Battle of Songhu, also known as the Battle of Shanghai, was the first engagement between China and Japan, and also the largest of the entire war, and both parties did not declare war on each other. After the July 7 Incident, China aimed to force Japan to adopt an east-to-west direction of attack, in order to gain long-term strategic advantage, and thus counterattacked Japanese troops in Shanghai. During the fierce three-month battle, about 800,000 Chinese soldiers fought against about 200,000 Japanese soldiers. The battle caused 330,000 Chinese casualties and 100,000 Japanese casualties. China suffered a huge loss of manpower, but successfully frustrated Japanese ambition of overcoming China in three months.

中国抗日战争暨世界反法西斯战争胜利七十周年特展

An Exhibition Dedicated to 70th Anniversary of Victory of War of Resistance against
Japanese Aggression and World Anti-fascist War

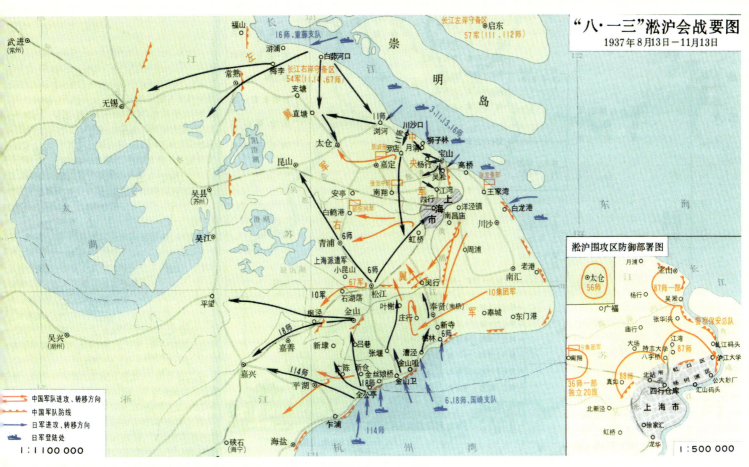

"八·一三"淞沪会战要图
1937年8月13日—11月13日

引自武月星主编:《中国现代史地图集(1919–1949)》, 中国地图出版社, 2000年。

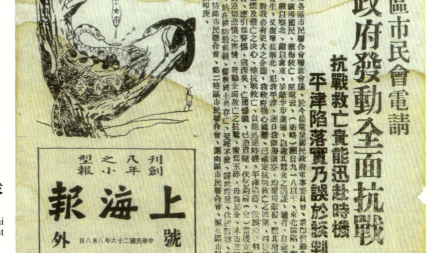

《上海报》号外上海人民电请政府发
动全面抗战

An extra to Shanghai Paper reading that Shanghai
residents ask the government to launch an all-out
was of resistance

1937年8月8日
纵24.7、横29.4 厘米
香港翰墨轩(香江博物馆)藏

大家看報

27.
廿七年十月五日
—第八集團軍戰地服務隊編—

注意清潔　保重身体

天氣遠很熱，蒼蠅到處飛，飛到食物上和狗屎牛屎著不管，要生病。蚊子多得很，實在吃不了就生病，氣味臭薰薰，聞了要暈頭，身體最要緊，就得講衛生，房屋掃乾淨，不要蒼蠅停，處處講清潔，永久不害病。

◎軍民合作◎

各位父老兄弟姊妹：殺人放火的日本鬼子快要打到我们的頭上来了！我们是中國人，住的是中國土地，我们的姊妹兄弟能不能讓日本鬼子隨便強殺死呢？不能！我们生在這裡，長在這裡，誰要搶去一尺一寸土地，我们就跟他拼！大家起来想辦法，保衛自己保衛國家！軍隊是替老百姓打仗的，是為我们拼命的，我们应該帮助他们，应該同他们合作，燒茶水，挑担子，領路，挖戰壕……都是我们出力帮忙的方法，我们盡力的做去，然後打勝仗才有辦法。大家不有好日子過。

—軍民合作歌—

我们都是中國人，不分軍隊老百姓，
人民帮助軍隊，軍隊愛護人民，
相親相愛，萬众一心，
我们軍民合作，打倒強盜小日本，
我们抗戰到底，趕走強盜享太平。

＝躲飛機的方法＝

「日本飛機太可惡，專門炸我们老百姓，房子被他燒個光，大家要學躲避法，第一當心白衣服，第二莫要隨便跑，第三莫辞抬頭看飛機炸彈丟下時，卧倒地下不出聲，鬼子炸彈等於零。」

「人人照著這樣做」

"放小腳"

我說啦你那大姑娘太愚蠢，腳板本是天生就，何必包得像顆針，走路不方便，做事也不行，出門也不好見客人，再說時代已超新，哪個另男要個尖尖脚，更何況鬼子快要打到大门口，男女都要當兵，大姑娘，勸你趕快把腳放，勸伯娘趕快打東洋。

—老百姓是異厚愛國的新聞—

鬼子怕了我们的地方，總要吃虧，不信且往下看，山西河津縣有個張民……

請識字的人唸給不識字的人聽，講給不識字的人聽。

抗战墙报《大家看报》

News for All, a wall newspaper spreading anti-Japanese ideas

1938年10月5日
第八集团军战地服务队编
纵72、横69厘米
香港翰墨轩（香江博物馆）藏

抗战爆发后，第八集团军总司令朱绍良请郭沫若帮忙筹建战地服务队。在周恩来指示下，上海中共党组刘晓、潘汉年、钱亦石、夏衍等鼓动文化界人士和热血青年参加战地服务队。首任队长是周恩来推荐的湖北咸宁钱亦石。该墙报在湖北阳新编制，由共产党员郭弼昌、杨治明手写，沈振黄插画。本件乃为国共合作共同抗战的实物。

中国抗日战争暨世界反法西斯战争胜利七十周年特展
An Exhibition Dedicated to 70th Anniversary of Victory of War of Resistance against
Japanese Aggression and World Anti-fascist War

淞沪抗战纪念章
A medal for the Battle of Shanghai

抗战时期
4.3、横3.2厘米
湖北省博物馆藏

刷在墙上的抗战标语
Anti-Japanese mobilizing slogans painted on the wall

黄浦江上的日本军舰
Japanese warship on the Huangpu River

淞沪会战期间的我军阵地
Our positions during the battle of Songhu

我军某部正在阵地前沿紧张地进行通讯联络

A unit of our army was busy communicating on the frontal position

罗店我军缴获敌人的步枪与轻机枪

Enemies' rifles and light machine-guns captured by our soldiers at Luodian

淞沪会战期间，海军鱼雷快艇突袭黄浦江日舰

Chinese torpedo boats launch surprise attacks on Japanese ships in the Battle of Shanghai

中国抗日战争暨世界反法西斯战争胜利七十周年特展
An Exhibition Dedicated to 70th Anniversary of Victory of War of Resistance against
Japanese Aggression and World Anti-fascist War

1-2 四行仓库和八百壮士
800 Heroes in Defense of Sihang Warehouse

　　淞沪会战后期，苏州河以北仅剩八十八师五二四团副团长谢晋元所率的第一营。该营因减员临时补充了由湖北通城保安大队改编的湖北第五保安团的半数士兵，兵力约四百人，坚守四行（金城、中南、大陆及盐业银行）仓库4日，谢对外宣称八百人。激战中，女童子军队员杨慧敏深夜将一面国旗送到四行仓库。天亮后，数万上海民众看到仓库楼顶飘扬的国旗，极大鼓舞了全国人民的抗战精神。八百壮士后退到租界。谢晋元于1941年4月遭汉奸刺杀殉国。

　　At the end of the Battle of Shanghai, only the First Battalion of the 524th Regiment of the 88th Division stationed to the north of Suzhou River, under Xie Jinyuan, deputy regimental commander of the 524th Regiment. Due to heavy casualties in the battle, the battalion requested reinforcement from the Hubei Fifth Regiment adapted from the Tongcheng Garrison. In the end, about 400 Chinese soldiers engaged in the four-day defense of Sihang Warehouse, a concrete building built jointly by four banks (Jincheng, Zhongnan, Dalu and Yanye)—hence the name Sihang (literally "Four Banks"), although Xie provided an exaggerated number of 800 people. Yang Huimin, a member of the Girl Scouts, secretly delivered a Republic of China flag to the warehouse late at night, and at the next daybreak it was flying atop the building before thousands of watching eyes, which proved inspiring to Chinese soldiers and civilians. The defenders finally had to retreat to the concessions, and Xie was assassinated in April 1941.

四行仓库外景
The Sihang Warehouse
国民党党史馆提供

孤军据守四行仓库
The isolated army garrisoned at the Sihang Warehouse

谢晋元团长及所部四位连长
Regimental Commander Xie and Company Commander of the isolated 4th company

谢团长领导部属举手宣誓，将生命奉献于国家与民族
As a leader, Regimental Commander Xie raised his hand and took an oath to sacrifice his life

2 南京保卫战（1937.12.1-12.13）
Defense of Nanjing (1937.12.1-12.13)

淞沪会战失利后，日军于1937年12月1日下令其华中方面军与海军攻占南京。唐生智主动请战，被蒋介石任命为首都卫戍部队司令。12月5日，南京外围开战。10日，日军攻城。12日，唐生智下令撤退，军队秩序大乱。13日，日军第6、第114师团入城，战役即告结束。日方公布伤亡2600余人。据战后远东国际军事法庭的调查，随后6周，日军在南京屠杀30万以上中国军民。2014年2月27日，中国政府决定，每年12月13日为南京大屠杀死难者国家公祭日。

After the Battle of Songhu, Japan's Central China Area Army and navy attacked Nanjing on December 1, 1937. Tang Shengzhi volunteered for a battle assignment and was appointed by Chiang Kai-shek as the commander of the Nanjing garrison. The battle started on December 5 on the outskirts, and Japanese troops conquered Nanjing on December 10. Tang had to order a general retreat on December 12, which turned out to be a complete rout. The battle ended the next day with the entrance of the Japanese 6th and 114th divisions into Nanjing. Japan claimed that more than 2,600 soldiers were killed and injured in the battle. The investigation of the International Military Tribunal of the Far East revealed that in the next six weeks, Japanese troops murdered about 300,000 Chinese soldiers and civilians. On February 27, 2014, the Chinese government designated December 13 as a national memorial day to commemorate those killed by Japanese aggressors during the Nanjing Massacre.

国府主席林森与美国驻华大使在南京合影
Lin Sen, Chairman of the KMT government, and the American ambassador in Nanjing

1930年代
纵16.7、横21.7厘米
香港翰墨轩（香江博物馆）藏

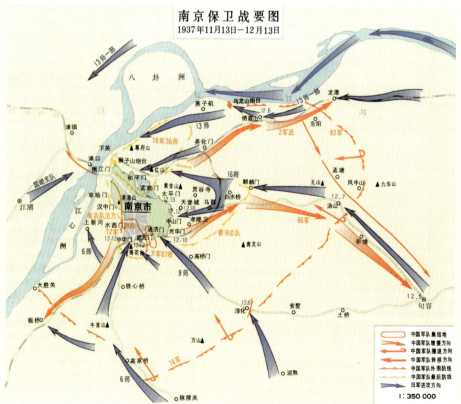

南京保卫战要图
1937年11月13日—12月13日

引自武月星主编：《中国现代史地图集（1919-1949）》，中国地图出版社，2000年。

中国抗日战争暨世界反法西斯战争胜利七十周年特展
An Exhibition Dedicated to 70th Anniversary of Victory of War of Resistance against
Japanese Aggression and World Anti-fascist War

日本军司令官劝降传单 "告中央军将士诸君"

To Officials and Soldiers of the Central Army, a leaflet issued
by Japanese army to persuade Chinese troops to surrender

1930年代
纵14.2、横10.4 厘米
香港翰墨轩（香江博物馆）藏

防守南京的中国炮兵
Artillery positions of protecting Nanjing

参加南京保卫战的我第23军148师的炮兵阵地
Artillery positions of the 148th division of the 23rd Corps
which participated in battles protecting Nanjing

南京街道旁的抗战标语
Anti-Japanese mobilizing slogans next to the street in Naking

121

国军将领在前线视察战情
Leaders of the Nationalist Party Army were visiting the frontal line

日军的坦克向我进攻
Japanese tanks attacked us

日军在南京挹江门举行入城仪式
Japanese troops entering Yijiang Gate of Nanjing in a grand ceremony

中国抗日战争暨世界反法西斯战争胜利七十周年特展
An Exhibition Dedicated to 70th Anniversary of Victory of War of Resistance against
Japanese Aggression and World Anti-fascist War

3－1 太原会战（1937.9.13－11.8）
Battle of Taiyuan (1937.9.13-11.8)

　　1937年9月，日军为确保主力南下作战的侧翼安全并获取煤炭等战略物资，以华北方面军第5师团、关东军察哈尔派遣兵团进攻山西。国军第二战区包括八路军在内的部队同日军在山西北部、东部和中部地区进行了包括天镇、平型关、忻口、娘子关和太原保卫战等大规模的防御战役，日军伤亡2.6万人，此后华北正面战场的战争基本结束。

　　In September 1937, the 5th Division of the North China Area Army and the Chahar Expeditionary Corp of Kwantung Army attacked Shanxi to protect Japanese troops advancing southwards and obtain coal supply. Chinese troops in the 2nd War Area, including the Eighth Route Army, organized defense in northern, eastern and central Shanxi and caused 26,000 Japanese casualties in large-scale combats in Tianzhen, Pingxing Pass, Xinkou, Niangzi Pass and Taiyuan. After the war no major battle occurred in the frontline battlefields in northern China.

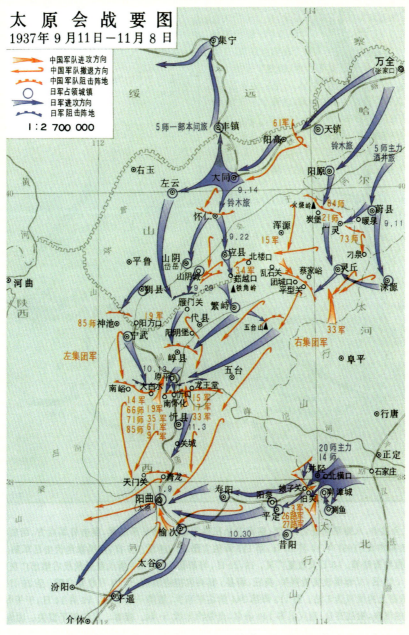

引自武月星主编：《中国现代史地图集（1919-1949）》，中国地图出版社，2000年。

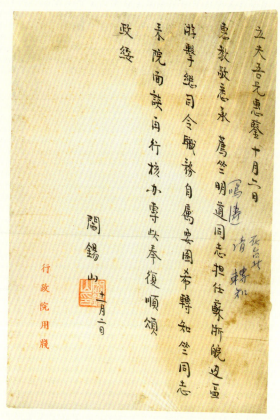

阎锡山致陈立夫书函

A letter written by Yan Xishan to Chen Lifu

纵、横厘米
台湾中华海峡两岸文化资产交流促进会名誉理
事长王水衷藏，台湾美术馆提供

阎锡山（1883-1960），山西五台人，抗战期
间，任第二战区司令长官。陈立夫（1900-
2001），浙江吴兴人。抗战中任教育部长，为
承续中华文脉有重大贡献，晚年主张两岸和平
统一。

太原会战被中国军队伏击毙命的日军部队

Japanese troops ambuscaded by the Chinese army in Taiyuan Battles

太原会战奔赴战场的我军

The Chinese army setting off to battlefields in Taiyuan Battles

太原会战中对空射击的中国军队机枪手

Chinese machine-gunners shooting in the air in Taiyuan Battles

中国抗日战争暨世界反法西斯战争胜利七十周年特展
An Exhibition Dedicated to 70th Anniversary of Victory of War of Resistance against
Japanese Aggression and World Anti-fascist War

3－2 平型关大捷
Battle of Pingxing Pass

　　八路军在太原会战中为了配合友军作战，第一一五师在师长林彪、副师长聂荣臻指挥下，在平型关伏击日军板垣师团的辎重队，歼敌1000余人，缴获汽车60余辆，九二步兵炮一门和大量枪支弹药。平型关大捷打破了日军不可战胜的神话，振奋了中国人民抗战精神和必胜的信念。八路军也通过此次战斗明确了今后开展"独立自主的山地游击战"的正确战略方针。

　　To assist Chinese forces engaged in the Battle of Taiyuan, the 115th Division of the Eighth Route Army under the command of Lin Biao and Nie Rongzhen, ambushed Japanese troops under Itagaki Seishiro. They caused 1,000 Japanese casualties and captured more than 60 vehicles, one type-92 infantry cannon and sufficient arms and ammunition. The battle was the first victory of Chinese troops, providing a major boost in morale and confidence to the Chinese people. And in this battle, the Eighth Route Army established the strategic principle of mountain-based independent guerrilla warfare.

平型关战役中林彪率部前进
Lin Biao and his troops advancing to the frontlines in the Battle of Pingxing Pass

八路军一一五师师长林彪
Lin Biao, commander-in-chief of the 115th Division of the Communist 8th Route Army

林彪（1907–1971），湖北黄冈人。红军改编后任八路军一一五师师长。

平型关战役中的聂荣臻
Nie Rongzhen in the Battle of Pingxing Pass

平型关战役中的一一五师阵地上我军严阵以待
Chinese soldiers of the 115th Division on alert in the Battle of Pingxing Pass

平型关战役中八路军缴获的武器
Japanese weapons captured by the Eighth
Route Army in the Battle of Pingxing Pass

中国抗日战争暨世界反法西斯战争胜利七十周年特展
An Exhibition Dedicated to 70th Anniversary of Victory of War of Resistance against
Japanese Aggression and World Anti-fascist War

4－1 徐州会战（1938.1－5）
Battle of Xuzhou (1938.1-5)

　　1938年初，日军为了打通津浦铁路，连接华北与华中战场，采取南北对进的方针，夹击徐州。中日双方在以江苏省徐州为中心的津浦（天津至浦口）、陇海（宝鸡至连云港）铁路地区开展大规模防御战役，其中毙伤日军1万余人的台儿庄大捷给日军以沉重打击，大大迟滞了日军西进的步伐，为我部署武汉会战赢得了时间。

　　In early 1938 Japan attacked Xuzhou on the north and south sides, in order to ensure smooth operation of the Tianjin-Pukou railway line and connect the battlefields in northern and central China. Chinese and Japanese troops engaged in large-scale defense along the Tianjin-Pukou railway, Baoji-Lianyungang railway, both of which centered on Xuzhou. Chinese troops caused 10,000 Japanese casualties in the Battle of Tai'erzhuang, held back Japanese troops advancing westward, and more importantly, allowed China more time for the preparation of the defense of Wuhan.

引自武月星主编：《中国现代史地图集（1919–1949）》，中国地图出版社，2000年。

徐州会战中奔赴前线的我军
The Chinese army setting off to battlefields in Xuzhou Battles

徐州会战中日军过浮桥
Japanese troops crossing a raft bridge in the Battle of Xuzhou

日军渡微山湖
Japanese troops crossing the Weishan Lake

中国抗日战争暨世界反法西斯战争胜利七十周年特展
An Exhibition Dedicated to 70th Anniversary of Victory of War of Resistance against
Japanese Aggression and World Anti-fascist War

我军重机枪扫荡村庄内藏匿之日军
Sweeping enemies hidden in the village with heavy
machine-guns

我军排炮阵地
Our artillery position

**山东前线，我军在用黏土构筑的工事
上关注敌情**
Chinese troops on alert at the defense works built
with clay in Shandong

4-2 台儿庄大捷
Battle of Taierzhuang

　　台儿庄为徐州水、陆运输大动脉要地。日军为打通南北战场，占领武汉，以矶谷、板垣师团分由津浦线南北夹击徐州。1938年3月20日，矶谷师团濑谷支队攻克枣庄、韩庄后，孤军突进台儿庄。第五战区司令官李宗仁令第二集团军孙连仲部守台儿庄，第二十军团汤恩伯部诱敌深入，待机破敌。板垣师团主攻临沂，矶谷师团主攻滕县、临城、台儿庄均遭失败，台儿庄战役尤其惨烈。4月3日，汤恩伯部与孙连仲部会师后，对被包围于台儿庄的日军发起进攻，至4月7日结束，歼敌万余。台儿庄战役是正面战场的首次胜利，为武汉会战赢得宝贵时间。

　　Tai'erzhuang was the main artery for land and water transportation of Xuzhou. Japanese troops led by Rensuke Isogai and Itagaki Seishiro attacked Tai'erzhuang from both the north and south along the Tianjin-Pukou railway line, in a move to link up northern and southern theaters and make preparation for attacks on Wuhan. On May 20, 1938, a regiment of Isogai Rensuke's division drove deep into Tai'erzhuang alone, after the capture of Zaozhuang and Hanzhuang. Li Zongren, commander of the 5th War Area, gave the responsibility of defending Tai'erzhuang to Sun Lianzhong, who led the 2nd Army Group, and of luring Japanese troops into the city to Tang Enbo, who led the 20th Army. On the Japanese side, Itagaki Seishiro's troops lost the battle in Linyi; Rensuke Isogai's division failed to conquer Teng County, Lincheng, and Tai'erzhuang in which they met bloody resistance. On April 3, Sun Lianzhong and Tang Enbo arrived in Tai'erzhuang with their forces, and began to attack Japanese troops that besieged the city. The battle ended on April 7 with more than ten thousands Japanese casualties. The battle of Tai'erzhuang was the first major Chinese victory of the war in the frontline battlefields, and allowed more time for the preparation of the defense of Wuhan.

李宗仁将军在台儿庄
General Li Zongren in Taierzhuang

1938年3月，我军在台儿庄车站集结
In 1938 March, China troops gathered at Taierzhuang station

台儿庄会战中的我军炮兵
Our artillery in the battle of Taierzhuang

我军增援部队奔赴台儿庄阵地
Our reinforcement army rushing to the Taierzhuang position

中国抗日战争暨世界反法西斯战争胜利七十周年特展
An Exhibition Dedicated to 70th Anniversary of Victory of War of Resistance against
Japanese Aggression and World Anti-fascist War

我军攻入台儿庄与敌巷战

Our troop entered Taierzhuang fighting enemies
in alleys

台儿庄大捷，汉口举行胜利大游行

Hankou people held a spectacular procession
for the great victory of Taierzhuang Battles

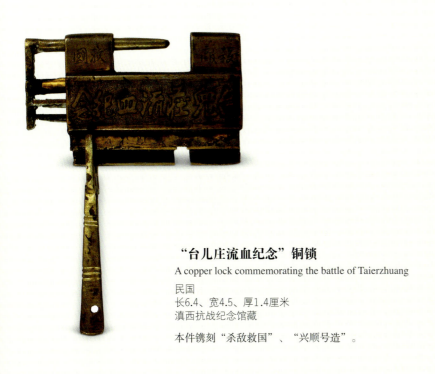

"台儿庄流血纪念"铜锁

A copper lock commemorating the battle of Taierzhuang

民国
长6.4、宽4.5、厚1.4厘米
滇西抗战纪念馆藏

本件镌刻"杀敌救国"、"兴顺号造"。

台儿庄（三幕剧）

The script of Taierzhuang

1938年
湖北省博物馆藏
王莹、舒群等著，汉口读书生活书店出版。

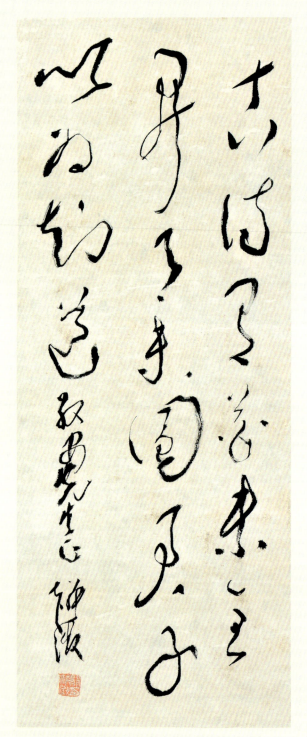

关麟征 草书条幅

A scroll in cursive script, by Chinese general Guan Linzheng

纵75.3、横30厘米

香港翰墨轩（香江博物馆）藏

关麟征（1905－1980），陕西户县人。抗日期间任第五十二军军长、第三十二军团军团长、第十五集团军总司令、第一方面军副总司令（总司令卢汉），参加台儿庄、武汉、长沙等会战。1949定居香港。书云：“古诗有云，花未全开月未圆，君子以为知道。敬安先生正。麟征”。

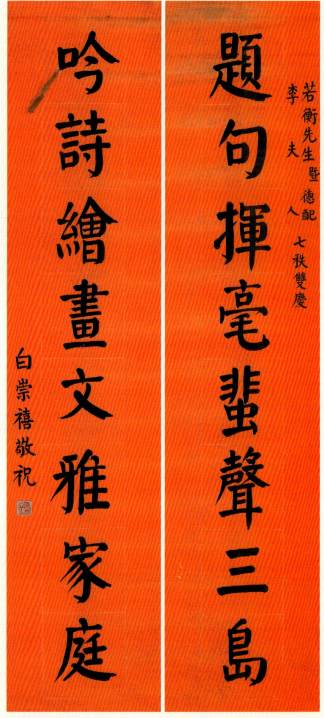

白崇禧楷书八言联

1965年

纸本立轴

纵150、横34厘米

鲁荡平旧藏，台湾董良彦先生提供

白崇禧（1893－1966）广西桂林人，抗战中任副参谋总长、军训部部长、第五战区代理司令长官、第四战区司令长官等，其中协同指挥台儿庄、昆仑关战役等沉重打击了日寇。鲁荡平（1895－1975），字若衡。鲁涤平之弟，教育家。

中国抗日战争暨世界反法西斯战争胜利七十周年特展
An Exhibition Dedicated to 70th Anniversary of Victory of War of Resistance against
Japanese Aggression and World Anti-fascist War

5－1 武汉会战（1938.6.12－10.24）
Battle of Wuhan (1938.6.12-10.24)

南京沦陷后，武汉成为全国抗战中心。日军以华中派遣军第2、第11军共约140个大队，约120艘舰艇，300架飞机，共25万人进攻武汉。国民政府军事委员会则调集14个集团军，约200架飞机，30余艘舰艇，总兵力近110万人保卫武汉。会战在安徽、江西、河南、湖北等省发生大小战斗数百次。中国空军和苏联志愿航空队共击落日机78架，炸沉日舰23艘。中国海军也击沉日舰多艘。此役我方阵亡将士25万余，杀敌3.55万，粉碎日寇速胜的梦想，中国抗战从此进入相持阶段。

After the fall of Nanjing, Wuhan became the center of China's war effort. Japan deployed about 140 battalions from the 2nd and 11th armies of the Central China Expeditionary Army, and 120 warships and 300 planes to attack Wuhan. A total of 250,000 Japanese troops engaged in the battle. In response, the National Military Council of the KMT government mustered 14 army groups, 200 planes, 30 warships and 1.1 million troops for defense. The battle included hundreds of fights in Anhui, Jiangxi, Henan and Hubei. The Chinese Air Force and the Soviet Volunteer Group shot down 78 Japanese planes and destroyed 23 Japanese warships. In addition, Chinese navy sank several Japanese warships. The battle resulted in 250,000 Chinese casualties and 35,500 Japanese casualties. It smashed Japanese ambition of quick and decisive victory, and since then, the war reached stalemate.

引自武月星主编：《中国现代史地图集（1919–1949）》，中国地图出版社，2000年。

武汉保卫战时第五战区司令长官李宗仁（左）、第九战区司令长官陈诚（右）

Li Zongren (left), Commander of No. 5 Military Region and Chen Cheng, Commander of No. 9 Military Region during the Battle of Wuhan

武汉保卫战中，信阳我军向敌发射迫击炮

Our army garrisoning Xinyang fired mortars to attack enemies in battles defending Wuhan

武汉会战日军101师团使用毒气攻击我军

The soldiers of Japan's No. 101 Division using gas attack

中国机械化部队

China mechanized troops

1938年3月7日
纵23.5、横17.7厘米
香港翰墨轩（香江博物馆）藏

中国抗日战争暨世界反法西斯战争胜利七十周年特展
An Exhibition Dedicated to 70th Anniversary of Victory of War of Resistance against
Japanese Aggression and World Anti-fascist War

5-2 马当要塞保卫战
Defense of Madang Stronghold

马当要塞地处长江南岸江西彭泽县境，与北岸安徽宿松小孤山互为犄角。此处江面狭窄，水流湍急，形势险要，是长江中游战略要冲。全面抗战爆发后，国民政府为保九江、武汉安全，耗巨资构筑马当要塞并广布水雷、沉船，阻止日军从水上进攻武汉。6月22日，日军波田支队与海军第11战队由安庆进攻马当，遭到中国空军和要塞炮火的重创，日军被迫放弃从江上展开进攻的计划，改由陆路迂回攻击。因援军行动迟缓，26日日军攻占马当。

Madang Stronghold was located in the county of Pengze, Jiangxi, on the southern bank of the Yangtze River, opposite Xiaogushan of Susong, Anhui, on the northern bank. The river was narrow, and water rapid there. Madang was a very important strategic stronghold on the middle reaches of the river. After the war broke out in full scale, the National Government spent huge amount of money to build the stronghold with torpedoes and sunken ships to defend Jiujiang and Wuhan from Japanese attack along the river. On June 22, a detachment and navy No. 11 brigade attacked Madang from Anqing. Severely damaged by Chinese air force and artilleries, the Japanese had to give up the attack plan from the river. Later, they hit from the land and occupied Madang on June 26 due to the slow support of the Chinese army.

中国士兵在马当要塞严阵以待
Chinese troops were ready to fight at Madang Stronghold

马当炮台遗址
The remains of Madang Fort

5-3 海军御敌
Navy's contribution

抗日战争爆发后，我海军协同陆军、空军抗击日本侵略者。在武汉保卫战中，海军将舰艇上的舰炮拆卸下安装在沿江要塞防御敌舰，同时在长江布放大量的水雷，阻遏敌舰。在武汉保卫战中，虽然我舰艇伤沉殆尽，但粉碎了敌舰沿长江进攻武汉的计划。

After the war broke out, the Chinese navy joined the army and air force to battle the Japanese invaders. During the Battle of Wuhan, the navy dismantled the cannons from the warships and set them up on the forts along the river. They also laid a large number of torpedoes in the river. Although the Chinese warships were mostly destroyed, they helped smashed the invaders' plan to attack Wuhan from the river.

5-4 中山舰
Zhongshan Warship

1938年10月24日，中山舰奉命巡防武昌县金口，遭日机轰炸。舰长萨师俊两腿被炸断，仍镇守望台，后与舰上官兵一同殉国。

On October 24, 1938, Zhongshan Warship was ordered to patrol at Jinkou, Wushang County. It was bombed by Japanese planes. Sa Shijun had his two legs broken but still stuck to the post. He died with all the crew of the ship.

1995年11月，国家文物局正式批准"中山舰"由湖北组织打捞。1997年1月28日，"中山舰"整体打捞出水

In November 1995, the State Administration of Cultural Heritage approved the salvage of Zhongshan Warship in Hubei. On January 28, 1997, the warship was refloated

中国抗日战争暨世界反法西斯战争胜利七十周年特展
An Exhibition Dedicated to 70th Anniversary of Victory of War of Resistance against
Japanese Aggression and World Anti-fascist War

5-5 万家岭大捷（1938.8-10）
Battle of Wanjialing(1938.8-10)

1938年8-10月，日军一部沿长江南岸向瑞昌方向进攻、日军106师团沿南浔线南犯与薛岳兵团在德安县磨溪乡万家岭一带经过包围和反包围，战况惨烈，经过反复搏杀，我军几乎全歼日军106师团及101师团一部共计1万余敌。万家岭大捷是抗战以来首次几乎全歼日本师团，极大的鼓舞了中国军民的抗日斗志。

From August to October 1938, a unit of the Japanese army invaded toward Ruichang on the southern bank of the Yangtze River. Its No. 106 Division moved along Nanxun Railway and confronted the corps of Xue Yue at Wanjialing, Moxi township in De'an County. As a result of close fighting, the Chinese troops killed more than 10,000 Japanese troops and almost annihilated Japan's No. 106 Division and No. 101 Division.

万家岭战役总指挥薛岳
Xue Yue, Commander-in-chief of the Battle of Wanjialing

薛岳（1896-1998），广东韶关人，是抗战歼敌最多的将领，参加过淞沪会战，指挥了武汉会战、徐州会战、长沙会战。武汉会战任第九战区第一兵团总司令，在万家岭战役中，他率军几乎全歼日军106师团。

薛岳行书
Running script by Chinese general Xue Yue

纵74、横33厘米
香港翰墨轩（香江博物馆）藏

书云："惠长志兄：自诚明，谓之性。诚则明矣。弟薛岳"。

5-6 武汉空战（1938.8-10）
Air Battle of Wuhan

1937年8月21日至1938年10月25日，日军飞机空袭武汉共72次，投弹3030枚，炸死炸伤4798人，炸毁房屋3437栋。为了援助中国的抗战，苏联空军志愿队来到武汉，配合中国空军阻击日军飞机。武汉会战期间，中苏空军共击落日机80多架，击伤9架。

From August 21, 1937 to October 25, 1938, Japanese planes air-raided Wuhan 72 times with 3,030 bombs, killing and injuring 4,798 people and destroying 3,437 houses. The Soviet volunteer team came to help the Chinese air force. During the battle, Chinese and Soviet air forces downed more than 80 planes and injured nine.

遭日机轰炸后的汉口
Hankou was bombed by Japanese bombers
国民党党史馆提供

5-6-1 2.18空战

1938年2月18日，日军飞机38架空袭武汉。我空军第四大队在苏联志愿航空队配合下迎敌，击落日机14架，我方损失4架飞机。第四大队大队长李桂丹及吕基淳、巴清正、王怡之、李鹏翔5人殉国。

On February 18, 1938, a total of 38 Japanese planes attacked Wuhan. The Fourth Group of the Chinese Air Force and the Soviet Volunteer Group destroyed 14 Japanese aircraft at a loss of four. Li Guidan, captain of the 4th Group, and pilots Lv Jichun, Ba Qingzheng, Wang Yizhi and Li Pengxiang died in the battle.

2.18空战牺牲的李桂丹烈士
Li Guidan, head of No. 4 team of Chinese air force, died in the February 18 air battle

李桂丹（1914-1938），辽宁新民人。在抗战初期的空战中，曾先后击落敌机8架。在2.18空战保中，他击落敌机3架，后不幸被日寇击中殉国，时年24岁。

中国抗日战争暨世界反法西斯战争胜利七十周年特展
An Exhibition Dedicated to 70th Anniversary of Victory of War of Resistance against
Japanese Aggression and World Anti-fascist War

5-6-2 4.29空战

4.29空战是武汉会战期间中日双方最大规模的空战。1938年4月29日是日本天皇生日，39架日机空袭武汉。我空军及苏联志愿航空队63架飞机严阵以待，击落敌机21架，我军飞机损失5架。陈怀民在座机受伤的情况下，放弃跳伞，驾机与敌机同归于尽。

The April 29 Air Battle is the largest air battle during the Battle of Wuhan. On April 29, 1938, a total of 39 planes of the Japanese air force launched air strikes on Wuhan to celebrate Emperor Hirohito's birthday. The Chinese Air Force and the Soviet Volunteer Group were well prepared, and shot down 21 Japanese planes at a loss of five of their 63 planes. In the battle the pilot Chen Huaimin crashed a damaged aircraft into a Japanese aircraft, though he could escape from the plane with a parachute.

武汉民众热烈庆祝4.29空战大捷
Wuhan residents celebrated the victory of
April 29 air battle
国民党党史馆提供

4.29空战牺牲的陈怀民烈士
Chen Huaimin, a Chinese pilot, died in the April 29 air battle

陈怀民（1916-1938），江苏镇江人。1938年武汉4.29空战中，陈怀民身受重伤后驾机撞向敌机，是世界空战史上与敌机对撞的第一人，表现了中国军人视死如归的气概。

6 中国空军远征日本
Chinese Air Force over Japan

　　1938年5月19日，中国空军第14队队长徐焕升、第8大队第19队副队长佟彦博各驾飞机一架，飞临日本长崎、福冈、久留米、佐贺及九州各城市投洒《告日本国民书》等传单近百万张，震动了日本和世界。

　　On May 19, 1938, Xu Huansheng, captain of the 14th Group of the Chinese Air Force, and Tong Yanbo, deputy captain of the 19th Group of the 8th Regiment, flied to Japan, and dropped nothing but about one million copies of an anti-war leaflet A Letter to the Japanese People, over Japanese cities, including Nagasaki, Fukuoka, Kurume, Saga and Kyushu. The mission sent shock waves to Japan and the rest of the world.

徐焕升远征凯旋
Team leader Xu Huansheng returned from a successful long-distance journey

徐焕升（右）、佟彦博（左）、蒋纯禹（中）
Xu Huansheng (right), Tong Yanbo (left) and Jiang Chunyu (center)
国民党党史馆提供

徐焕升驾驶的马丁139W轰炸机
Xu Huansheng's Martin 139W bomber

中国抗日战争暨世界反法西斯战争胜利七十周年特展
An Exhibition Dedicated to 70th Anniversary of Victory of War of Resistance against
Japanese Aggression and World Anti-fascist War

远征日本的我空军飞行员
Our air force pilots over Japan

中国空军远征日本胜利归来后，周恩来、董必武、邓颖超、边章五、李涛代表八路军到空军司令部慰问并赠送锦旗
Dong Biwu, Deng Yingchao, Bian Zhangwu and
Li Tao presented a pennant to the pilots returning
from Japan at the air force headquarters

武汉各界向飞往日本作人道远征归来的徐焕升、佟彦博献旗致敬
Wuhan residents presented pennants to Xu
Huansheng and Tong Yanbo, who returned from a
humanitarian flight to Japan

国民党党史馆提供

7 随枣会战（1939.5.1–5.24）
Battle of Suixian–Zaoyang (1939.5.1-5.24)

1939年5月，武汉会战之后，日军第十一军司令官冈村宁次为解除国军对平汉线的威胁，以第三、第十三、第十六师团和骑兵第二、第四旅团等向随县、枣阳进攻。第五战区李宗仁部队编为左、右两个集团军和江防守军进行防御反击。至24日，国军先后收复枣阳、随县。日军未能达到预定的战略目标，退回钟祥、应山，恢复战前态势。是役毙敌1.3万人。

In May 1939 after the Battle of Wuhan, to relieve some pressure of the NRA on the Beijing-Hankou railway, Yasuji Okamura, commander in chief of the 11th Army, sent the 3rd, 13th, 16th divisions and the 2nd and 4th brigades of Japanese Calvary to attack Suixian and Zaoyang. Two army groups and armed forces defending the Yangtze River in the 5th War Area organized counter-offensives under the command of Li Zongren. By May 24, Chinese troops had retaken Zaoyang and Suixian, while Japanese troops failed to achieve its objectives and retreated to Zhongxiang and Yingshan, with a total of 13,000 casualties.

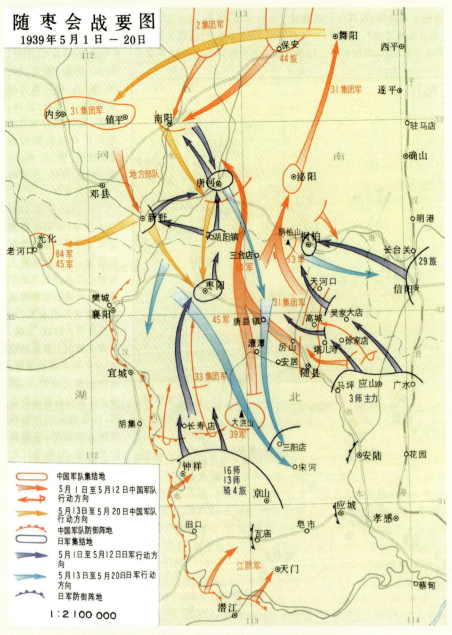

引自武月星主编：《中国现代史地图集（1919–1949）》，中国地图出版社，2000年。

中国抗日战争暨世界反法西斯战争胜利七十周年特展
An Exhibition Dedicated to 70th Anniversary of Victory of War of Resistance against
Japanese Aggression and World Anti-fascist War

第一次长沙会战薛岳部与敌激战

The troop led by Xue Yue fought enemies fiercely in the 1st
Changsha battle

**第一次长沙会战中，国军士兵以重机枪向敌
军猛烈扫射**

The Nationalist Revolutionary Army firing heavy machine
guns in the first battle of Changsha

第一次长沙会战中中国军队在巷战中

Chinese soldiers fighting in alleys in the 1st Changsha battle

9-1 桂南会战（1939.11.13-1940.10.30）
Battle of Southern Guangxi (1939.11.13-1940.10.30)

　　1939年11月，日军第5师团、台湾混成旅团、第5舰队为打击中国国际交通线并威胁西南大后方，在广西南宁等地区展开作战，先后攻陷防城、南宁、龙州。国民革命军第五、第九十九、第三十六军增援广西。第五军在杜聿明指挥下取得昆仑关大捷。是后，日军反击重占昆仑关，我军遭重挫，但是役毙伤日军1.2万余人。

　　In November 1939, the Japanese 5th Division, the Taiwan Mixed Brigade, and the 5th Fleet launched attacks on Nanning, Guangxi, in order to cut off China's international communication line and make a threat to southwestern China. They captured Fangcheng, Nanning, and Longzhou. The 5th, 99th and 39th armies of the NRA were deployed to support Chinese forces in Guangxi, and the 5th Army under Du Yuming achieved victory in the battle of Kunlun Pass. Although Japanese troops recaptured the pass and inflicted heavy casualties on China, more than 120,000 Japanese soldiers died in the battle.

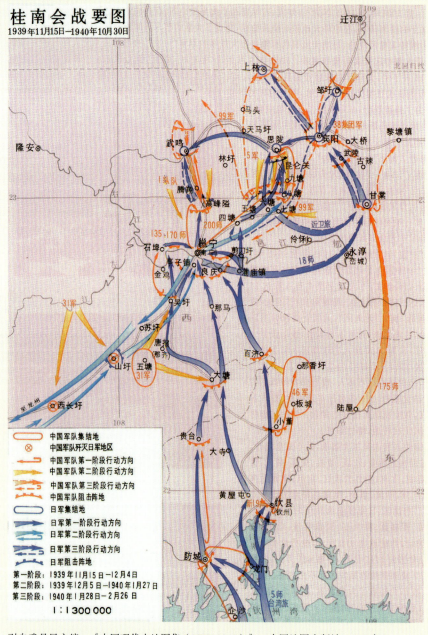

引自武月星主编：《中国现代史地图集（1919-1949）》，中国地图出版社，2000年。

中国抗日战争暨世界反法西斯战争胜利七十周年特展
An Exhibition Dedicated to 70th Anniversary of Victory of War of Resistance against
Japanese Aggression and World Anti-fascist War

桂南会战中我军新式炮兵
Our newly-equipped artillery in south Guilin Battles

我军坦克部队向前进击
Our tank troops advanced on

9-2 昆仑关战役（1939.12.18-1940.1.11）
Battle of Kunlun Pass (1939.12.18-1940.1.11)

昆仑关战役为桂南会战组成部分，是国民革命军唯一的机械化部队第五军与日军号称"钢军"的第5师第21旅团对决。是役歼灭第21旅团5000余人，少将旅团长中村正雄也毙命。

Part of the Battle of Southern Guangxi, the Battle of Kunlun Pass was fought between the Chinese 5th Army, the only mechanized force of the NRA, and the Japanese 21st Brigade of the 5th Division, the so-called "Army of Steel". The battle caused more than 5,000 Japanese casualties and Major General Masao Nakamura died in action.

我军参加昆仑关战役的英制维克斯坦克
Chinese army's Vickers tanks in the battle of Kunlun Portal

昆仑关大捷中，我军发起冲锋
For the great victories of the Kunlun Portal, Chinese army launched an assault

中国抗日战争暨世界反法西斯战争胜利七十周年特展
An Exhibition Dedicated to 70th Anniversary of Victory of War of Resistance against
Japanese Aggression and World Anti-fascist War

我军夺回昆仑关后欢呼胜利
Our soldiers hailed for the triumph after recovering the KunLun Portal

驻守昆仑关
Our army garrisoning the KunLun Portal

昆仑关大捷，我官兵展示所缴获的日本军旗
Our soldiers show seized the Japanese flag after the victory of Kunlun Portal

10-1 枣宜会战（1940.5.1-6.18）
Battle of Zaoyang – Yichang (1940.5.1-6.18)

日军为打击第五战区部队、切断通往重庆运输线，集结30万兵力发动枣宜会战。会战以枣阳为中心和以宜昌为中心分为两个阶段。第一阶段，日第11军第39师团进攻枣阳，我第三十三集团军总司令张自忠将军率部与敌交战，在宜城南瓜店殉国。第二阶段日军渡过汉水占领宜昌。枣宜会战是武汉会战之后日军在正面战场最大规模的战役，我军投入56个师的兵力，阵亡就达36983人，仅毙伤敌军七千余人。

The battle started when 300,000 Japanese troops launched attacks on Chinese troops in the 5th War Area, in order to cut off the transportation line into the relocated Chinese capital, Chongqing. It centered on Zaoyang and Yichang. The 39th Division of the Japanese 11th Army attacked the 33rd Army Group under General Zhang Zizhong, who died in Nanguadian of Yicheng. And then Japanese troops crossed the Hanjiang River and occupied Yichang. The battle was the largest frontal engagement after the battle of Wuhan. A total of 56 Chinese divisions were involved and suffered 36,983 casualties, as opposed to 7,000 Japanese casualties.

引自武月星主编：《中国现代史地图集（1919-1949）》，中国地图出版社，2000年。

德安附近激战中，我军重机枪阵地向敌扫射
Our heavy machine-guns were firing towards enemies in fierce battles near De'an

中国抗日战争暨世界反法西斯战争胜利七十周年特展
An Exhibition Dedicated to 70th Anniversary of Victory of War of Resistance against
Japanese Aggression and World Anti-fascist War

10-2 张自忠将军
General Zhang Zizhong

张自忠（1891-1940），山东临清人。七七事变后，日方企图利用张自忠，一时被国人认作"汉奸"。抗战中，他先后参与徐州、武汉、随枣会战与枣宜会战。1940年5月，日军发动枣宜会战，他亲自率部2000余人渡河杀敌，不幸殉国。他是世界反法西斯战场殉国的最高将领。国民政府在重庆为张自忠举行国葬，追晋为陆军二级上将，新中国人民政府亦追认为革命烈士。

Zhang Zizhong (1891-1940) was born in Linqing, Shandong. After the July 7 Incident, Japan attempted to lure him to its advantage, thus making him a traitor in the eyes of the Chinese. In the war against Japan, he was involved in the battles in Xuzhou, Wuhan, Suixian-Zaoyang, and Zaoyang-Yichang. In May 1940 when the Japanese launched the Zaoyang-Yichang Battle, he led over 2,000 soldiers to fight, and unfortunately, he died in the battle. Zhang Zizhong was one of the highest-ranked Allied officers that was killed in action in World War II. The KMT government organized state funeral for him in Chongqing and promoted him to Full General. The government of the People's Republic of China recognizes him as a revolutionary martyr.

张自忠将军
General Zhang Zizhong

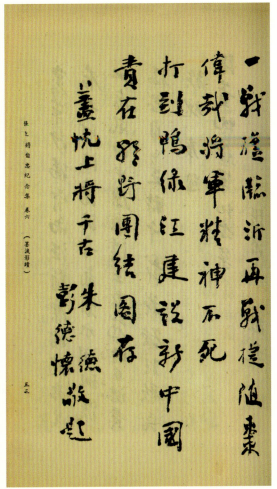

朱德、彭德怀为张自忠题辞
Inscriptions written by Zhu De and Peng Dehuai for Zhang Zizhong

蒋介石题辞
Inscriptions written by Chiang Kai-shek

《张上将自忠纪念集》
" General Zhang Zizhong Memorial"

纵14.5、横5.7厘米
香港翰墨轩（香江博物馆）藏
1948年9月出版。

林森题辞
Inscriptions written by Lin Sen

张自忠遗体权厝重庆北碚梅花山麓，蒋介石、冯玉祥、孔祥熙等前往致祭
Chiang Kai-shek, Feng Yuxiang, and Kong Xiangxi visiting the temporary tomb of Zhang Zizhong at the foot of the Meihua Mountain, Beibei District, Chongqing

11 豫南会战（1941.1.30－3.1）
Battle of Southern Henan (1941.1.30-3.1)

　　1941年1月，日军为消灭豫南地区第五战区主力，解除对信阳日军的威胁，以华中派遣军第11军为主，在华北方面军一部的配合下，以7个师、1个骑兵旅、3个坦克团发起豫南会战。第五战区司令长官李宗仁避实击虚，留少数兵力正面抗击，主力转向两翼，待日军进攻兵力分散之时，从其两侧及背后围歼。是役，日军一度攻占安徽界首和太和，但在伤亡9000人后最终撤退。

　　In January 1941, the Japanese 11th Army of the Central China Expeditionary Army and the Unit 1 of the Northern China Area Army attacked southern Henan, in an attempt to eliminate Chinese main forces of the 5th War Area and ease the pressure on Japanese troops in Xinyang. Seven Japanese divisions, one cavalry brigade and three tank regiments were involved in the battle. Li Zongren, commander of the 5th War Area, deployed only a few troops in the frontline, and sent the main forces to outflank and siege the Japanese when they launched frontal attacks. Although Japanese troops conquered Jieshou and Taihe of Anhui province, they had to retreat due to 9,000 casualties.

中国抗日战争暨世界反法西斯战争胜利七十周年特展
An Exhibition Dedicated to 70th Anniversary of Victory of War of Resistance against
Japanese Aggression and World Anti-fascist War

12 上高会战（1941.3.15－4.9）
Battle of Shanggao (1941.3.15-4.9)

　　1941年初，日军为加强华北治安战，调驻江西安义地区的第33师团往华北，调动之前对驻江西上高地区的第九战区第十九集团军发动进攻，以巩固南昌外围安全。日军第33、第34师团及第20混成旅团，分北、中、南三路合击上高。中路第34师团占领高安后冒进，被第十九集团军总司令罗卓英率部围歼于高安地区。是役是抗战中中方取得全面胜利的战役，歼敌9000余人，何应钦称之为"抗战以来最精彩的一战"。

　　In early 1941, the Japanese 33rd Division in Anyi, Jiangxi was deployed to northern China to improve local security. Before their departure, the division attacked the Chinese 19th Army Group of the 9th War Area in Shanggao, Jiangxi, in order to strengthen security around Nanchang. The 33rd and 34th divisions and the 20th Mixed Brigade attacked Shanggao on the northern, central and southern fronts. After the capture of Gaoan, the 34th Division in the central section drove deeper into China-controlled areas, and was encircled and annihilated by the troops under Luo Zhuoying, commander in chief of the 19th Army Group. China achieved total victory in the battle and killed 9,000 Japanese soldiers, and He Yingqin said that it was "the most impressive battle of the war."

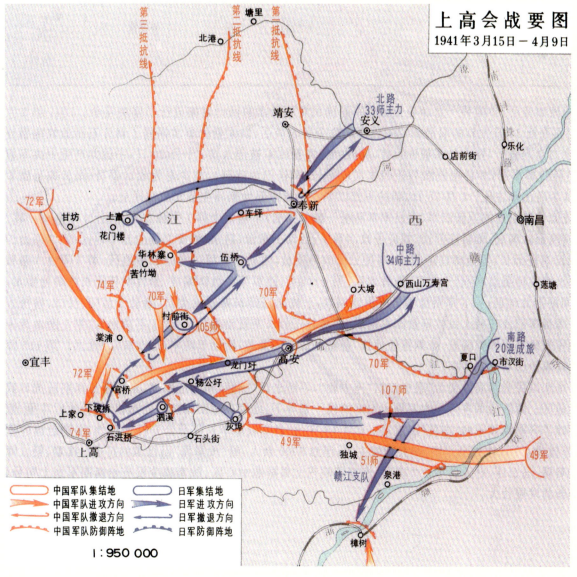

引自武月星主编：《中国现代史地图集（1919–1949）》，中国地图出版社，2000年。

清之同志

罗卓英敬赠 廿六年

罗卓英将军
General Luo Zhuoying

罗卓英（1896-1961），广东大埔人。抗战中历任第十六军团司令、国民革命军第十五集团军总司令、南京卫戍副司令长官、第九战区前敌总司令、第九战区副司令长官、国民革命军第十九集团军总司令、太平洋战区中国远征军第一路司令长官，先后参加淞沪抗战、南京保卫战、南昌会战、上高会战、长沙会战、平满纳会战等。

王耀武将军
General Wang Yaowu

王耀武（1904-1968），山东泰安人。抗战中参加淞沪、南京、武汉、长沙等多次重大会战，上高会战率七十四军痛歼日军。

上高会战中的日军坦克
Japanese tanks in the battle of Shang-gao

中国抗日战争暨世界反法西斯战争胜利七十周年特展
An Exhibition Dedicated to 70th Anniversary of Victory of War of Resistance against
Japanese Aggression and World Anti-fascist War

13 晋南（中条山）会战（1941.5.7－5.27）
Battle of Southern Shanxi (Zhongtiao Mountains) (1941.5.7-5.27)

　　1941年5月7日，日军在华北方面军司令官多田骏统一指挥下，调集6个师团、3个旅团共10余万人，企图消灭中条山地区第1战区部队主力。第一战区调集约18万人由何应钦指挥应战。日军在空军支持下，由东、北、西三个方向全面进攻。国军准备不足，仓皇对敌，伤亡4.2万余人，被俘3.5万余人，而日军仅伤亡约3000人。是役为山西正面战场唯一的大规模对日作战，被蒋介石称为"抗战史上最大之耻辱"。

　　On May 7, 1941, more than 100,000 Japanese soldiers from six divisions and three brigades under Hayao Tada, commander in chief of the North China Area Army, attacked Chinese troops in the 1st War Area in the Zhongtiao Mountains region. He Yingqin deployed 180,000 soldiers to counterattack. Supported by air forces, Japanese troops attacked the Chinese from the east, north and west. The ill-prepared Chinese troops suffered 42,000 casualties, and 35,000 were captured, while the Japanese suffered only 3,000 casualties. The battle was the only frontal engagement with Japanese troops in Shanxi and Chiang Kai-shek called it "the biggest shame of the war."

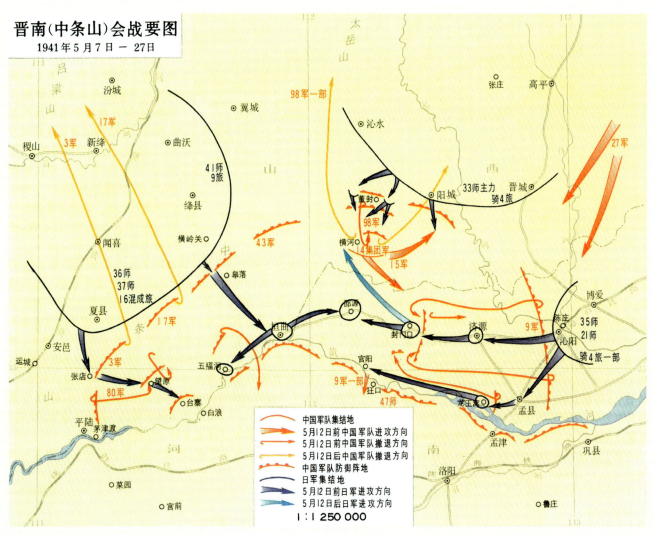

引自武月星主编：《中国现代史地图集（1919-1949）》，中国地图出版社，2000年。

155

我骑兵由侧翼猛烈攻击，敌由南阳溃退
Our cavalry attacked the wings of enemies fiercely, and the enemy withdrew in disorder at Nanyang

太行山游击队扰击敌人
Guerrilla forces around the Taihang Mountain harassed enemies cautiously

我军高级将领在官桥视察敌阵地
A senior officer of our army was inspecting the position of the enemy in Guanqiao

我军军官在掩蔽所查看地图，指挥作战
Our commanders were studying maps in a military shelter and commanding

中国抗日战争暨世界反法西斯战争胜利七十周年特展
An Exhibition Dedicated to 70th Anniversary of Victory of War of Resistance against
Japanese Aggression and World Anti-fascist War

14 第二次长沙会战（1941.9.17-10.9）
The Second Battle of Changsha (1941.9.17-10.9)

　　1941年苏德战争爆发，新任中国派遣军总司令畑俊六反对日本进攻苏联，主张彻底摧毁中国抗战意志，遂集结4个师团和4个旅团共12万余人，发动第二次长沙会战，意图消灭我第九战区的部队。第九战区的11个军加上中央直辖的2个军和第六、第七战区各调1个军约30万人参战。战争历时一个月，日军伤亡约7000人，我军伤亡失踪7万人。

Despite the outbreak of the Russo-German War in 1941, Shunroku Hata, commander-in-chief of the China Expeditionary Army, opposed Japanese attacks on the Soviet Union; instead, he insisted on destroying the Chinese intention of resistance. He deployed 120,000 soldiers from four divisions and four brigades to launch the second attack on Changsha in an attempt to eliminate Chinese troops in the 9th War Area. A total of 300,000 Chinese soldiers from the 11 armies in the 9th War Area, two centrally-managed armies and two armies from the 6th and 7th war areas, engaged in the battle. The one-month engagement caused 7,000 Japanese casualties and 70,000 Chinese casualties.

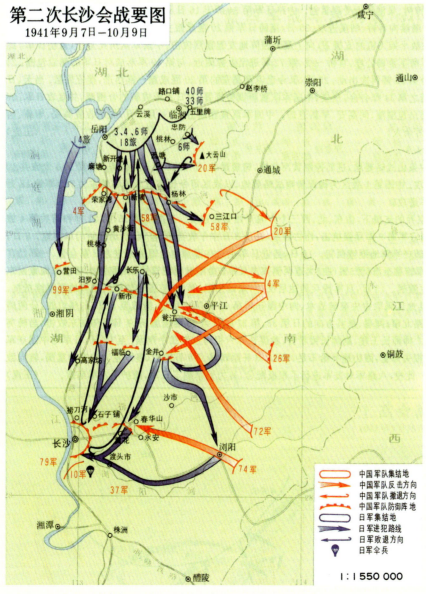

第二次长沙会战要图
1941年9月7日-10月9日

引自武月星主编：《中国现代史地图集（1919-1949）》，中国地图出版社，2000年。

1941年6月22日，莫斯科居民在红场收听德国进攻苏联消息

Moscow residents listen to news of German attacks on the Soviet Union at the Red Square, June 22, 1941

尤金·迦勒底（Евгений Халдей）摄，俄罗斯俄中友协提供

我军与日军激战中，炮火连天

Covered by shellfire in battles with Japanese army

我军在废墟中阻击敌人

Chinese army was fighting the Japanese enemies fiercely in alleys and relic

我军凭险坚守洞庭湖

Our soldiers guarding at the bank of the Dongting Lake at advantageous positions

奔赴长沙迎战敌军的中国军队

Chinese armies rushing to Changsha to fight enemies

中国抗日战争暨世界反法西斯战争胜利七十周年特展
An Exhibition Dedicated to 70th Anniversary of Victory of War of Resistance against
Japanese Aggression and World Anti-fascist War

15第三次长沙会战（1941.12.24-1942.1.6）
The Third Battle of Changsha (1941.12.24-1942.1.6)

　　太平洋战争爆发后，日本第11军司令阿南惟几为策应攻击香港的日军，率6万兵力向第九战区薛岳30个师约30万兵力发动牵制性攻击。阿南惟几因进兵顺利，于是进攻长沙。薛岳采用坚壁清野，诱敌深入战略，合围日军。日军苦战，伤亡6000余人后得以逃脱。是役为太平洋战争爆发后盟军的首场战役胜利。

Despite the outbreak of the Russo-German War in 1941, Shunroku Hata, commander-in-chief of the China Expeditionary Army, opposed Japanese attacks on the Soviet Union; instead, he insisted on destroying the Chinese intention of resistance. He deployed 120,000 soldiers from four divisions and four brigades to launch the second attack on Changsha in an attempt to eliminate Chinese troops in the 9th War Area. A total of 300,000 Chinese soldiers from the 11 armies in the 9th War Area, two centrally-managed armies and two armies from the 6th and 7th war areas, engaged in the battle. The one-month engagement caused 7,000 Japanese casualties and 70,000 Chinese casualties.

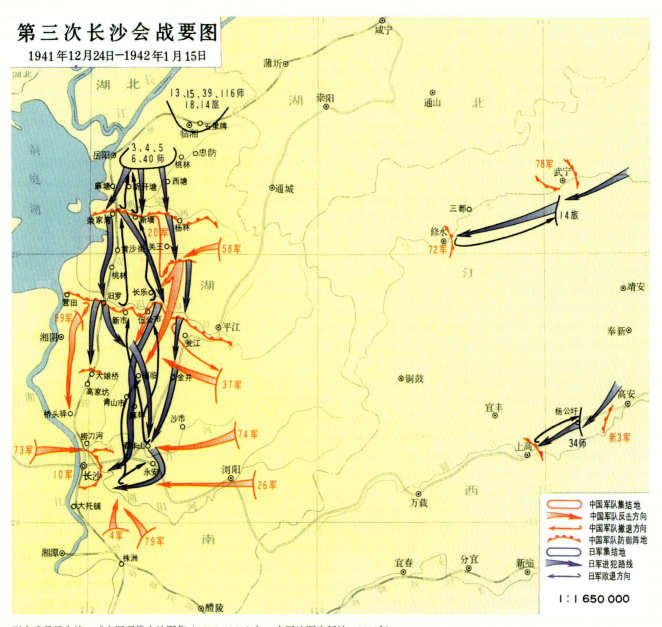

引自武月星主编：《中国现代史地图集（1919-1949）》，中国地图出版社，2000年。

159

1941年12月7日，日本袭击珍珠港，太平洋战争爆发
In December 7, 1941, the Japanese attack on Pearl Harbor, the Pacific War broke out

薛岳指挥三次长沙会战取得胜利后接受战地采访
Xue Yue accepted an interview in the battlefield after commanding and winning the three Changsha Battles

第三次长沙会战后清理战场
Cleaning up the battlefield after the three Changsha Battles

第三次长沙会战战利品
Booty of the 3rd Changsha Battle

中国抗日战争暨世界反法西斯战争胜利七十周年特展
An Exhibition Dedicated to 70th Anniversary of Victory of War of Resistance against
Japanese Aggression and World Anti-fascist War

16 浙赣会战（1942.4.25－7.28）
Zhejiang and Jiangxi Campaign (1942.4.25-7.28)

　　太平洋战争爆发后，1942年4月18日，日本本土首次遭美机空袭，美机飞至浙江衢州等地机场降落。日军为摧毁浙江的前进机场，以5个师团兵力向国军第三战区主力发动攻击。中方第九、第三战区约30万兵力应战。日军的进攻基本摧毁浙赣两省的我方机场，打通浙赣铁路，实现战役目标。我军伤亡7万余人，人民财产蒙受巨大损失。日军也伤亡1.7万人。

Following the outbreak of the Pacific War, the United States launched the first air attack on Japan's mainland on April 18, and some American aircraft landed in Chinese airfields, including those in Quzhou of Zhejiang. To destroy the Qianjin Airport in Zhejiang, Japan's five divisions attacked Chinese troops in the 3rd War Area. China responded with the deployment of about 300,000 soldiers from the 9th and 3rd war areas. Japanese troops destroyed almost all the airfields in Zhejiang and Jiangxi and linked up the Zhejiang-Jiangxi railway line, both of which were its strategic goals. The battle resulted in 70,000 Chinese casualties and an enormous economic loss as well as 17,000 Japanese casualties.

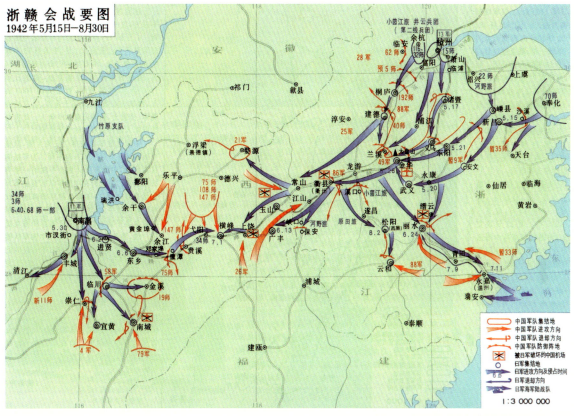

引自武月星主编：《中国现代史地图集（1919-1949）》，中国地图出版社，2000年。

装甲列车

Armored Train

1942年
纵27.5、横20.8厘米
香港翰墨轩（香江博物馆）藏

17-1 鄂西会战(1943.5-6)
Battle of Western Hubei (1943.5-6)

　　1943年5月至6月，日军为打通长江上游航线并摧破重庆门户，以3个师团、2个旅团向鄂西第六战区部队攻击。第六战区以10个军的兵力迎敌。日军用各个击破的战术重创第二十九、第十集团军和江防军。会战历时月余，我军歼敌4000余人。其中，第十八军十一师胡琏率部死守石牌要塞，成为抗战胜利的一个转折点。

　　In May and June of 1943, Japan's three divisions and two brigades attacked Chinese troops in the 6th War Area in western Hubei, in order to secure shipping in the upper reaches of the Yangtze River and breach the defense of Chongqing. China responded with the deployment of ten field armies. The Japanese army inflicted heavy casualties on the 29th and 10th army groups and armed forces defending the Yangtze River, one by one. The battle lasted for about a month, with 4,000 Japanese casualties. The 11th Division of the 18th Army, led by Hu Lian, succeeded in defending the Shipai fortress, which became a turning point of the war.

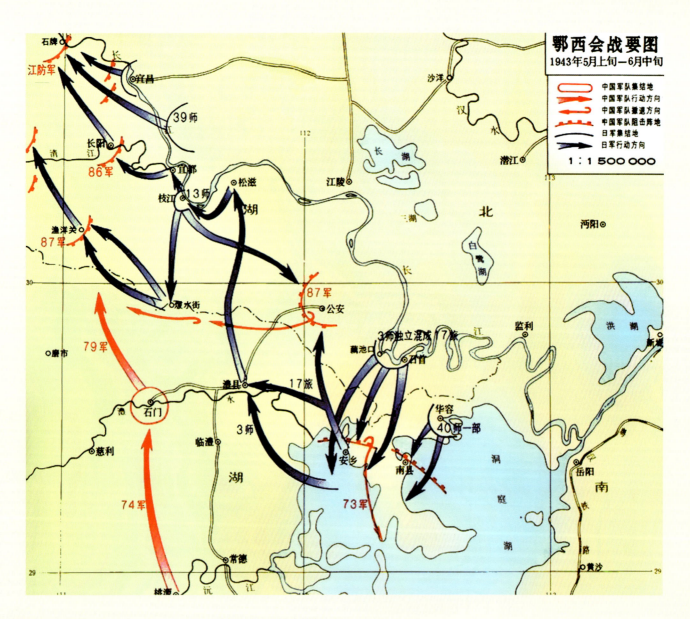

中国抗日战争暨世界反法西斯战争胜利七十周年特展
An Exhibition Dedicated to 70th Anniversary of Victory of War of Resistance against
Japanese Aggression and World Anti-fascist War

17-2 石牌保卫战（1943.5.5-6.18）
Defense of Shipai (1943.5.5-6.18)

　　武汉沦陷后，1939年3月，我军在宜昌三斗坪镇石牌村构筑第一道要塞以保卫重庆。鄂西会战中，日军约15万人企图攻占石牌。我军以1万余人伤亡代价，毙伤日军约2.5万人。是役被国际媒体称为"东方的斯大林格勒保卫战"。中日军队伤亡比例也由此转变。

　　After the fall of Wuhan, Chinese troops built a strong fortress in Shipai Village of Sandouping, Yichang in March 1939, to fight against Japanese offensive towards Chongqing. And in the Battle of Western Hubei, about 150,000 Japanese soldiers tried in vain to seize Shipai. In the Defense of Shipai, Chinese troops caused 25,000 Japanese casualties at a loss of 10,000. The battle was named as the Battle of Stalingrad in the East by international media. And after the war Chinese troops suffered fewer casualties than before.

石牌要塞保卫战我军指挥序列
Military command sequence of Defense of Shipai

第六战区司令长官：	陈　诚（兼）孙连仲（代）
副司令长官：	吴奇伟　王缵绪
长江上游江防军总司令：	吴奇伟（兼）
副总司令：	曾以鼎　李及兰
第十八军（军长方天）辖：	第十一师（师长胡琏）
	第十八师（师长罗广文）
	暂编第三十四师（师长彭巩英）
第八十六军（军长朱鼎卿）辖：	第十三师（师长曹金轮）
	第六十七师（师长罗贤达）
第三十二军（军长宋肯堂）辖：	第一三九师（师长孙定超）
	第五师（师长刘云瀚）
海军宜巴要塞区司令：	方　天（兼）
第十集团军总司令：	王敬玖
第二十六集团军总司令：	周　岩
第二十九集团军总司令：	王缵绪（兼）
第三十三集团军总司令：	冯治安

石牌保卫战日军作战序列
Military command sequence of Japan

第11军（兵力约10万人）司令官：横山勇中将
参谋长：小圆江邦雄少将
辖：第3师团（日本甲种师团，师团长山本三男中将）
第13师团（日本甲种师团，师团长赤鹿理中将）
第34师团（师团长伴健雄中将）
第39师团（师团长澄田睐四郎中将）
第40师团（师团长青木成一中将）
第58师团（师团长毛利末广中将）
第68师团（师团长佐久间为人中将）
第17独立旅团（旅团长岸川健一少将）

胡涟将军石牌决战的祭天誓词
General Hu Lian's oath on heaven worship of the battle at Shipai

誓词曰："陆军第十一师师长胡涟谨以至诚昭告山川神灵：我今率堂堂之师,保卫我祖宗坚苦经营遗留吾人之土地。汉贼不两立，古有明训。华夷须严辨，春秋存义。生为军人，死为军魂。后人视今，亦尤今人之视昔。吾何惴焉！今贼来犯，决予痛歼。力尽，以身殉之。然吾坚信苍苍者天，必佑忠诚，吾人于血战之际，胜利即在握。此誓。中华民国三十二年五月二十七日正午"。

石牌保卫战阵亡士兵墓碑

Gravestones of soldiers that died in the Defense of Shipai

1943年
湖北省宜昌石牌文物保护委员会供图

中国抗日战争暨世界反法西斯战争胜利七十周年特展
An Exhibition Dedicated to 70th Anniversary of Victory of War of Resistance against
Japanese Aggression and World Anti-fascist War

鄂西会战中驻守长江关隘，保卫陪都重庆的我军

Chinses army defending the provisional capital of Chongqing
on the battle of West Hubei Three Gorges pass

1943年，我军在鄂西地区渡口集结备战

Chinese troops gather at a ferry in the Three Gorges region in
western Hubei, 1943

豫西、鄂北会战俘获的敌兵

Enemy soldiers captured in the west Henan and north Hubei Battles

石牌抗战遗址远景

Shipai Site Vision

石牌保卫战长江上游江防军总司令吴奇伟
将军（1891-1953）
General Wu Qiwei

我军在石牌战役中冒敌轰炸，奋勇前进
Move forward! Chinese Army fought under enemy flery bombardment

石牌抗战U形防空洞
U-shaped dugout of Shipai

中国抗日战争暨世界反法西斯战争胜利七十周年特展
An Exhibition Dedicated to 70th Anniversary of Victory of War of Resistance against
Japanese Aggression and World Anti-fascist War

石牌防空洞
Dugout of Shipai

鼎锅田炮台
Fort of Shipai

石牌碉堡
Bunker of Shipai

石牌弹药库
Ammunition depots of Shipai

18 常德会战（1943.11.2–12.20）
Battle of Changde (1943.11.2–12.20)

常德是华中、西南物质集散地。日军为牵制国军对云南的反攻，并掠夺战略物资，以7个师团约10万人进攻常德。国军以第六战区和第九战区的16个军约21万人迎敌。 是役我军以伤亡约6万人的代价，毙伤日军4000余人，最后收复常德。

Changde was a center of supply for central and southwestern China. In order to impede the NRA's attacks on Japanese troops in Yunnan and ensure ample supply, Japan deployed about 100,000 soldiers from seven divisions to attack Changde, which was defended by about 210,000 Chinese soldiers from 16 corps of the 6th and 9th war areas. Chinese troops killed 4,000 Japanese at a loss of 60,000, and retook Changde.

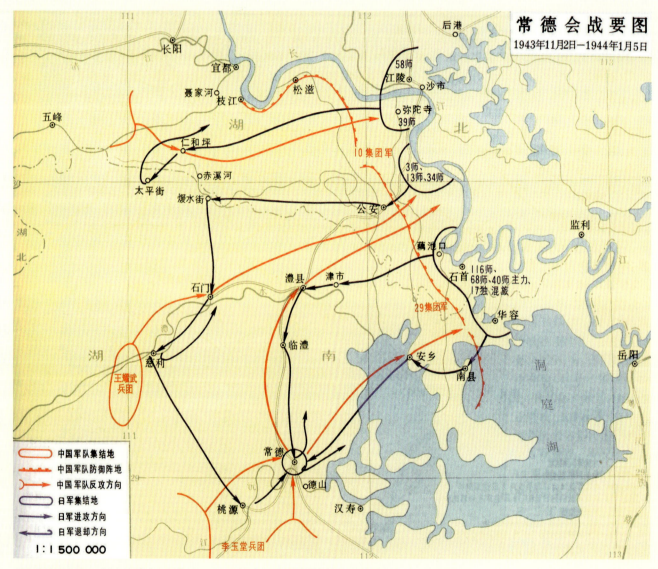

引自武月星主编：《中国现代史地图集（1919–1949）》，中国地图出版社，2000年。

中国抗日战争暨世界反法西斯战争胜利七十周年特展
An Exhibition Dedicated to 70th Anniversary of Victory of War of Resistance against
Japanese Aggression and World Anti-fascist War

常德会战中我军在常德市区对日军阵地发起攻坚行动

In the Changde battle, Chinese army in the downtown of Changde stormed the fortification of the Japanese army

常德会战中我军在废墟中与日军激烈巷战

In the Changde battle, Chinese army was fighting the Japanese enemies fiercely in alleys and relic

我军克复常德后入城

Our army was entering the city after recovering Changde

常德会战中中国军队重机枪阵地向日军猛烈扫射
In the Changde battle, Chinese soldiers in the heavy machine-gun position were shooting the Japanese enemy heavily

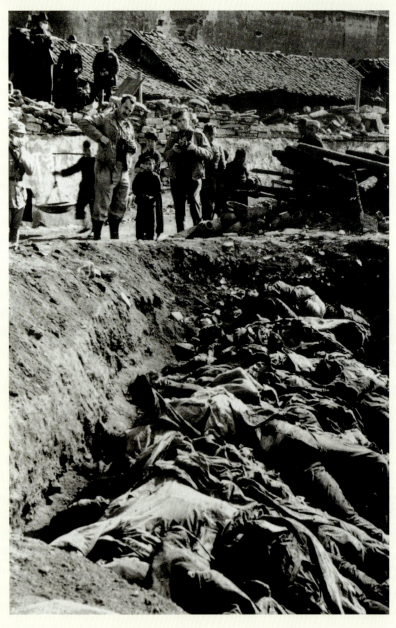

常德会战结束后中国军队清理战场，掩埋日军尸体
Chinese army cleaned up the battlefield and buried the bodies of Japanese soldiers after the Changde battle

中国抗日战争暨世界反法西斯战争胜利七十周年特展

An Exhibition Dedicated to 70th Anniversary of Victory of War of Resistance against
Japanese Aggression and World Anti-fascist War

19 豫中会战（1944.4.17–6.19）
Battle of Central Henan (1944.4.17-6.19)

日军为打通大陆交通线和歼灭中国西南部空军基地制定1号作战（中方称豫湘桂会战）计划，豫中会战是其一部分。从4月初始，日军华北方面军司令官冈村宁次指挥从东北、华北抽调5个师团、5个旅团约15万兵力，分三路向豫中进攻，打通平汉线南段，击败第一战区蒋鼎文、汤恩伯部8个集团军约40万军队，洛阳沦陷。我军伤亡4万，敌军仅伤亡3千多，可谓惨败。

The Battle of Central Henan was the first offensive in the Japanese Operation Ichi-Go (Battle of Henan-Hunan-Guangxi by Chinese side) during the war, in which Japan attempted to establish a land transportation route from the Japanese occupied territories and to destroy the airbases in southwestern China. From early April, about 150,000 Japanese soldiers from five divisions and five brigades in the northeast and north began to attack central Henan on three fronts, led by Yasuji Okamura, commander in chief of the North China Area Army. They occupied the southern section of the Beijing-Hankou railway, and defeated 400,000 Chinese soldiers from eight army groups led by Jiang Dingwen and Tang Enbo in the 1st War Area. And Luoyang was lost. The battle resulted in 40,000 Chinese casualties and 3,000 Japanese casualties.

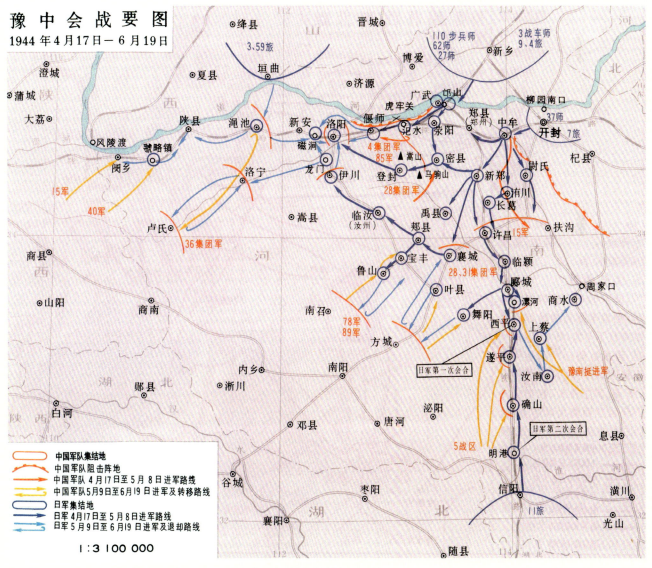

豫 中 会 战 要 图
1944 年 4 月 17 日 — 6 月 19 日

引自武月星主编：《中国现代史地图集（1919-1949）》，中国地图出版社，2000年。

171

20 长（沙）衡（阳）会战（1944.5.23-9.14）
Battle of Changsha-Hengyang (1944.5.23-9.14)

长衡会战是豫湘桂会战的第二部分。日军动员10个师团约28万人，我军16个军参战，约38万人。日军参战兵力之多、作战地域之广，创下记录。是役以衡阳保卫战重创了日军 著称，但战役未能阻止日军实现控制粤汉、湘桂铁路的企图，而我军伤亡 9万余人，日军只伤亡不足2万人，可谓惨败。

The Battle of Changsha-Hengyang was the second part of the Battle of Henan-Hunan-Guangxi. Japan deployed about 280,000 troops from ten divisions to attack the 380,000 Chinese troops from 16 armies. The operation involved more Japanese troops and a larger battlefield than any other campaign in the war. Although Chinese troops inflicted heavy casualties on Japan, they failed to prevent Japanese troops from occupying the Guangzhou-Hankou railway and the Hengyang (Hunan)-Guilin railway. In fact China suffered a crushing defeat with 90,000 casualties, compared to less than 20,000 casualties on the part of Japan.

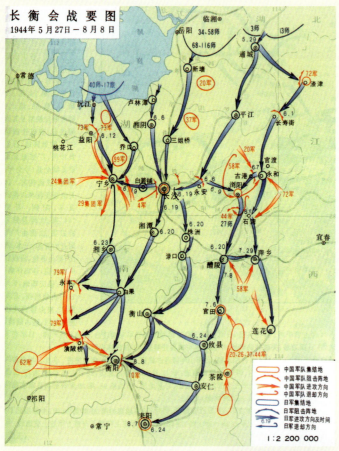

引自武月星主编：《中国现代史地图集（1919-1949）》，中国地图出版社，2000年。

与日军寸土必争的衡阳保卫战
Hengyang Defending Battles in which every inch of land was indispensable

中国抗日战争暨世界反法西斯战争胜利七十周年特展
An Exhibition Dedicated to 70th Anniversary of Victory of War of Resistance against
Japanese Aggression and World Anti-fascist War

21 桂（林）柳（州）会战（1944.8–12.10）
Battle of Guilin–Liuzhou (1944.8-12.10)

　　日军为挽回太平洋战争的失败发动桂柳会战，以摧毁大西南的空军基地，打通平汉路经湘、桂两省至越南的陆路交通线，该会战也是豫湘桂会战的第三部分。日军调集第11、第23军团约16万人，国军9个军约20万人迎敌。结果日军以伤亡1.5万的代价完成战役目标。日军在豫、湘、桂会战中，摧毁中、美空军7个基地、36个机场，占领了豫、湘、桂大片土地，打通了大陆交通线。国军这次惨败也影响到美英苏盟国对华政策的调整。

　　To reverse the downward trend since its defeat in the Pacific War, Japan decided to destroy airbases in southwestern China and connect the line of communications through Hunan, Guangxi and Vietnam. This battle was the third part of the Battle of Henan-Hunan-Guangxi. About 160,000 Japanese soldiers from the 11th and the 23rd armies launched attacks on 200,000 Chinese soldiers from nine divisions of the NRA. In the end Japan achieved its strategic goals with 15,000 casualties. And in the Battle of Henan-Hunan-Guangxi, Japanese troops destroyed seven airbases and 36 airfields of Chinese and American air forces, occupied larger territories of Henan, Hunan and Guangxi, and opened a land transportation route from the Japanese occupied territories. The defeat of the NRA resulted in changes of the Allied policy towards China.

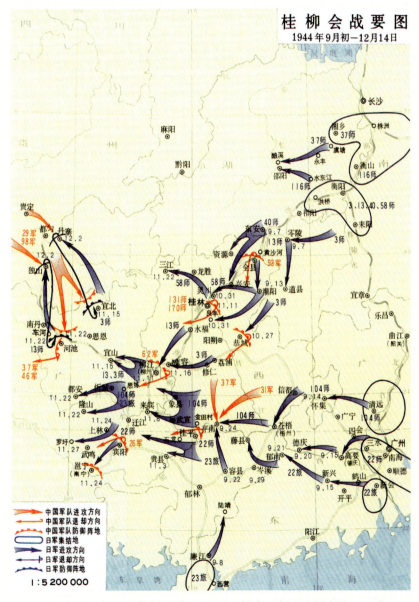

引自武月星主编：《中国现代史地图集（1919–1949）》，中国地图出版社，2000年。

参加豫湘桂会战的广西抗战女兵
Chinese women troops from Guangxi in the Battle of Henan-Hunan-Guangxi

被轰炸后的桂林市区
Guilin City after the bombing

中国抗日战争暨世界反法西斯战争胜利七十周年特展
An Exhibition Dedicated to 70th Anniversary of Victory of War of Resistance against
Japanese Aggression and World Anti-fascist War

22 湘西会战（1945.4.9–6.7）
Battle of Western Hunan (1945.4.9-6.7)

　　湘西会战是中国抗战的最后一次会战。日军战役目的是夺取芷江空军基地。日军5个师团10万余人，我方9个军18万余人参战，战线长达200余公里。在王耀武指挥下，湘西会战取得了雪峰山大捷。战役以我军获胜结束，毙伤日军2.6万余人。湘西会战的胜利标志着中国抗战由防御转入了反攻。

　　The Battle of Western Hunan is the last major battle between China and Japan. In order to seize the Zhijiang military airbase, more than 100,000 Japanese soldiers from five divisions were deployed to fight against 180,000 Chinese soldiers from nine divisions on a land of 200 kilometers. Chinese troops under the command of Wang Yaowu defeated the enemy on Xuefeng Mountain. The battle ended in a victory for China, inflicting 26,000 Japanese casualties. After the battle, China began to launch nationwide counterattacks on Japan.

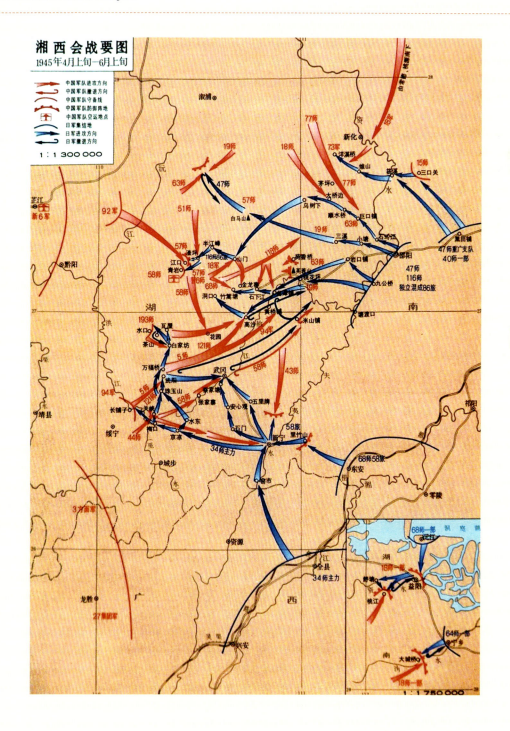

国民政府第二次军事委员会参谋长会议合照
Group photo of the Second National Government Conference of the Chief of General Staff of Military Committee

1941年
周海圣先生捐赠，湖北省博物馆藏

前排正中蒋介石右手起为冯玉祥、唐生智、陈绍宽、俞飞鹏、？、何键、万耀煌、？、？、郭寄峤。蒋介石左手起为何应钦、徐永昌、张治中、？、何成浚、熊斌，第十一人为叶剑英，第十七人为张云逸。二排左一为贺衷寒。

中国抗日战争暨世界反法西斯战争胜利七十周年特展
An Exhibition Dedicated to 70th Anniversary of Victory of War of Resistance against
Japanese Aggression and World Anti-fascist War

浩如代表八秩华诞

蒋中正
蒋宋美龄 敬祝

蒋介石、宋美龄楷书寿字

The regular-script character "Longevity", handwriting
by Chiang Kai-shek and Soong May-ling

纸本立轴
纵65.5、横39厘米
曾宝荪旧藏
台湾董良彦先生提供

熊斌 隶书
Official script, handwriting by Xiong Bin

纵82.5、横37厘米
台湾董良彦先生提供

熊斌（1894-1964），湖北大悟人，曾任湖北军政府北伐第一军参谋抗战中任军令部次长兼战时新闻检查局局长、陕西省政府委员兼省政府主席兼陕西省保安司令等。书云："於穆我君，既敦既纯。雪白之性，孝友之仁。纪行来本，兰生有芬。克岐有兆，绥御有勋。利器不觌"（张迁碑）。

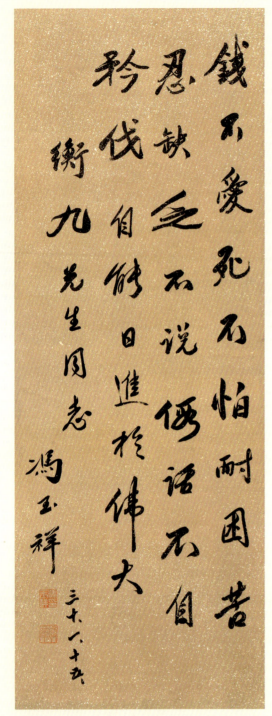

冯玉祥 行书
Running script by Feng Yuxiang

1941年
纵98、横36 厘米
香港翰墨轩（香江博物馆）

冯玉祥（1882-1948），安徽巢县人。抗日战争爆发后，他历任第三、第六战区司令长官、第三战区督导长官、国防最高委员会委员、军政部部长、军政部陆海空军抚恤委员会委员长等职。书云："钱不爱，死不怕，耐困苦，忍缺乏，不说假话，不自矜伐，自能日进于伟大。"

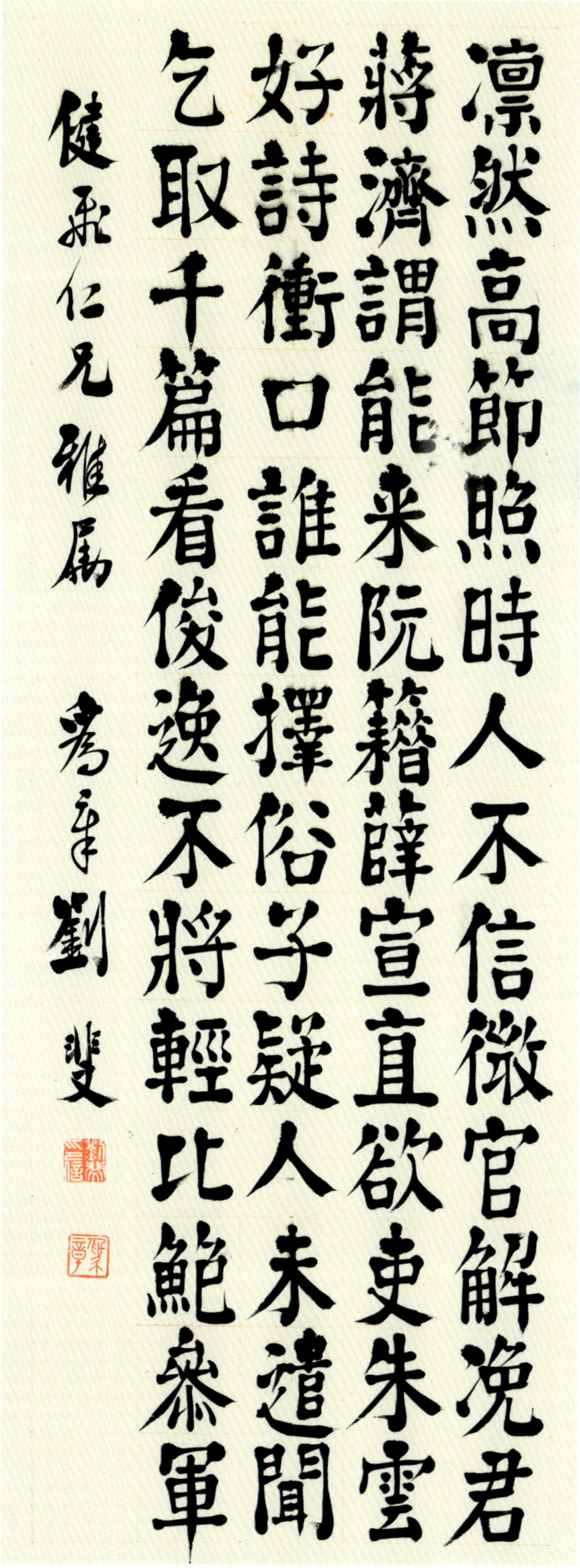

中国抗日战争暨世界反法西斯战争胜利七十周年特展
An Exhibition Dedicated to 70th Anniversary of Victory of War of Resistance against
Japanese Aggression and World Anti-fascist War

凛然高節照時人不信微官解浼君
蔣濟謂能来阮籍薛宣直欲吏朱雲
好詩衝口誰能擇俗子疑人未遣聞
乞取千篇看俊逸不將輕比鮑參軍

健飛仁兄雅屬 秀峰 劉斐

刘斐楷书七言诗

Seven-character regular script, handwritingby liu Fei

纵112、横42.5厘米
台湾董良彦先生提供

刘斐（1898-1983），湖南醴陵人。抗战时期任国防部参谋次长，全面负责作战部的实际指挥。中华人民共和国成立后，在香港通电起义，任全国政协副主席等职。钞苏轼诗云："凛然高节照时人，不信微官解浼君。蒋济谓能来阮籍，薛宣直欲吏朱云。好诗冲口谁能择，俗子疑人未遣闻。乞取千篇看俊逸，不将轻比鲍参军。"

贺衷寒楷书四言联

Four-character couplet in regular
script, handwriting by He Zhonghan

纵126.5、横33.3厘米
台湾董良彦先生提供

贺衷寒（1900–1972），湖南岳阳
人，黄埔一期毕业。抗战时任国
民政府军事委员会政治部第一厅
厅长、政治部秘书长。

钱大钧 篆书四言诗

Four-character couplet in seal script, handwriting
by Qian Dajun

纸本立轴
纵67、横29厘米
熊斌旧藏
台湾董良彦先生提供

钱大钧（1893–1982），江苏吴县人，抗战
中任航空委员会主任、军政部政务次长、军
事委员会委员长侍从室第一处主任兼军事委
员会调查统计局局长。
书云："敬慎威仪，君子有谷。为此春酒，
以介景福。"（集《诗经》句）

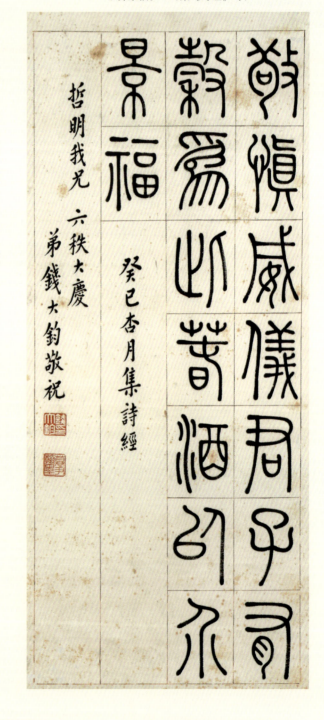

中国抗日战争暨世界反法西斯战争胜利七十周年特展
An Exhibition Dedicated to 70th Anniversary of Victory of War of Resistance against
Japanese Aggression and World Anti-fascist War

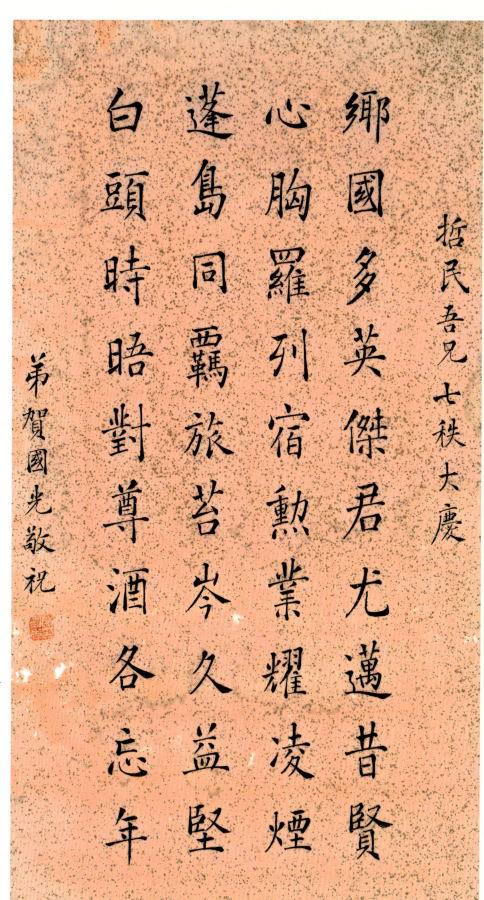

贺国光 楷书五言诗

Five-character couplet in regular script, handwriting by He Guoguang

纸本立轴
纵58.2、横32.2厘米
熊斌旧藏
台湾董良彦先生提供

贺国光（1885-1969），湖北蒲圻人，抗战中代理四川省主席、重庆宪兵司令、防空司令、军事委员会办公厅主任等，为防御日机轰炸有重要贡献。熊斌字哲明。诗云：
"乡国多英杰，君尤迈昔贤。心胸罗列宿，勋业耀凌烟。蓬岛同羁旅，苔岑久益坚。白头时晤对，尊酒各忘年。"

抗戰殉國將領 （來源依據 何應欽上將《日軍侵華八年抗戰史》、忠烈祠入祀名冊，共計 268 名）

依姓氏筆畫順序

國軍上將 佟麟閣、郝夢齡、陳安寶、唐淮源、張自忠、饒國華

國軍中將 寸性奇、方叔洪、王甲本、王　竣、王銘章、王鳳山、王鳳閣、石作衡、朱世勤、朱鴻勳、吳克仁、李必藩、李守維、李成林、李忍濤、李宜煊、李家鈺、李國良、李漢卿、周　復、武漢卿、邵存誠、姜玉貞、段朗如、唐聚五、孫明瑾、徐鎮國、秦　霖、翁　達、馬玉仁、高致嵩、張培梅、張誠德、張維良、張譜行、張鵬飛、張鑾基、許國璋、陳　烈、彭士量、馮安邦、萬　舞、鄧　洪、趙登禹、劉家麒、劉震東、樊　劍、蔣志英、鄧鐵梅、鄭作民、蕭山令、賴傳湘、鮑　剛、戴民權、戴安瀾、鍾　毅、闞維雍

國軍少將 丁永緒、于思元、毛岱鈞、王立業、王自衡、王松元、王保忠、王禹九、王庭麟、王振東、王淦塵、王　湘、王傅綬、王殿華、王劍岳、王輝武、王儒欽、司徒非、左　權、任景讓、朱　赤、朱炎輝、朱芝榮、朱家麟、江春炎、余子武、吳廕恕、吳繼光、呂公良、呂旃蒙、岑家焯、岑　鏗、李文開、李文煥、李世平、李仲寰、李岐山、李果諶、李恆華、李春農、李席九、李紹嘉、李　儉、李翰卿、李錦榮、李懷功、李蘭池、周　元、周致中、周致遠、周鴻賓、宮惠民、易安華、林光偉、林英燦、武士敏、邱中度、邱毓楨、邵恩三、金光灼、金鏡清、姚中英、姚建新、姜宏勛、姜寶德、段推三、洪鋤非、紀鴻儒、胡式禹、胡旭旰、胡金波、胡　越、胡義賓、胡鳳林、苑培民、郁仁治、韋　燦、夏子明、夏軍川、夏國璋、夏維禮、孫子高、孫堂臣、宮志沂、宰青雲、徐衍崑、徐積璋、柴意新、秦　墉、袁聘之、馬文彩、馬威龍、高克敏、高志航、高道光、尉遲鳳崗、張人傑、張世惠、張成義、張利堂、張致廣、張能忍、張國基、張眾佩、張惠民、張景南、張植桴、張　敬、張新階、張殿魁、張榮岡、張榮發、張劍虹、張慶樹、張毅中、張樹楨、張　駿、張鏡遠、扈先梅、曹直正、梁鏡齋、梁鑑堂、莫肇衡、許金臯、郭如嵩、郭貽衍、郭懷翰、陳中柱、陳文杞、陳宗祀、陳飛龍、陳師洛、陳紹堂、陳德馨、陳　範、陳濟垣、陳蘊瑜、陳鐘書、陸　領、傅忠貴、傅　楠、彭　璋、黃永淮、黃英誠、黃啟東、黃梅興、黃禎泰、黃福臣、黃德興、楊　生、楊秀峰、楊家騮、楊振西、楊　傑、溫健公、萬金聲、葛子厚、路景榮、雷　忠、廖孟仁、廖齡奇、趙　侗、趙清廉、趙渭濱、趙翔之、趙　銘、趙錫璋、齊學啟、劉金聲、劉眉生、劉桂五、劉啟文、劉景山、劉民民、劉　緯、蔡炳炎、鄭玉琢、鄧佐虞、鄧述恩、鄭廷珍、燕鼎九、盧尚秀、盧廣偉、蕭孝澤、蕭俊嶺、蕭健九、戴靜園、繆徵中、薄錫三、謝昇標、謝晉元、謝瓊珠、謝鐵男、鍾芳峻、韓忠義、韓炳宸、韓香齊、韓家麟、魏鳳韶、羅策群、龐泰峰、龐漢楨、嚴家訓、竇來庚、蘇世安

抗战胜利70周年《勇士国魂》月历
Heroes: Spirit of the Nation, a calendar issued in Taiwan to mark the 70th anniversary of the victory over Japan

台湾美术馆提供

为纪念抗战胜利70周年，台湾军方发行了《勇士国魂》月历，其中最引人注意的是月历提供台湾官方公布抗战阵亡将士名单中首次公开列入中共将领左权将军。这一做法引起海内外正面评价。

郝柏村为展览题辞
A soldier Hao Baicun writing an inscription for the exhibition

中国国民党前副主席郝柏村先生为《四万万人民——中国抗战暨世界反法西斯战争胜利70周年特展》在所著书籍上题辞为贺。

中国抗日战争暨世界反法西斯战争胜利七十周年特展
An Exhibition Dedicated to 70th Anniversary of Victory of War of Resistance against
Japanese Aggression and World Anti-fascist War

23 抗战英烈永垂不朽
Eternal Legacy of Heroes

　　近年来，在胡锦涛、连战会谈精神的指导下，两岸有关抗战的认识趋于理性。2015年，台湾军方公布的268名殉国将领中包括八路军的左权将军，引起关注。从中日双方公布的阵亡将领名单可以看出，中国抗战在中华民族的救亡图存史上，其力量之悬殊、战斗之惨烈、破坏之严重、牺牲之重大、民族之团结，堪称空前绝后。这些为中华民族牺牲的英烈永垂不朽！

Over recent years people across the Taiwan Straits have an increasingly sensible understanding of the War of Resistance against Japanese Aggression, illustrated by the outcomes of top-level meetings between the CPC and the KMT. In 2015, Taiwan announced 268 top Chinese military officials died in the war, including Zuo Quan from the Eighth Route Army, which attracted intense attention. An examination of the lists of deceased generals published by China and Japan reveals that during the war, China was weak and poor, and suffered devastating consequences and enormous sacrifice in the battles. Yet it witnessed an unprecedented national cohesion born out of the war. The heroes died, but their legacy lives on!

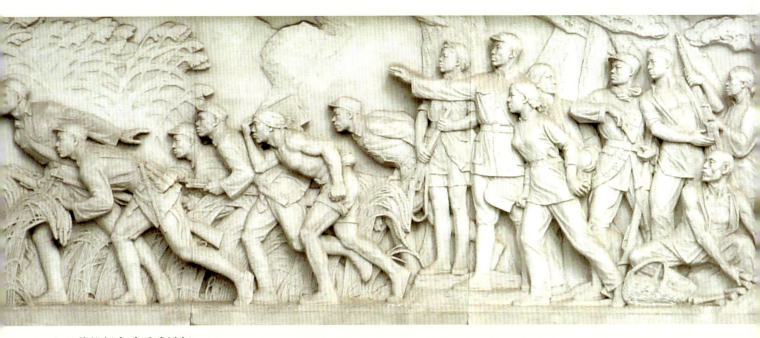

人民英雄纪念碑浮雕局部
Relief of People's Heroes Monument

二 中国士兵
II CHINESE SOLDIERS

在抗战中，国民革命军约有320个师，日军约40个师，双方兵力约8:1。国民革命军牺牲约400万人（含八路军、新四军约30万人），击毙日军约45万，比例约10:1。在正面战场22场会战中，双方战力平均差距为8:1。中国士兵80%是农民，文盲比例高达90%。美军参谋长马歇尔（George C. Marshall）相信，中国军人能吃饱、训练、装备和适当的领导，不输于任何国家。中国的普通士兵，在武器落后、供给匮乏、指挥无能、几无外援的情况下，以他们的坚韧、吃苦、服从、英勇和牺牲，筑起了捍卫民族生存的血肉长城，赢得了世界的尊敬。

About 320 divisions of the NRA were fighting against 40 Japanese divisions in the war. A total of 4 million Chinese soldiers died, 300,000 of whom were from the Eighth Route Army and the New Fourth Army, along with 450,000 Japanese casualties. In 22 major battles in the frontline, Japanese combat forces were seven times stronger than Chinese troops. And 80 percent of Chinese soldiers were peasants, and 90 percent of them were illiterate.George C. Marshall, Chief of Staff of the United States Army, was convinced that with enough food, training, equipment and right leadership, Chinese soldiers would be no weaker than those of any other countries. Despite low-tech weaponry, inadequate supply, weak leadership and little outside support, Chinese soldiers were persistent, gallant and ready to lie down for the country. And they have won global respect for their heroic efforts in defending the country they held dear.

24-1 中日国力
National Strength

日本明治维新后，经济迅速发展。经过甲午战争、庚子赔款、日俄战争，实力远超中国。从1931年到1945年生铁、钢和煤产量看（中国的数据不包括已沦陷的东北，日本数据仅包括其本土），中日国力极其悬殊。以军需看，日本战争期间生产了5.5万架飞机、4800辆坦克和244艘舰船。中国为零。太平洋战争后期，日本在原料匮乏情况下，1945年前8个月仍生产了4万挺机枪，超过中国战时的总和。

Japan saw a rapid economic growth in the wake of the Meiji Restoration. It became much stronger than China after the Sino-Japanese War of 1894-1895, the Boxer Indemnity, and the Russo-Japanese War of 1904-1905. Japan had an obvious edge over China between 1931 and 1945, as illustrated in the much higher production of pig iron, steel and coal on its main land than that of China (excluding the northeastern region). In terms of military supply, Japan produced 55,000 planes, 4,800 tanks and 244 warships throughout the war, as opposed to the zeroes in China. In the first eight months of 1945 when the Pacific War was coming to an end, Japan, short of raw materials, produced 40,000 machine guns, a figure much higher than the total number of China in the war.

年份	生铁（万吨）		钢（万吨）		煤（万吨）	
	中国	日本	中国	日本	中国	日本
1931		91.73		166.3	180	2452
1933	3.45		3		188	
1937	14	253.4	4	508		4526
1938	5.29	285.7	0.09	548.8	470	4868
1940	4.5	357.8	0.15	526.1	570	5731
1942	9.6	457.5	0.3	505	631.4	5718
1945	4.85	91.1	1.82	115.3	523.8	2234

中国抗日战争暨世界反法西斯战争胜利七十周年特展
An Exhibition Dedicated to 70th Anniversary of Victory of War of Resistance against
Japanese Aggression and World Anti-fascist War

24-2 中日军力
Military Strength

中央军满员师约1万人，步枪2千支，子弹每人每月20发，轻重机枪60挺，山炮5门，汽车20辆；日军甲种师团2.2万人，步枪9千支，轻重机枪600挺，汽车1千辆，山炮200门，装甲车20辆，子弹每人月耗300发。

A division of the Central Army had 10,000 soldiers, 2,000 rifles, 60 light-and-heavy machine guns, 5 pieces of mountain artillery, and 20 vehicles. Each solider had 20 bullets. In contrast, a top Japanese division had 22,000 soldiers, 9,000 rifles, 600 light-and-heavy machine guns, 1,000 vehicles, 200 pieces of mountain artillery, and 20 armored vehicles. Each soldier used 300 bullets on average each month.

西班牙摄影师卡帕摄：中国士兵，1938年摄于汉口
Chinese Soldiers by Robert Capa, Hankou,1938

1938年，卡帕随伊文思来华，在台儿庄、武汉等地拍摄《四万万人民》。其代表作"中国士兵"刊登于1938年5月18日美国的《生活》杂志，产生极大的影响。

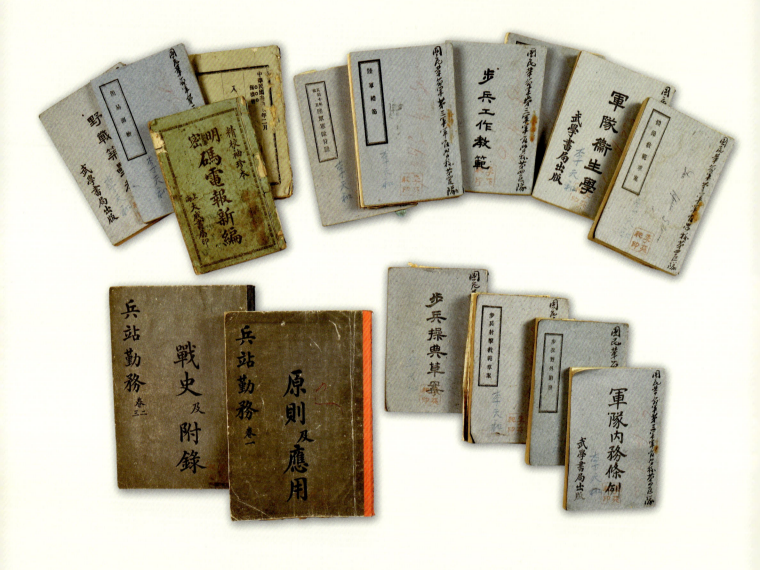

士兵教材

抗战期间，中日军力除了武器之外，还有军人待
遇、文化和训练的差距。太平洋战争爆发后，接
受现代军事训练的中国士兵素质大大增强，单兵
对抗能力由平均8比1，逐渐成1比1。

中国抗日战争暨世界反法西斯战争胜利七十周年特展
An Exhibition Dedicated to 70th Anniversary of Victory of War of Resistance against
Japanese Aggression and World Anti-fascist War

24-3 中国抗战徽章和纪念章
The badges and medals of the war of resistance against Japanese

云南省防空疏散委员会章
直径3.4厘米
滇西抗战纪念馆藏

北平联勤总部六四后方医院荣军纪念章
直径3厘米
滇西抗战纪念馆藏

天津市民敬赠国之干城荣誉铜章
高2.6、宽2.3厘米
滇西抗战纪念馆藏

救国安民荣誉铜证章
直径3厘米
滇西抗战纪念馆藏

抗战反战干团"精干"铜校徽
直径2厘米
滇西抗战纪念馆藏

徽章背后有"抗战反战干团"，"战干团"是战时工作干部训练团的简称。

军官教育程度统计表

类别	人数	百分比
黄埔军校	43018	31.6%
陆军小学堂	20033	14.7%
陆军中学堂	11493	8.4%
保定陆军军官学校	6575	4.8%
各种军官团	5621	4.1%
工兵学校	2175	1.6%
军需学校	2175	1.6%
外国军事学校	1922	1.4%
军医学校	1414	1.0%
特种兵科学校	1075	0.8%
伦家大学	992	0.7%
兵工学校	237	0.2%
行伍	39744	29.4%
总计	136474	100%

（资料来源：张瑞德著《抗战时期的国军人事》，中研院近代史所专刊68，1993年）

抗战时期士兵教育程度表

	陆军第14军（1945）	陆军荣誉第2师（1946）
文盲	29%	5.2%
初识字	46%	45.0%
小学	22%	49.0%
初中	3%	0.5%
高中	0%	0.3%
总计	100%	100%

（资料来源：张瑞德著《抗战时期的国军人事》，中研院近代史所专刊68，1993年）

军训部1944年陆军中下级军官素质统计表

	总计	步	骑	炮	工	辎	通	机
已受养成教育者	31724	25867	227	1722	780	288	2198	631
	27.0%	27.3%	33.8%	48.4%	29.0%	6.8%	21.0%	44.6%
已受召集教育者	44283	42322	264	423	499	---	234	443
	37.6%	44.6%	39.3%	11.9%	18.6%	---	2.3%	31.3%
行伍	38704	26662	181	1410	1410	967	7734	340
	32.9%	28.1%	26.9%	39.7%	52.4%	22.9%	76.0%	24.0%
其他	2968	---	---	---	---	2968	---	---
	2.5%	---	---	---	---	70.30%	---	---
总计	117579	94860	672	3555	2689	4223	10166	1414
	100%	100%	100%	100%	100%	100%	100%	100%

（资料来源：张瑞德著《抗战时期的国军人事》，中研院近代史所专刊68，1993年）

中国抗日战争暨世界反法西斯战争胜利七十周年特展
An Exhibition Dedicated to 70th Anniversary of Victory of War of Resistance against
Japanese Aggression and World Anti-fascist War

三　中国抗战报道
III WAR NEWS IN CHINA

中国抗战期间，在新闻报道出版等宣传上，也进行激烈的斗争。那些揭露日伪罪行，歌颂英烈事迹，真实描述正面战场和敌后战场的抗战报道，鼓舞了人民，打击了敌人；那些吹嘘日军战绩，美化侵略的报道则成为历史的罪证。

An invisible war was fought in news reports of the war in China. On one hand, many news reports provided a morale-boost to the Chinese people and a heavy blow to Japanese troops, because they exposed crimes committed by Japan and the collaborators, celebrated the heroes, and gave a real picture of war in the frontlines and behind enemy lines. On the other hand, some reports were evidence of Japanese crimes, because they highlighted Japanese military performance and whitewashed the aggression.

丁玲、舒群主编抗战刊物《战地》（半月刊）

Battlefild magazine (semi-monthly), editors Ding Ling and Shu Qun

1938年
湖北省博物馆藏

1938年3月20日《战地》在武汉创刊，由上海杂志公司总店发行。

苏联列明著，孙冶方译《中国抗战与国际关系》

"China's Anti-Japanese War and International Relations", written by Soviet Union's Remin, translated by Sun Yefang and published by Liming Bookstore in March 1938

1938年
湖北省博物馆藏

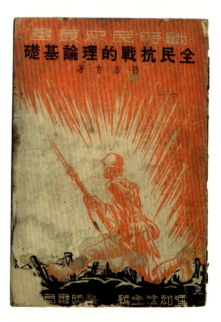

孙冶芳著《全民抗战的理论基础》

Theoretical Foundation of National Resistance, by Sun Yefang

抗战时期
湖北省博物馆藏

本件为第五战区出版。

美国周报《Yank》
(1944年11月11日)
纵35、横25.8厘米

昆明市博物馆藏

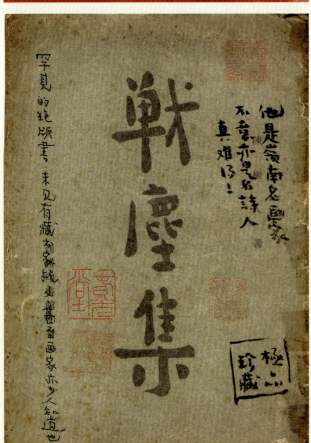

陈树人《战尘集（抗战心史）》
Dust of War, by Chen Shuren

纵20.5、横14.8厘米
香港翰墨轩（香江博物馆）藏

陈树人（1884–1948），广东番禺人，政治活动家、岭南画派创始人之一。本件为战时出版的诗集。1946年7月商务印书馆重庆初版，12月上海初版。

中国抗日战争暨世界反法西斯战争胜利七十周年特展
An Exhibition Dedicated to 70th Anniversary of Victory of War of Resistance against
Japanese Aggression and World Anti-fascist War

日刊《周报》"汉口沦陷"
Fall of Hankou of Japan's Weekly

1938年
纵21、横14.8 厘米
阮鹏
湖北省博物馆藏

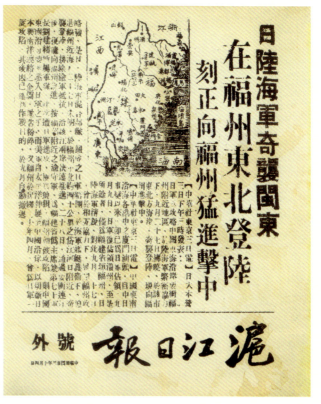

《华北新报》号外
An extra to Huabei New Paper

1944年10月23日
纵29.5、横20.7厘米
香港翰墨轩（香江博物馆）藏

《华北新报》是日本侵华期间华北地区
乃至全国有影响的最后一份亲日报纸。

《沪江日报》号外
An extra to Hujiang Daily

1944年10月4日
纵26.5、横22 厘米
香港翰墨轩（香江博物馆）藏

《沪江日报》是抗战期间上海的日伪报纸。

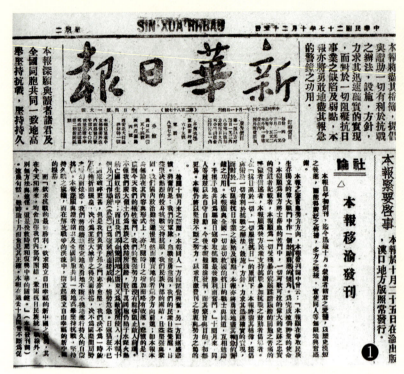

1938年10月25日，创刊于武汉的《新华日报》停刊，同日在重庆出刊，发表《本报移渝发刊》社论

Xinhua Daily stops publication in Wuhan and publishes a statement about its relocation in its new office in Chongqing, October 25, 1938

抗战时期的《新华日报》营业部（现位于渝中区民生路240号）

The office of the Xinhua Daily during the war, at today's 240, Minsheng Road, Yuzhong District Life Bookstore, established by Zou Taofen, is relocated to 157, Minsheng Road, Chongqing, and continued to be published there, 1938

邹韬奋创办的生活书店于1938年底迁至重庆民生路157号继续出版

Life Bookstore, established by Zou Taofen, is relocated to 157, Minsheng Road, Chongqing, and continued to be published there, 1938

中国抗日战争暨世界反法西斯战争胜利七十周年特展
An Exhibition Dedicated to 70th Anniversary of Victory of War of Resistance against
Japanese Aggression and World Anti-fascist War

四 抗战中的宋美龄
IV SOONG MAY-LING IN THE WAR

宋美龄（1897–2003），海南文昌人。抗战期间，她作为中国的第一夫人，发挥了巨大作用。西安事变爆发后，她亲临西安，敦促西安事变的和平解决。抗战期间她出任航空委员会秘书长，被称为"中国空军之母"。她是第一位在美国国会发表演说的中国人，为美国了解和支持中国抗战发挥了不可替代的作用。

Soong May-ling (1897-2003), born in Wenchang, Hainan, was the First Lady of the Republic of China during the war in which she played a prominent role. In Xi'an Incident, she arrived in Xi'an and urged for a peaceful resolution of the incident. She acted as the secretary-general of Chinese Aeronautical Affairs Commission, thus known as the "Mother of Chinese Air Force". Soong was the first Chinese ever to address both houses of the US Congress, and played an irreplaceable role in increasing American understanding and support of the war of Chinese people's resistance against Japanese aggression.

蒋介石宋美龄抗战期间合照
Chiang Kai-shek and Soong May-ling during the war

1940年代
纵27.1、横21.5厘米
香港翰墨轩（香江博物馆）藏

1940年4月18日，宋氏三姐妹参加中美文化协会招待会
The Soong Sisters: Soong May-ling, Soong Ai-ling, and Soong Ching-ling at the reception of the Sino-American Cultural Society on April 18, 1940

1943年2月，宋美龄在美国国会发表演说，为争取美援助、加强同盟关系发挥了重要作用
Soong May-ling addressing the American Congress to seek American support and strengthen the Allied relations, February 1943

第三单元 世界反法西斯同盟

SECTION III
THE WORLD ANTI-FASCIST ALLIANCE

法西斯主义是20世纪20年代兴起的一股反共、反民主、反自由的极权主义和军国主义的政治运动，分别在意大利、德国、日本取得成功。1931年日本侵华，中国最先抵抗日本法西斯。二战爆发后，英、法等国组成联盟抵抗德、意、日轴心国。苏德战争、太平洋战争爆发后，中、美、苏也加入同盟国，美国总统罗斯福则称同盟国为"联合国"。1942年1月1日，26国签署了《联合国共同宣言》誓言取得反法西斯战争的完全胜利。至此，中国抗战成为世界反法西斯战争的重要组成部分。

Fascism, rising in the 1920s, is a political movement that is anti-communist, anti-democratic, anti-liberal totalitarianism and militarism. Fascism was well received in Italy, Germany and Japan. In 1931 Japanese troops invaded China, and China was the first to fight against the Japanese fascists. During World War II, Britain, France and other countries formed an alliance to resist the Axis Powers: Germany, Italy, and Japan. After the outbreak of Russo-German War and the Pacific War, China, the United States, and the Soviet Union joined the Allies. US President Franklin D. Roosevelt named the allied countries "United Nations." On January 1, 1942, a total of 26 countries signed the Declaration by the United Nations and pledged for a total victory over Fascism. Thus the War of Resistance against Japanese Aggression became an important part of the world anti-fascist war.

中国抗日战争暨世界反法西斯战争胜利七十周年特展
An Exhibition Dedicated to 70th Anniversary of Victory of War of Resistance against
Japanese Aggression and World Anti-fascist War

一 得道多助
I FOREIGN SUPPORTS

1931年日本侵略我东三省，当时的国际联盟只是派出调查团对中国表示同情。七七事变爆发后，日本法西斯的残暴侵略和中国的英勇抗战赢得了世界的广泛同情。世界各国纷纷伸出援助之手，支持中国抗战。

When Japan invaded China's three northeastern provinces in 1931, the then League of Nations just sent an investigation group to express sympathy. After the Lugou Bridge Incident, China's heroic resistance to the brutal aggression of Japanese fascists won worldwide sympathy as well as supports from many foreign countries.

1 国际反侵略大会
International anti-invasion conference

国际反侵略大会是一个具有广泛影响的国际组织，1938年1月23日国际反侵略大会中国分会在汉口市商会礼堂成立。1938年2月，该会在英国伦敦召开援华大会，中国驻法国大使顾维钧代表宋庆龄担任大会名誉主席。

International Anti-Invasion Conference is an extensively influential international organization. The China sub-conference was established in the auditorium of Hankou Chamber of Commerce on January 23, 1938. In February 1938, the conference held a meeting to support China in London. Chinese ambassador to France Gu Weijun participated as honorary chairman on behalf of Soong Ching Ling.

1938年1月23日国际反侵略大会中国分会在汉口市商会礼堂（今中山大道489号，武汉市工商业联合会所在地）成立

On January 23, 1938, China sub-conference of International Anti-Invasion Conference was established in the auditorium (No. 489 Zhongshan Dadao, Wuhan Federation of Industry and Commerce) of Hankou Chamber of Commerce

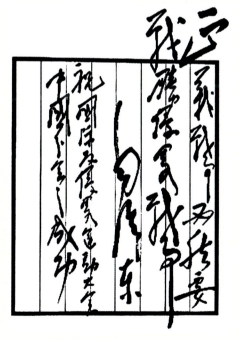

毛泽东为国际反侵略运动大会中国分会两周年题词

The inscription by Mao Zedong for the second anniversary of the China sub-conference of International Anti-Invasion Conference

195

国际反侵略大会中国分会出版的期刊《反侵略》
The periodical "Anti-Invasion" published by the China sub-conference of International Anti-Invasion Conference

2 世界学联
World Students Association

抗日战争爆发后，世界学生联合会一直积极支援中国人民抗击日本法西斯的正义斗争。1938年世界学联派遣代表团抵达战时首都武汉，受到武汉各界热烈欢迎。

After the war broke out, the World Students Association had been actively supporting the Chinese people's just struggle against the fascist invaders. In 1938, the association sent a delegation to the wartime capital Wuhan and was welcomed by various circles of the city.

1938年5月，世界学联代表团抵汉，受到武汉各界热烈欢迎。图为中共和八路军代表欢迎世界学联。

1938年，中共和八路军代表欢迎世界学联代表团抵汉
In 1938, representatives of CPC and the Eighth Route Army welcomed the delegation of World Students Association

中国抗日战争暨世界反法西斯战争胜利七十周年特展
An Exhibition Dedicated to 70th Anniversary of Victory of War of Resistance against
Japanese Aggression and World Anti-fascist War

3-1 尤里斯·伊文思
Joris Ivens

尤里斯·伊文思（Joris Ivens，1898-1989），荷兰人，世界著名纪录片电影导演。1938，伊文思第一次来华，经香港到达汉口，拍摄了代表作《四万万人民》，记录了中国人民抗日战争。在汉期间，他将一部电影摄影机赠给延安的电影工作者吴印咸，这是人民电影事业的第一部摄影机。

Joris Ivens (1898-1989), a native of the Netherlands, is world-famous film director of documentaries. In 1938, Ivens first came to Wuhan through Hong Kong. He shot his masterpiece "400 Million Chinese People" which recorded the war of resistance against Japanese aggression. During his stay in Wuhan, he gave a film camera to Wu Yinxian, a film worker in Yan'an, as a gift. This is the first film camera for the people's film making industry.

周恩来、邓颖超在伊文思赠送给八路军的电影机前留影

Zhou Enlai and Deng Yingchao took a photo by the film camera donated by Ivens to the Eighth Route Army

197

3-2 路易·艾黎与工合
Rewi Alley and Industrial Cooperative Movement

路易·艾黎（Rewi Alley，1897～1987），新西兰人。作家、教育家和社会活动家，伟大的国际主义战士。1927年来到中国，直到去世，为中国人民的解放和建设事业奋斗了整整60年。抗日战争时期，他积极参加并发起组织了工业合作社运动（简称工合），1938年8月5日，中国工业合作协会在武汉正式成立。路易·艾黎任代理总干事。工合成为抗战时期失业工人和难民生产自救、支援抗战的一支独特的经济力量。它为供应战时军需民用特别是援助中国共产党领导下的人民游击战争做出了重要贡献。

Rewi Alley (1897-1987), from New Zealand, is writer, educator, social activist and great international fighter. He came to China in 1927 and had lived here till his death, devoting 60 years to China's liberation and construction. During the war, he initiated the Industrial Cooperative Movement. On August 5, 1938, China Industrial Cooperative Association was founded in Wuhan with Alley as the acting secretary-general. The association became a unique economic power during the war to help jobless workers and refugees and support the resistance. It made great contributions to the supply of military and civil logistics, especially the people's guerilla war.

路易·艾黎与工合的工友一起劳动
Rewi Alley worked with workmates at the Industrial Cooperative Association

中国抗日战争暨世界反法西斯战争胜利七十周年特展
An Exhibition Dedicated to 70th Anniversary of Victory of War of Resistance against
Japanese Aggression and World Anti-fascist War

抗战时期的路易·艾黎（右三）
Rewi Alley during the war (third right)

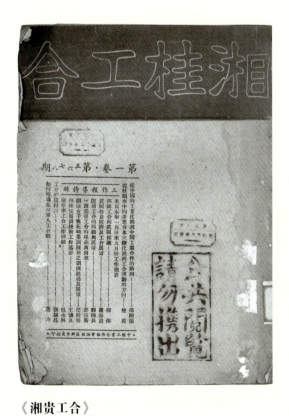

《湘贵工合》
"Hunan and Guizhou Industrial Cooperative Movement"

工合证章
Badge of Industrial Cooperative Movement

4 国际志愿医疗队
International volunteer medical team

抗日战争爆发后，中国军队恶劣的医疗条件引起世人关注。在国内外爱好和平的人士的努力下，1938年以白求恩大夫为首的加拿大、美国志愿医疗队和以爱德华大夫为首的印度志愿医疗队陆续来到武汉，再由武汉奔赴抗战前线。其后，又有许多来自德国、英国、法国、荷兰、捷克斯洛伐克、波兰和奥地利等国家的医务工作者，为支援中国人民的反法西斯战争，来到中国，并送来了一批批医药和器械。

After the war broke out, the harsh medical conditions of the Chinese troops aroused the attention of the world. In 1938, the Canadian-American Volunteer Medical Team headed by Doctor Henry Norman Bethune and Indian Volunteer Medical Team headed by M. M. Atal came to Wuhan. And from there, they went on to other parts of the battlefronts. Medical workers from Germany, UK, France, the Netherlands, Czechoslovakia, Poland and Austria came to support China in the war against Japanese aggression. Along with them were also medicines and equipment.

1938年1月8日，率加美医疗队来华的白求恩（左一）在"亚洲女皇号"上

On January 8, 1938, Dr. Bethune (first left) who headed the Canadian-American medical team on the ship Asian Queen

亨利·诺尔曼·白求恩（Henry Norman Bethune，1890–1939）是加拿大共产党党员。抗战爆发后率领加拿大、美国医疗队于1938年初来武汉，3月底到达延安，不久赴晋察冀边区。因急救手术时受感染，于1939年11月12日在河北省唐县逝世。毛泽东曾为他写下著名篇章《纪念白求恩》。

武汉八路军办事处欢迎印度援华医疗队在屋顶花园的合影

Wuhan No. 8 Office welcomed Indian medical team on the roof garden

印度国大党领袖尼赫鲁的组织成立了印度援华医疗队，在队长爱德华（M. M. Atal）率领下于1938年1月抵达汉口。1939年，医疗队先后到达延安和山西八路军总部。该队柯棣华(D. S. Kotnis，1910–1942)医生于1941年1月任白求恩国际和平医院院长，1942年12月9日不幸因病殉职。

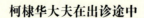

毛泽东会见印度援华医疗队全体成员。毛泽东（右四）、爱德华（右二）、卓克华（右一）、柯棣华（左二）、巴苏（左一）、木克华（左四）

Mao Zedong (fourth right) met members of Indian medical team: B.K. Basu (first left), D. S. Kotnis (second left), M.M.Atal (second right) and M.R.Cholkar (first right)

柯棣华大夫在出诊途中
Dr. Kotnis on the way to visiting patients

中国抗日战争暨世界反法西斯战争胜利七十周年特展
An Exhibition Dedicated to 70th Anniversary of Victory of War of Resistance against
Japanese Aggression and World Anti-fascist War

5 三S在武汉
Three S in China

　　美国著名进步记者埃德加·斯诺、艾格尼丝·史沫特莱和安娜·路易斯·斯特朗三人姓氏的第一个英文字母都是S，所以统称三S。他们三人长期致力于向全世界宣传和介绍中国人民解放事业。1938年，三S汇集到当时的抗战中心武汉，为中国人民的抗战事业奔走呼号，向世界报道中国军民抗击日本侵略者的斗争。

　　Edgar Snow, Agenes Smedle and Anna Louis Strong, the three famous American journalists were called "Three S" for they all had the letter "S" in their surnames. They devoted themselves in introducing and promoting the Chinese anti-war action to the world. In 1938, they gathered in the then anti-war center Wuhan to report the Japanese brutal aggression to China, and called on support to the Chinese people.

1938年周恩来在武汉与史沫特莱等合影

In 1938, Zhou Enlai was with Agenes Smedle inWuhan

艾格尼丝·史沫特莱(Agenes Smedle，1892-1950)，1938年初至1938年10月史沫特莱在汉口，以英国《曼彻斯特卫报》记者和中国红十字会志愿人员的身份，一面报道中国抗战，一面积极募捐和争取国际医疗援助，动员并组织了白求恩、印度援华医疗队等来华支援中国抗战。

1938年周恩来、邓颖超和斯诺在武汉大学珞珈山的合影

Zhou Enlai and Deng Yingchao were with Edgar Snow at Luojiashan in 1938

抗战时期宋庆龄与斯诺的合影

Soong Ching Ling was with Edgar Snow during the war

周恩来与斯特朗的合影

Zhou Enlai was with Anna Louis Strong

6 日本反战人士
Japanese anti-war people

1938年，政治部三厅组织日本反战人士开展对日宣传，他们与中国人民一道，为抗击日本侵略者做出了特殊的贡献。

鹿地亘（1903～1982），日本著名反战作家。抗日战争期间，在中国国统区积极领导和组织了在华日人的反战活动，为中国人民的抗战事业做出了独特的贡献。 1938年3月，鹿地亘和夫人池田幸子应三厅厅长郭沫若邀请抵达武汉，接受国民政府军委会设计委员聘书，参加第七处工作。帮助指导三厅七处的对日宣传工作。

Kaji Wataru (1903-1982), famous Japanese anti-war writer. During the war, he took an active part in organizing anti-war activities among the Japanese in China in the Kuomintang-ruled areas, making great contributions to the Chinese people's war against Japanese aggression. In March 1938, Kaji Wataru and his wife were invited by Guo Moruo to come to Wuhan and accepted the invitation to work as a plan member of Military Committee under the National Government. They worked at No. 7 Division to help with the publicity work toward Japan.

鹿地亘在前线作反战宣传
Kaji Wataru worked in the battlefront

日本友人鹿地亘（左一）、池田幸子（左二）
夫妇是三厅对敌宣传方面的顾问

绿川英子与丈夫刘仁
Verda Majo and her husband Liu Ren

绿川英子（1912-1947），本名长谷川照子。早年参加了左翼文化运动和反对日本军国主义的斗争，后与中国留学生刘仁结婚。1937年来到中国参加中国抗战活动。1938年7月来到临时首都武汉，担任中国电台的日语播音。周恩来曾对她说："日本军国主义把你称为'娇声卖国贼'，其实你是日本人民忠实的好女儿，真正的爱国主义者。"

中国抗日战争暨世界反法西斯战争胜利七十周年特展
An Exhibition Dedicated to 70th Anniversary of Victory of War of Resistance against
Japanese Aggression and World Anti-fascist War

二 苏联援华志愿航空队
II SOVIET AIR FORCE VOLUNTEER GROUP

1937年11月苏联组成志愿航空队援华作战，直至苏联卫国战争爆发，先后派遣2000余人来华参战。从1937年12月在南京上空秘密参战，到1939年底基本撤出，有700多名志愿队员直接参加了保卫南京、武汉、南昌、成都、重庆、兰州等地的25次战役，出动飞机千余架次，击落日机数百架，炸沉日军各类船舰70余艘。苏联志愿航空队200多名官兵献出了生命。

In November 1937, the Soviet Union organized a Volunteer Air Force Group; more than 2,000 volunteers were sent to support China before the outbreak of the Great Patriotic War. From the secret air aid over Nanjing in December 1937 to the end of withdrawal in 1939, more than 700 volunteers directly participated in 25 campaigns, defending Nanjing, Wuhan, Nanchang, Chengdu, Chongqing, and Lanzhou; they carried out more than a thousand of missions, shot down hundreds of Japanese planes, and sank more than 70 Japanese warships of various types. More than 200 military officers and soldiers from the Soviet Air Force Volunteer Group lost their lives in action.

自1938年2月18日起，日本对重庆进行长达五年半的狂轰滥炸，企图瓦解我军民的抗敌意志
Japan begins to launch heavy air attacks on Chongqing, February 18, 1938, to force Chinese troops and civilians to surrender, and the attacks lasts for a total of five years a half

苏联援助中国的SB-2轰炸机
SB-2 bomber provided to China by the Soviet Union

苏联在抗战初期派遣了2000多航空志愿队员，并向中国提供
飞机援助。图为苏联援助中国的SB-2轰炸机。

抗战初期来华助战的苏联航空志愿队I-16战斗机
I-16 fighter of the volunteers of Soviet Air Force at the early days of the war

库里申科

库里申科（ригорий Акимович Кулишенко，
1903–1939），苏联援华飞行员。1939年10月
14日，库里申科与日机在武汉上空激战，飞机
受损。返航中，飞机被迫停在万州境内的江
面，库里申科因疲劳无法出舱，溺水牺牲。

1938年武汉市民仰头观看空战的情形
Wuhan residents looked up at the air battle in 1938

中国抗日战争暨世界反法西斯战争胜利七十周年特展
An Exhibition Dedicated to 70th Anniversary of Victory of War of Resistance against
Japanese Aggression and World Anti-fascist War

7-1 苏联志愿航空队轰炸日军松山基地
Soviet Air Force Volunteer Group Bombing the Japanese Base in Songshan

位于台北的松山机场是日军用来攻击江浙各地的基地。中国空军和苏联志愿航空队获悉日本一支运载新飞机的船队刚抵达台北，决定奇袭松山机场。1938年2月23日，28架С Б-2飞机轰炸松山机场，炸毁日机40架，我飞机全部返回。

Songshan Airport, located in Taipei, was the Japanese base to attack the area around Jiangsu and Zhejiang. When informed a new fleet of Japanese aircraft had just arrived in Taipei Songshan Airport, China and the Soviet Air Force Volunteer Group decided to launch a surprise attack. On February 23, 1938, twenty-eight СБ-2 planes bombed Songshan Airport, destroying 40 Japanese aircraft with no loss on China's side.

志愿航空队的架С Б-2(SB-2)轰炸机在汉口机场进行挂弹
The СБ-2 planes of Soviet Air Force Volunteer bomber is hanging bombs in Hankou airport

7-2 南昌空战
Nanchang Combat

1938年2月至7月，苏联空军志愿队与中国空军在江西省南昌与日机多次交战。2月25日击落日机8架，击伤日机4架，损失飞机7架。6月26日，击落击伤日机6架。7月4日，击落日机7架。7月18日，击落日机4架。

From February to July in 1938, the Soviet Air Force Volunteer Group and the Chinese Air Force had several combats with Japanese troops in Nanchang, Jiangxi Province. On February 25, eight Japanese aircraft were shot down, four Japanese aircraft were damaged, and seven aircraft were lost on our side. On June 26, six Japanese aircraft were shot down or damaged. On July 4, seven Japanese aircraft were shot down. On July 18, four Japanese aircraft were shot down.

日军飞行员村宽一三的座机，在南昌空战中被中国空军打掉了二分之一机翼
Japanese pilot Murahiro Kazumi's plane, half of which is destroyed by Chinese fighters in the air battle over Nanchang

7-3 兰州空战
Lanzhou Combat

1939年2月，中国空军和苏联空军志愿队在甘肃兰州与日机空战，击落敌机40多架，尾随敌机在山西运城机场炸毁敌机40多架，极大地打击了日寇的嚣张气焰。10个月后，敌机又于1939年12月26、27、28日连续3天再袭兰州。日陆海军航空队联合先后共出动90多架，又被我军击落10架。

In February 1939, the Soviet Air Force Volunteer Group and the Chinese Air Force combated Japanese air force in Lanzhou, Gansu Province. More than 40 Japanese aircraft were shot down and more than 40 aircraft were blown up in Yuncheng airport, which was a great blow to the arrogant Japanese invaders. Ten months later, Japanese air force once again attacked Lanzhou in three consecutive days from December 26 to 28 in 1939. The Joint Air Force of Japanese Army and Navy dispatched more than 90 planes, out of which 10 were shot down

空战英雄之一的徐华江与I-15座机合影
Xu Huajiang and his I-15 fighter. Xu Huajiang was a hero in air battles against Japan

中国抗日战争暨世界反法西斯战争胜利七十周年特展
An Exhibition Dedicated to 70th Anniversary of Victory of War of Resistance against
Japanese Aggression and World Anti-fascist War

7-4 空袭汉口日军机场
Air Raids on Japanese Military Airport in Hankou

　　1939年10月，第一次长沙会战期间，为打击日本空军，中国空军及苏联志愿航空队9架DB3轰炸机由成都起飞攻击日军汉口机场，炸毁日军飞机24架及正在修理中的日军飞机10架。14日，以20架DB3飞机再次攻击日军汉口机场，炸毁日军飞机50架，击落日军飞机2架，给日军华中陆军航空队以重大打击。库里申科在这次空袭中牺牲。

　　During the first battle of Changsha in October 1939, in order to combat the Japanese air force, nine DB3 bombers from the Chinese Air Force and the Soviet Volunteer Group took off from Chengdu Airport and attacked Japanese Hankou airport, destroying 24 Japanese aircraft and 10 under-repair aircraft. On October 14th, 20 DB3 aircraft, in another raid on Japanese Hankou airport, bombed 50 Japanese planes and shot down two Japanese planes. These raids caused serious damage to the Japanese Army Air Corps in Central China. Curry Tymoshenko sacrificed in the air combat.

包雷宁上将

包雷宁（Полынин Федор Петрович，1906–1981），苏联英雄，空军上将。1938年2月23率机轰炸松山机场，创无损凯旋记录。包雷宁也因此获苏联英雄金星勋章。

顾边科

顾边科 (Губенко Антон Алексеевич, 1908–1939)，苏联英雄。从5.31空战开始顾边科在华较为时间短暂的抗战中总共起飞了50多次，总共空战飞时超过60小时，八战七胜，共击落敌机七架。

珂拉夫钦科

珂拉夫钦科（Кравченко Григорий Пантелеевич，1912–1943）因在援华抗战时击落敌机10架，成为获得两次苏联英雄奖章。1940年11月，刚满28岁的珂拉夫钦科被授予空军中将军衔。1943年牺牲后葬于红场。

何留金上将

何留金上将（Хрюкин Тимофей Тимофеевич, 1910–1953），双重苏联英雄（1939, 1945），苏联空军上将，苏联空军副总司令。1938年3月至11月作为第五批苏联抗日志愿军航空队成员赴华参加抗战。曾获国民政府政府颁授特种襟绥云麾勋章。

阿列克谢·谢尔盖耶维奇·报喜

阿列克谢·谢尔盖耶维奇·报喜（Алексей Сергеевич Благовещенский, 1909–1994），苏联英雄。1938年11月14日他因在华空战的英雄事迹被授予苏联英雄奖章。苏联卫国战争期间任第二歼击航空兵团后备司令，中将。后转入航空业负责新飞机研发。本照片系作者家属提供。

崔可夫元帅

崔可夫元帅 (Vasily Ivanovich Chuikov, 1900–1982)，1940年，崔可夫作为苏联最后一任顾问团团长来华。

国民政府发给苏联援华志愿航空队的救护符
Ambulance symbo issued by Chinese government

中国抗日战争暨世界反法西斯战争胜利七十周年特展
An Exhibition Dedicated to 70th Anniversary of Victory of War of Resistance against
Japanese Aggression and World Anti-fascist War

8 汉口苏联空军志愿队烈士墓
Soviet Air Force Volunteer Group Memorial Monument in Hankou

1938年，当中国抗战最激烈时，苏联派出最优秀的儿女苏联空军志愿队援华，许多名志愿队员血洒长空。在汉口解放公园内有15位苏联空军志愿队的烈士墓。

In 1938, the Soviet Union assembled the best personnel and sent the Soviet Air Force Volunteer Group to support China during the most intensified battle against Japanese invasion; as many volunteer members died in the missions, a memorial monument for 15 heroes of the Soviet Air Force Volunteer Group was built in the Hankou Liberation Park.

记事碑碑文如下：

1938年，当中国人民正遭到日本法西斯疯狂侵略的时候，苏联人民无私的派遣了自己的优秀儿女——苏联空军志愿队来到中国，援助了中国人民反抗日本法西斯侵略的伟大的正义的斗争。

苏联空军志愿队与中国人民一道在反击日本法西斯的斗争中创立了无数的英雄战绩。他们以武汉为基地，曾远征台北，猛烈地轰击过长江中的敌舰，并顽强地参加了保卫武汉的斗争，严重地打击了日寇的疯狂气焰，鼓舞了中国人民的战斗意志。

在激烈的战斗中有许多名志愿队员献出了自己的生命。其中有重轰炸机大队长库里申科和战斗机大队长拉赫曼诺夫。为了中国人民的解放事业，苏联空军志愿队的烈士们的鲜血和中国人民的鲜血溶结在一起了。他们将永远活在中国人民的心里。

让这种属于工人阶级的高贵的国际主义精神永远发展和牢固的中苏两国人民兄弟般的牢不可破的友谊。烈士们永垂不朽！

一九五六年三月

2013年5月14日俄罗斯总统全权代表巴比奇拜谒苏联空军志愿队烈士墓
Mikhail Viktorovich Babich, Plenipotentiary of the Russian President, visits a cemetery of volunteers of Soviet Air Force, May 14, 2013

汉口苏联空军志愿队烈士墓15位烈士
15 martyrsof Soviet Air Force Volunteer Force in Hankou

姓名	生卒时间	军衔	荣誉
米哈伊尔·德米特里耶维奇·希什洛夫 Михаил Дмитриевич Шишлов	1908–1938.2.8	二级军事技术员	
莫伊谢伊·伊萨阿科维奇·基吉里什登 Моисей Исаакович Кизильштейн	1913–1938.2.15	初级指挥官	1938年被授予红旗勋章
弗拉基米尔·伊万诺维奇·帕拉莫诺夫 Владимир Иванович Парамонов	1911–1938.2.15	二级军事技术员	1938年被授予红星勋章
瓦连京·谢尔盖耶维奇·科兹洛夫 Валентин Сергеевич Козлов	1912–1938.2.15	初级指挥官	1938年被授予红星勋章
瓦西里·瓦西里耶维奇·佩索茨基 Василий Васильевич Песоцкий	1907–1938.2.15	中尉	被授予红旗勋章
德米特里·巴甫洛维奇·马特维耶夫 Дмитрий Павлович Матвеев	1907–1938.7.16	中尉	
伊万·伊里奇·斯图卡洛夫 Иван Ильич Стукалов	1905–1938.7.16	上尉	
马克·尼古拉耶维奇·马尔琴科夫 Марк Николаевич Марченков	1914–1938.7.9	初级指挥官	获"苏联英雄"称号，并获列宁勋章
德米特里·伊万诺维奇·库列申 Дмитрий Иванович Кулешин	1914–1938.8.21	初级指挥官	
列昂尼德·伊万诺维奇·斯科尔尼亚科夫 Леонид Иванович Скорняков	1909–1938.8.17	上尉	
弗拉基米尔·格拉西莫维奇·多尔戈夫 Владимир Герасимович Долгов	1907–1938.7.16	上尉	
菲利普·杰尼索维奇·古里耶 Филипп Денисович Гулый	1909–1938.8.12	上尉	
柯西扬·柯西扬诺维奇·楚里亚科夫 Хасьян Хасьянович Чуряков	1907–1938.8.12	上尉	
尼古拉·米哈伊洛维奇·捷列霍夫 Николай Михайлович Терехов	1907–1938.8.12	上尉	
伊万·尼基福罗维奇·古罗夫 Иван Никифорович Гуров	1914–1938.8.3		

中国抗日战争暨世界反法西斯战争胜利七十周年特展
An Exhibition Dedicated to 70th Anniversary of Victory of War of Resistance against
Japanese Aggression and World Anti-fascist War

三 中国空军美国志愿援华航空队
III AMERICAN VOLUNTEER GROUP (AVG) OF THE CHINESE AIR FORCE

七七事变后，美飞行教官陈纳德接受宋美龄的意见，在美国召募飞行员组建中国空军美国志愿援华航空队，正式名称为美籍志愿大队（American Volunteer Group）。由于飞机头部画有飞虎，故称飞虎队。太平洋战争爆发后，飞虎队归入美军编制为第23航空大队，也称美国驻华空军特遣队。1943年扩编为美国陆军航空兵第14航空队，陈纳德任少将司令。至战争结束，第十四航空队共击落日敌机2600架，自己损失500架，仅驼峰航线就牺牲近3000人，为中国抗战和世界反法西斯战争做出了巨大贡献。

After the Lugou Bridge Incident, the American flight instructor Chennault, accepting Soong May-ling's suggestion, recruited pilots and established the US Air Force Volunteer Group of the Chinese Air Force, formally known as the American Volunteer Group. The aircrafts were painted with tiger heads, hence named the Flying Tigers. After the outbreak of the Pacific War, the Flying Tigers was absorbed into the 23rd Fighter Group of the US Army Air Forces, also known as US Special Air Unit in China, and was later expanded to Fourteenth Air Force of the United States Army Air Forces with General Chennault as commander. To the end of the war, the Fourteenth Air Force shot down 2,600 Japanese aircrafts but lost 500 planes; the Hump alone lost nearly 3,000 people, a sacrifice that made great contributions to the Chinese people's anti-Japanese war and the World Anti-Fascist War.

9 中国军民援救美军飞行员
Chinese people saving the American pilot

1944年5月6日，美军第十四航空队（飞虎队）飞行员格林·本尼达（Green E. Beneda）驾驶P-51野马战机攻击日军在武汉的目标返航时，被监利白螺机场起飞的日机击落于监利周老嘴罗家村下凤湖。格林被村民营救，送至江陵赵家垴的新四军第五师第三军分区襄南指挥部。

Glen E. Beneda was a P-51 Mustang pilot of the American 14th Air Force (Flying Tigers). On May 6, 1944, on his way back after attacking the Japanese-occupied Wuhan, he was shot down by Japanese planes taking off from Bailuo Airport in Jianli. After crash-landing in the Xiafeng Lake in Luojia Village, Zhoulaozui Town, Jianli, Hubei, he was rescued by local residents and sent to the headquarters of the Third Sub-region of the Fifth Division of the New Fourth Army in Zhaojianao, Jiangling.

格林·本尼达驾驶的P51战机起落架
The landing gear of P-51 Mustang by Glen E. Beneda
1944年
监利县博物馆藏

《飞虎情缘》
Touching the Tigers

2002年，格林·本尼达来华参加在北京举办的二战中美老兵的座谈会。他接到了一位监利县女士的电话。她获悉本尼达的故事，她祖父就参与过救助本尼达。2005年，本尼达再次来华遇到了李小林。李小林被本尼达的故事以及他与父亲李先念之间的渊源深深感动。她帮本尼达安排了一次回到拯救过他的村庄的"朝圣之旅"。2005年，监利千余名民众夹道欢迎英雄回归，并为本尼达举办了欢庆会。他们还制作了特殊的竹椅，抬着他前往飞机坠落的湖泊。本尼达居然发现人群中还有当年救助过他的乡亲。2011年4月12日，讲述本尼达与中国人民结缘的故事的纪录片《飞虎情缘》（Touching the Tigers）在美国首都华盛顿中国驻美大使馆首映。前中国国家主席李先念之女、时任中国人民对外友好协会副主席李小林是该片的制片人。当年正是在李先念的安排下，本尼达从救助他的村庄处被安全地转移到了飞虎队当时在重庆的驻地。

中国抗日战争暨世界反法西斯战争胜利七十周年特展
An Exhibition Dedicated to 70th Anniversary of Victory of War of Resistance against
Japanese Aggression and World Anti-fascist War

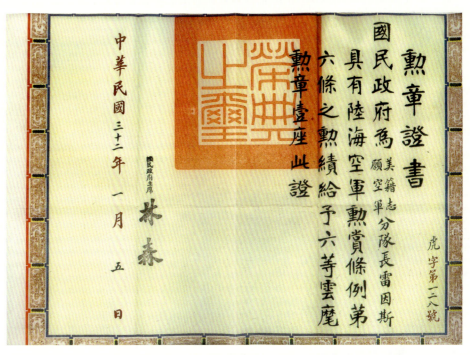

国民政府颁发给飞虎队员的六等云麾勋章证书
Medal and certificate issued to the Flying Tigers by the KMT government

纵48、横41.5厘米
昆明博物馆藏

中央飞机制造公司与飞虎队员签订的雇佣合约
An employment contract signed between the Central Aircraft
Manufacturing Company and the Flying Tiger pilots

纵42、横28厘米
昆明博物馆藏

太平洋战争之前，美国志愿队是以平民身份参战，由美国
联邦中央飞机制造公司与之签订合同。该合约每月支付飞
行员雷恩600美元工资。

美军飞虎队皮质圆形标志
The circular mark of Flying Tigers

直径13厘米
昆明博物馆藏

美军飞虎队徽章
Insignia of Flying Tigers

直径6.7 厘米
昆明博物馆藏

飞虎队求救护符
A "blood chit" of the Flying Tigers to seek
Chinese help in case of emergency

纵27、横20.6厘米
昆明博物馆藏

美飞虎队成员个人用品
Personal articles of Flying Tigers' members

昆明市博物馆藏

中国抗日战争暨世界反法西斯战争胜利七十周年特展
An Exhibition Dedicated to 70th Anniversary of Victory of War of Resistance against
Japanese Aggression and World Anti-fascist War

10 驼峰航线
The Hump

　　"驼峰航线"是二战时期中国和盟军一条主要的空中通道，始于1942年，终于二战结束。它西起印度阿萨姆邦，向东横跨喜马拉雅山脉、高黎贡山、横断山进入云南，航线全长500英里。中美双方共有84000多人参与，运送85万吨的战略物资、军队3.3万余人。美军共损失飞机1500架以上，牺牲飞行员近3000人。

　　"The Hump" refers to a major airlift passage for China and the Allies from 1942 till the end of World War II. This passage spanned 500 miles, and started from Assam of India to Yunnan province across the eastern end of the Himalayas, Gaoligong Mountains and the Hengduan Mountains. A total of 84,000 people from China and US took part in transporting 850,000 tons of strategic supplies and 33,000 military personnel. The U.S. Army lost more than 1,500 aircraft and nearly 3,000 pilots in total.

驼峰航线美国援华物资运送情况统计表
American supplies delivered to China through the Hump

航线长度（印度阿萨姆邦–中国昆明）	882公里
飞行总架次	80000多架次
飞行总时间	150万小时
1942年5–12月运送	4732吨
1943年运货量	109177吨
1944年运货量	231219吨
1945年运货量	435546吨
美国航空队运货总量	736374吨
中国航空队运货总量	44300吨
1942–1945年运货总量	780674吨
损失飞机	609架
损失飞行员	1579人
中航运人印度物质总量	20472吨
运送人员去印度	33477人

驼峰航线沿线的景色
View of the mountains along the hump rout

中美共同开辟了自印度汀江到昆明的空中运输航线即著名的"驼峰航线"
Chinese and American pilots open a line of communication between Dinjan of India and Kunming of China: the Hump

经驼峰航线运往中国供B-29远程轰炸机使用的燃油
Fuel oils for B-29 heavy bombers delivered to China through the Hump

1942年，美国志愿航空队"地狱天使"中队队员们在P-40飞机前合影，飞机上贴有5面日本国旗，表明已击落了5架日机
The Third Squadron "Hell's Angels" of the American Volunteer Group and a P-40 fighter. The five Japanese flags on the plane indicate that the pilot shots down five Japanese planes

中国抗日战争暨世界反法西斯战争胜利七十周年特展
An Exhibition Dedicated to 70th Anniversary of Victory of War of Resistance against
Japanese Aggression and World Anti-fascist War

第16战斗机中队安装用竹子和鱼胶制作的副油箱
The 16th Fighter Squadron install an auxiliary fuel tank made of
bamboos and fish bladders

等待起飞
Waiting to take off

支援地面部队
Support of ground forces

修建机场
Construction of airport

飞行员Theodore B Marxson和战机

Pilot Theodore B Marxson and a fighter

1943年
纵14、横10厘米
昆明博物馆藏

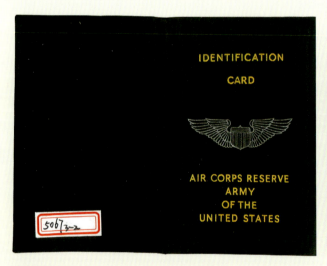

飞行员Theodore B Marxson的飞行证

The pilot license of Theodore B Marxson

1942年
纵10.2、横6.2厘米
昆明博物馆藏

中国抗日战争暨世界反法西斯战争胜利七十周年特展
An Exhibition Dedicated to 70th Anniversary of Victory of War of Resistance against
Japanese Aggression and World Anti-fascist War

11 陈纳德将军
General Chennault

陈纳德（ClaireLeeChennault，1893-1958），抗战时期任美国援华空军飞虎队队长。1936年他任中央航空学校飞行教官，后被宋美龄任命为空军顾问。全面抗战爆发后，他参加了淞沪、南京和武汉会战。1941年8月，他组建中国空军美国志愿航空队任上校队长。飞虎队转为美国陆军第14航空队后任少将司令。同年被聘为中国空军参谋长。

Chennault (Claire Lee Chennault, 1893-1958), served as the captain of Flying Tigers, the United States Army Air Forces (USAAF) Aid to China, during the anti-Japanese war. In 1936 he served as the flight instructor at the central aviation school, and was later appointed air advisor by Madam Chiang. After the outbreak of the War of Resistance against Japanese Aggression, he participated in the battles of Shanghai, Nanjing and Wuhan. In August 1941, he created the American Volunteer Air Force of the Chinese Air Force and served as colonel captain. He was appointed Major General when the Flying Tigers were absorbed into the US Army Fourteenth Air Force and took office as the Chief Advisor of the Chinese Air Force in the same year.

二战期间，飞虎队陈纳德和蒋介石夫妇在重庆
General Claire Lee Chennault, WW II leader of the "Flying Tigers" and Chiang Kaishek and Mme. Chiang (Soong Meiling) in Chongqing

陈纳德亲笔签名照
Autographed photo of Chennault

1941年
周海圣先生捐赠，湖北省博物馆藏

本件为陈纳德赠送周至柔将军的亲笔签名照。

四 中缅印战区
IV THE CHINA-BURMA-INDIA THEATER

太平洋战争爆发后，日军进攻缅甸击败英军，以切断中国唯一与外界联系的运输通道。美国希望中国出兵与英美军队共同作战。盟国于是在亚洲战场把缅甸、泰国、越南、印度与中国战区合并，成立盟军"中缅印战区"，由蒋介石出任总司令，美国史迪威将军任参谋长。1942年2月，中国远征军正式出兵缅甸，开启了中美英联合作战。

After the outbreak of the Pacific War, the Japanese army attacked Burma and defeated the British troops, cutting off China's only transport corridor. The United States wanted China to join the British and American military endeavor. So the allied countries merged the battlefields in Asia, including those in Burma, Thailand, Vietnam, India and China, and set up the China-Burma-India Theater (CBI) with Chiang Kai-shek as Commander in Chief and US General Stilwell as Chief of Staff. In February 1942, Chinese Expeditionary Force sent troops to Burma and officially commenced the joint operation with the United States and Britain.

中缅印战区区域示意图
A map of the China-Burma-India Theater

中国抗日战争暨世界反法西斯战争胜利七十周年特展
An Exhibition Dedicated to 70th Anniversary of Victory of War of Resistance against
Japanese Aggression and World Anti-fascist War

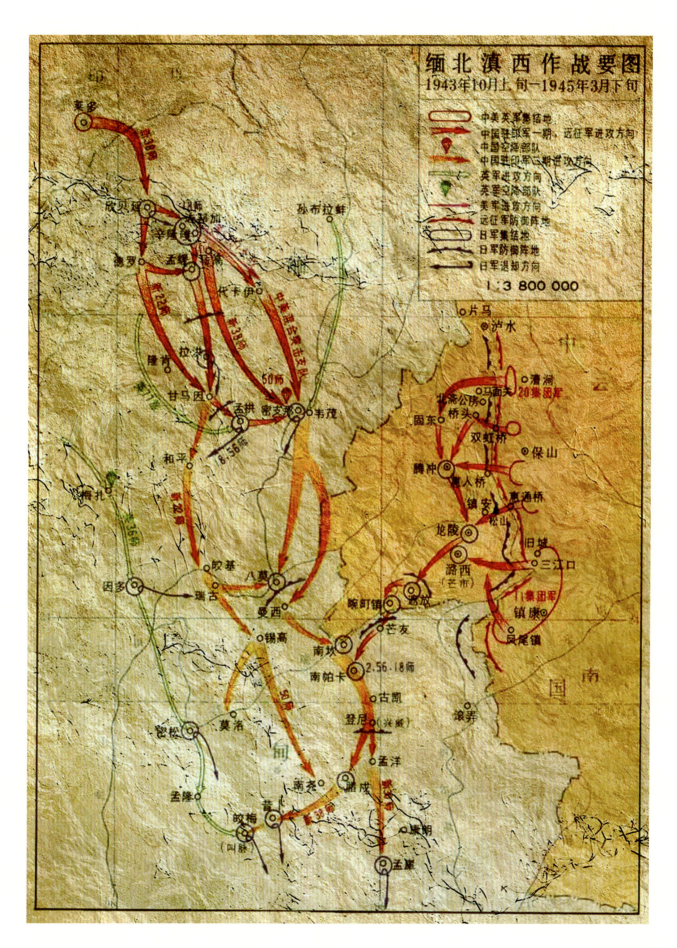

中国远征军入缅作战序列
Order of battle of Chinese Expeditionary Force in Burma

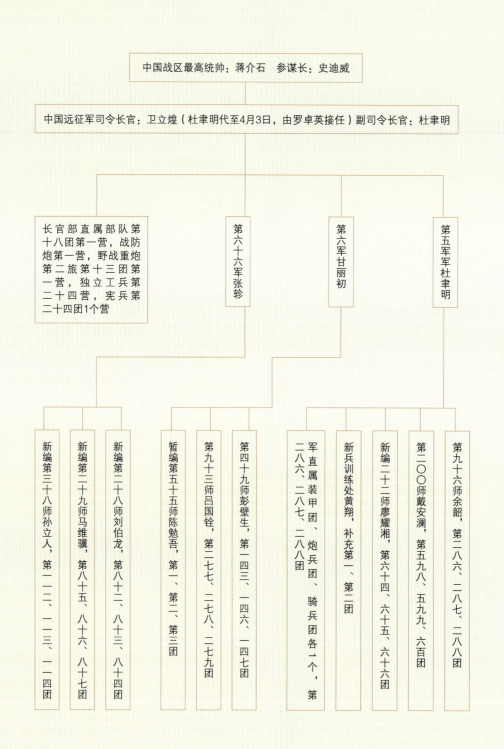

中国战区最高统帅：蒋介石　参谋长：史迪威

中国远征军司令长官：卫立煌（杜聿明代至4月3日，由罗卓英接任）副司令长官：杜聿明

长官部直属部队第十八团第一营，战防炮第一营，野战重炮第二旅第十三团第一营，独立工兵第二十四营，宪兵第二十四团1个营

第六十六军张轸

第六军甘丽初

第五军军杜聿明

新编第三十八师孙立人，第一一二、一一三、一一四团

新编第二十九师马维骥，第八十五、八十六、八十七团

新编第二十八师刘伯龙，第八十二、八十三、八十四团

暂编第五十五师陈勉吾，第一、第二、第三团

第九十三师吕国铨，第二七七、二七八、二七九团

第四十九师彭璧生，第一四三、一四六、一四七团

军直属装甲团、炮兵团、骑兵团各一个，第二八六、二八七、二八八团

新兵训练处黄翔，补充第一、第二团

新编二十二师廖耀湘，第六十四、六十五、六十六团

第二〇〇师戴安澜，第五九八、五九九、六百团

第九十六师余韶，第二八六、二八七、二八八团

中国抗日战争暨世界反法西斯战争胜利七十周年特展
An Exhibition Dedicated to 70th Anniversary of Victory of War of Resistance against
Japanese Aggression and World Anti-fascist War

1942年1月2日，中国战区统帅部成立，蒋介石担任中国战区最高统帅，美国史迪威将军经马歇尔向罗斯福推荐，任中国战区统帅部参谋长。图为蒋介石、史迪威合影

Chiang Kai-shek and Joseph Stilwell in 1942. The Command for the China Theater was founded on January 2, 1942, with Chiang Kai-shek as the Supreme Commander. Joseph Stilwell was recommended to Roosevelt by Marshall, and was appointed as the Chief of Staff of the Command

1942年1月5日，蒋介石在重庆宣布就任中国战区最高统帅

Chiang Kai-shek assumes the post of Supreme Commander of the China Theater, January 5, 1942

1943年10月17日至20日，中、英、美军事代表会议在重庆召开，达成了收复缅北联合作战的协议。图为蒋介石夫妇与东南亚盟军总司令蒙巴顿勋爵、史迪威、美国总统特使萨姆维尔准将合影

Chiang Kai-shek and his wife Soong May-ling, Lord Louis Mountbatten as the Supreme Allied Commander South East Asia, Joseph Stilwell and Wendell Willkie as the American president Roosevelt's personal representative. Military representatives from China, the United Kingdom and the United States agree to launch joint campaigns to retake northern Burma, in meetings organized in Chongqing, October 17-20, 1943

中国抗日战争暨世界反法西斯战争胜利七十周年特展
An Exhibition Dedicated to 70th Anniversary of Victory of War of Resistance against
Japanese Aggression and World Anti-fascist War

中缅印银丝徽章

The silver-wire embedded badge of
China Burma India Theatre

1940年代
长8、宽5.7厘米
昆明市博物馆藏

美军航空队银丝徽章

The silver-wire embedded badge of US aircraft corps

1940年代
直径5.7厘米
昆明市博物馆藏

美军飞行员护目镜片

The lens of goggles of an US pilot

1940年代
长21、宽9.4厘米
昆明市博物馆藏

美军飞行员护目镜

The goggles of an US pilot

1940年代
长21、宽9.6厘米
昆明市博物馆藏

美军信号队R-14耳机

The earphone of US signal corps

1940年代
长18.4、宽14厘米
昆明市博物馆藏

11-1 第一次缅甸战役（1942.1.4-5）
Burma Campaign (1942.1.4-5)

1942年1月到5月，日军在缅甸对中、英盟军进攻，以切断滇缅公路，迫使中国屈服；并伺机进军印度，促其脱离英联邦。结果，日军占领缅甸并侵占云南省龙陵、腾冲等地。

From January to May in 1942, the Japanese army attacked the Allied forces of China and Britain in Burma, and pressed China to surrender by cutting off the Yunnan-Burma Road; meanwhile, Japanese army entered India to promote India's separation from the British Federation. As a result, the Japanese occupied Burma and parts of Yunnan Province, including Longling, Tengchong and other places.

日军在仰光登陆
Japanese troops landed in Yangon

新补入缅甸作战的中国远征军
Chinese Expeditionary Force to enter Burma

《入缅须知》
To enter Myanmar notice

1943年
军事委员会军令部编印
滇西抗战纪念馆藏

中国抗日战争暨世界反法西斯战争胜利七十周年特展
An Exhibition Dedicated to 70th Anniversary of Victory of War of Resistance against
Japanese Aggression and World Anti-fascist War

11-2 同古保卫战（1942.3.19-3.29）
Battle of Toungoo (1942.3.19-3.29)

　　国军二〇〇（戴安澜师）在仰光失陷后，掩护英军撤退，与拥有制空权的敌军苦战12天，歼敌5000余人，为远征军的后续部队赢得了时间，最后第二〇〇师全师安全转移。

After the fall of Yangon, the 200th Division of the NRA covered the safe retreat of the British army, and battled desperately for 12 days with the enemies who had the air superiority. The 200th Division wiped out more than 5,000 opponents, won time for the follow-up units of the Expeditionary Force, and finally transferred the division safely.

同登前线的我军炮兵
The Chinese artillerymen at the Toungoo front.

日军在坦克掩护进攻在同古战役中以二〇〇师阵地
Japanese troop attack the 200th division positions by tanks cover during battle of Toungoo

11-3 仁安羌大捷（1942.4.19）
Retreat in Northern Burma (1942.4.19-5)

1942年4月，中国远征军新编第三十八师刘放吾团在缅西仁安羌地区营救出被包围的英军7000余人，取得仁安羌大捷。

Under the command of Liu Fangwu, the 38th Division of the Chinese Expeditionary Amy achieved a resounding success in rescuing more than 7,000 British troops encircled in Yenangyaung, April 1942

仁安羌大捷战役现场
A scene of the Battle of Yenangyaung

刘放吾团长
Regiment commander Liu Fangwu

中国抗日战争暨世界反法西斯战争胜利七十周年特展
An Exhibition Dedicated to 70th Anniversary of Victory of War of Resistance against
Japanese Aggression and World Anti-fascist War

12-1 缅北大撤退（1942.4.19-5）
Retreat in Northern Burma (1942.4.19-5)

仁安羌战役后，英缅军第一师北撤无力再战，全线向印度撤退，远征军随即陷入日军包围，于是分路突围。杜聿明率主力翻越缅北野人山撤退回国，伤亡惨重。孙立人率一部撤退到印度。

After the battle of Yenangyaung, the 1st Division of British Burma Army force, greatly weakened, retreated to India. Before long, the Chinese Expeditionary Army also faced the encirclement of the Japanese forces and had to split to break through. Du Yuming led the main force to retreat to China through the savage mountain in the North Burma and suffered heavy casualties. Sun Liren led his troop to retreat to India.

12-2 戴安澜将军殉国
The Sacrifice of General Dai Anlan

戴安澜（1904-1942），安徽无为人。曾先后参加古北口、台儿庄、武汉会战、昆仑关战役。1942年5月18日在郎科地区指挥突围战斗中负重伤，26日在缅北茅邦村殉国。牺牲后追赠陆军中将，新中国成立后追认为革命烈士。

Dai Anlan (1904-1942), a native of Wuwei, Anhui Province, participated in battles of Gubeikou, Taierzhuang, Wuhan, and Kunlun Pass. While directing a breakout combat in Langke area on May 18, 1942, Dai was seriously wounded and martyred in Maobang Village in northern Burma on May 26. He was awarded posthumously Lieutenant General, and later the revolutionary martyr by the government of the People's Republic of China.

中国远征军第五军二〇〇师师长戴安澜
Dai Anlan, Commander of the 200th Division of the
Fifth Army of the Chinese Expeditionary Army

第二次缅甸战役中英两军士兵合影
British soldiers and Chinses soldiers in Second Burma Campaign

中国抗日战争暨世界反法西斯战争胜利七十周年特展
An Exhibition Dedicated to 70th Anniversary of Victory of War of Resistance against
Japanese Aggression and World Anti-fascist War

缅甸丛林中作战的我军士兵
Chinses soldiers fighting in the Burma jungle

在缅甸山地运送弹药的我炮兵运输队
Chinses artillery convoys transport ammunition in Burma mountain

13 胡康河谷战役（1943.12–1944.3）
Hukawng Valley Campaign (1943.12-1944.3)

该役是中国驻印军反攻缅北之战，以开辟中印公路（中国昆明－印度利多）和敷设输油管，最终连通滇缅公路。远征军驻印军第一军3.5万人及美军第5307团，对阵日军第18师团3余万人，我军大胜。

The battle is the counterattack in northern Burma launched by the Chinese Army in India in order to open up the Sino-Indian Road (Kunming of China – Ledo of India) and to lay the oil pipelines, a route ultimately reaching the Yunnan-Burma Road. The 35,000 soldiers of the First Chinese Expeditionary Army in India plus US Army 5307th Regiment successfully defeated more than 30,000 military personnel from the Japanese 18th Division.

我军在北缅甸战场打胜仗，押运日军俘虏
Chinese army sent Japanese captives under escort after wining a battle on the North Burma theatre

孙立人戎装照
The photo of Sun Liren in military uniform (with a signature "Present to Comrade Changming")
纵19.5、横16厘米
香港翰墨轩（香江博物馆）藏

中国抗日战争暨世界反法西斯战争胜利七十周年特展
An Exhibition Dedicated to 70th Anniversary of Victory of War of Resistance against
Japanese Aggression and World Anti-fascist War

14 密支那战役（1944.4.29-8.4）
Battle of Myitkyina (1944.4.29-8.4)

密支那战役为驻印远征军反攻缅甸战役中进行的一次城市进攻作战，以奇袭开始，以消耗战结束。最终占绝对优势的中美混合支队历时近100天，以伤亡6000余人的代价歼灭日军3000余人，并迫使剩余的日军800人退出。

The Battle of Myitkyina is one of the counteroffensives operated by the Chinese Expeditionary Force in India during the Sino-Japanese War, which started out as an assault but ended as a war of attrition. Eventually it cost the dominant US-China combined regiments nearly 100 days with more than 6,000 casualties to annihilate more than 3,000 Japanese soldiers and force the withdrawal of the remaining 800 Japanese soldiers.

我新三十师及第五十师部队两团，美步兵一团，由密里尔准将指挥奇袭缅北铁路终点密支那。此图为我坦克部队向密支那进攻

Two regiments of the 30th Division and 50th Division of New Fourth Army and a regiment of US infantry commanded by Brigadier General Merrill were raiding Myitkyina. The picture illustrates Chinese tank army attacking Myitkyina.

15 腾冲战役(1944.5.11−9.14)
Tengchong Battle (1944.5.11-9.14)

腾冲战役是滇西反攻三大战役之一。中国远征军在美、英盟军的协同下，在缅甸北部和云南省西部对日军缅甸方面军发动进攻。国军以伤亡1.9万的代价击毙日军3000人，打通中印公路，收复腾冲。

Tengchong Battle is one of the three major battles in western Yunnan counterattack. Chinese Expeditionary Force collaborated with the Allied forces of the United States and the Britain launched an attack against the Japanese army stationed in Burma from northern Burma and western Yunnan. At the cost of 19,000 casualties, the Chinese army killed 3,000 Japanese soldiers, opened the Sino-Indian Road to traffic and recaptured Tengchong.

我军用喷火器肃清腾冲城边残余敌军，腾冲于1944年9月14日收复
Our military eliminate residual enemy of Tengchong by flamethrower, Tengchong recover on September 14, 1944

中国抗日战争暨世界反法西斯战争胜利七十周年特展
An Exhibition Dedicated to 70th Anniversary of Victory of War of Resistance against
Japanese Aggression and World Anti-fascist War

16 松山战役（1944.6.4-9.7）
Songshan Battle (1944.6.4-9.7)

松山战役是滇西反攻三大战役之一。抗战后期为打通滇缅公路，远征军进攻龙陵县腊勐乡的松山。全歼日本守军一个联队3000多人，为最终打通滇缅公路奠定了基础。敌我伤亡比1: 6.2。

The siege of Songshan is one of the three major battles in western Yunnan counterattack. During the latter part of the anti-Japanese war, in order to get through the Burma Road, the Chinese Expeditionary Army launched an attack at Songshan, Lameng Township, Longling County. The battle wiped out a Japanese regiment of more than 3,000 defenders, laying the foundation for the ultimate opening up the Burma Road. The casualty ratio of both sides is 1: 6.2.

远征军司令卫立煌将军在怒江东岸炮兵阵地听取松山日军兵力部署报告

General Wei Lihuang, The Chief Commander of rhe Chinese Expeditionary Force, was listening to the report about dispositing of Japanese forces at the artillery position on the east bank of the Salween River

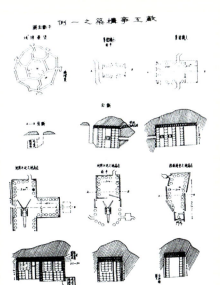

中国远征军绘制松山日军阵地工事结构图

The configuration map of Japanese fortication in Songshan Mount, draw by rhe Chinese Expeditionary Force

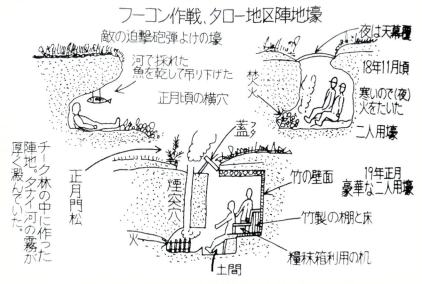

日军绘制松山阵地掩体剖面图（资料来源：日本防卫厅）

The profile map of shelters drawn by Japanese forces (The source of data, Minstry of Defense of Japan)

17 龙陵战役（1944.6.4–11.3）
Longling Battle (1944.6.4-11.3)

　　龙陵战役是滇西反攻三大战役之一，历时半年。龙陵县是连接保山、腾冲的交通枢纽，日军重点固守。1944年，我军于6月6日向驻龙陵日军发起进攻，在11月3日夺回龙陵要塞。是役毙敌1万余人，是滇缅战役消灭日军最多的，而我方也伤亡2.8万余人。

　　The six-month Longling Battle is one of the three battles in western Yunnan counterattack. Longling was the transportation hub that connected Baoshan and Tengchong, a key defensive position of the Japanese army. On June 6, 1944, the Chinese troops launched an attack against the Japanese army in Longling, which was recaptured on November 3. It caused more than 10,000 Japanese casualties, the largest number in western Yunnan counterattacks, while China also lost 28,000. people.

龙陵突击
Longling assault

攻克龙陵
Conquer Longling

中美盟军在芒友举行盛大会师庆典
Chinese and American troops organize a grand celebration in Mangyou

中国驻印军、中国远征军和盟军经过8个月的缅北滇西反攻作战，连克腾冲、松山、龙陵、芒市，中印公路遂完全打通。1945年1月27日，中国远征军与中国驻印军在芒友胜利会师。

中国抗日战争暨世界反法西斯战争胜利七十周年特展
An Exhibition Dedicated to 70th Anniversary of Victory of War of Resistance against
Japanese Aggression and World Anti-fascist War

18-1 史迪威公路
Stilwell Road

　　为了打通中印陆路交通线，盟军修筑从印度东北部雷多到昆明的中印公路（又称"史迪威公路"）。该路为中国抗战运送了5万多吨急需物资。该路至缅甸密支那后分成经缅甸八莫、南坎至中国畹町的南线和经过缅甸甘拜地、中国腾冲至龙陵的北线与滇缅公路相接。

　　In order to open the land transportation route between China and India, the Allied forces constructed the Sino-Indian Road (also known as "Stilwell Road"), which connected Ledo in northeastern India and Kunming in China. The functioning of this road made possible the delivery of over 50,000 tons of China-relief material during the China's resistance war. The route is split at Myitkyina into two parts: the southern route that passed through Bhamo and Namhkam in Burma and reached China's Wanting; the northern route that passed through Ganbaide in Burma, Tengchong and Longling in China and joined with the Yunnan-Burma Road.

1945年1月28日，在中缅边境畹町举行的"史迪威公路"通车典礼

The opening ceremony for the Stilwell Road in Wanding, a town close to the boundary between China and Burma, January 28, 1945

援华物资经滇缅公路到达昆明后，再经由贵州黔西南州晴隆县"二十四拐"，才能到重庆和前线。

在修建"史迪威公路"的同时，还修建了一条从印度加尔各答出发，沿"史迪威公路"进入中国境内的输油管道。图为中印输油管道及修建管道的士兵

Soldiers building an oil pipeline as part of the Stilwell Road

18-2 史迪威将军
General Joseph Warren Stilwell

约瑟夫·华伦·史迪威（1883-1946），美国陆军四星上将，曾经在二战期间任驻华美军司令、东南亚战区副司令、盟军中国战区参谋长等职务，1946年因胃癌在旧金山去世。

General Joseph Warren Stilwell (1883 -1946) was a United States Army four-star general known for service in the China Burma India Theater during World War II. He became the Chief of Staff to Generalissimo Chiang Kai-Shek, served as the commander of the China Burma India Theater responsible for all Lend-Lease supplies going to China, and later was Deputy Commander of the South East Asia Command. Unfortunately, despite his status and position in China, he soon became embroiled in conflicts over U.S. Lend-Lease aid and Chinese political sectarianism. He died after surgery for stomach cancer in 1946

史迪威将军
General Stilwell

史迪威将军与康复返回的中国远征军伤兵谈话
General Stilwell speaks with wounded Chinese veterans at a rehabilitation camp before their return to civilian life in July 1944

蒋介石夫妇和史迪威将军
Chiang Kai Shek and wife with Lieutenant General Stilwell

中国抗日战争暨世界反法西斯战争胜利七十周年特展
An Exhibition Dedicated to 70th Anniversary of Victory of War of Resistance against
Japanese Aggression and World Anti-fascist War

史迪威将军的传记影片

The move of General Stilwell

1945年
周海圣先生捐赠，湖北省博物馆藏

本件为美国陆军部寄给史迪威将军在滇缅战场的纪录片。史迪威去世后由其家属拍卖。周海圣先生捐赠本馆之前，该片尚未开封。

史迪威将军的木箱

The wooden case of General Stilwell

1945年
周海圣先生捐赠，湖北省博物馆藏

本件为史迪威将军在中国使用的木箱。史迪威去世后由其家属拍卖。

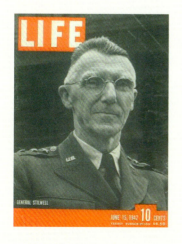

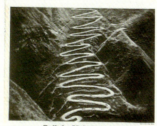

美国生活杂志

Life

1942年1月15日
纵35.6、横26.6厘米
昆明博物馆藏

18-3 南侨机工
Nanyang Overseas Chinese Mechanics

1939年至1942年间，3200多名南洋华侨汽车驾驶员和技术工人参加了南侨总会组织的"南洋华侨回国机工服务团"，为保障滇缅公路运输线做出了贡献。滇缅公路上超过三分之一的运输车量是由南侨机工驾驶，其中1000多名机工牺牲。

From 1939 to 1942, approximately 3,200 Nanyang Overseas Chinese (Southeast Asian Overseas Chinese) drivers and technicians joined the "Nanyang Overseas Chinese Mechanic Service Group" organized by the Nanyang Chinese Federation and made major contributions in safeguarding the transport line of the Yunnan-Burma Road. More than one third of the delivery trucks on this transportation artery were operated by Nanyang Chinese skilled workers, among whom more than 1,000 mechanics lost their lives.

南侨机工中的印度籍司机达拉星（中文名王亚能）
Dala Star or Wang Yaneng in Chinese Pinyin, an Indian driver among the volunteers from Nanyang(Southeast Asia)

华侨机工回国服务纪念章
Badge of Overseas Chinese Mechanic returned to service

1945年
直径2.3厘米
滇西抗战纪念馆藏

中国抗日战争暨世界反法西斯战争胜利七十周年特展
An Exhibition Dedicated to 70th Anniversary of Victory of War of Resistance against
Japanese Aggression and World Anti-fascist War

五　现代国际秩序的形成
V THE ESTABLISHMENT OF A NEW INTERNATIONAL ORDER

第二次世界大战中，以中、美、英、苏、法等国为代表的世界反法西斯盟国，为清算法西斯军国主义的罪行、维护胜利成果和持久和平，建立了以大国合作、大国一致为基础的联合国集体安全机制。在战时通过的《大西洋宪章》、《开罗宣言》、《波茨坦公告》、《联合国宪章》一系列文件成为今天国际法的基石。自1840年以来贫穷落后的中国获得大国地位，是中国抗战在世界反法西斯战争做出的巨大贡献和几千万军民浴血奋战的结果。

During World War II, the world anti-fascist allies, comprised of China, United States, Britain, the Soviet Union, France and other countries, in order to expose and criticize crimes resulted from fascist militarism and to maintain the fruits of victory and lasting peace, established the United Nations, which is a collective security mechanism based on the cooperation and consensus among major powers. A series of documents passed in the wartime, such as the Atlantic Charter, Cairo Declaration, Potsdam Proclamation, Charter of the United Nations, has become the cornerstone of international law today. China rose from a poor and underdeveloped country, an image coined in 1840, to a major power in the world, which is a result of the great contributions made by millions of soldiers and civilians' heroic act in numerous bloody battles against the world fascism.

19 （1943.11.22－26）
Cairo Conference (1943.11.22-26)

1943年11月，中、美、英三国政府首脑蒋介石、罗斯福、丘吉尔在埃及首都开罗举行会议，商讨联合对日作战计划及战后处置日本等问题。会议结束后发表的《开罗宣言》中明确宣告：在战争结束后，日本必须将东北三省、台湾和澎湖列岛归还给中国，朝鲜恢复独立。中国在会议上首次位列大国，并向世界宣告对台湾、澎湖列岛等拥有主权。

In November 1943, the leaders of the Chinese, American and British governments, represented by Chiang Kai-shek, Roosevelt and Winston Churchill (1874-1965), respectively attended a conference held in Cairo, Egypt, to discuss the plans for fight against and postwar treatment of Japan. The Cairo Declaration released at the end of the meeting explicitly declares: territories taken from China by Japan, including three provinces in northeast China, Taiwan, and the Penghu Islands, would be returned to the control of the China after the war ended; Korea regains independence. China was among the great powers in the conference and declared its sovereignty over Taiwan and Penghu Islands to the world.

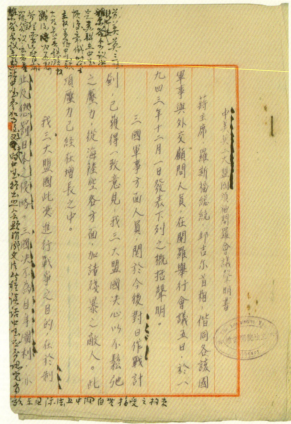
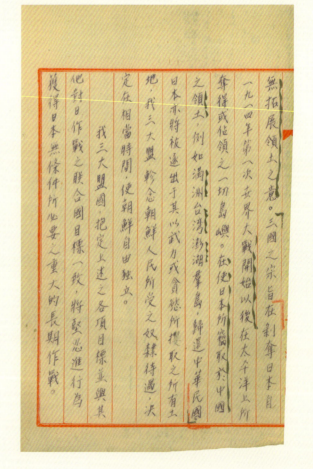

《开罗会议声明书》（《开罗宣言》）钞本

Copy of the Cairo Declaration

1943年
纵26.5、横19 厘米
香港翰墨轩（香江博物馆）藏

《开罗宣言》原件：一、美国。《开罗宣言》原文收录在美国国务院出版的《美国条约和其他国际协定汇编（1776-1949）》，原件现存于美国国家档案馆（RG59）；二、中国。《开罗宣言》原件由中华民国外交部保管。1949年后，原件保存于台湾，现收藏于台北故宫博物院，计英文一页。三、日本。日本因投降书承诺要实行开罗宣言，以《开罗宣言》为重要文件，其影印本保存于日本国立国会图书馆。本《开罗宣言》钞本与中文正本有个别字句差别，或为参加开罗会议中方人员记录本。本件约1949年后从国民政府立法院档案中流出。此钞本有力地反击了日本右翼否认《开罗宣言》文件存在的谎言。

中国抗日战争暨世界反法西斯战争胜利七十周年特展
An Exhibition Dedicated to 70th Anniversary of Victory of War of Resistance against
Japanese Aggression and World Anti-fascist War

美国保存的《开罗宣言》影印件
A copy of "Cairo Declaration" saved US

CONFIDENTIAL　　　　　CONFIDENTIAL　　　　　CONFIDENTIAL

HOLD FOR RELEASE　　　HOLD FOR RELEASE　　　HOLD FOR RELEASE

PLEASE SAFEGUARD AGAINST PREMATURE RELEASE OR PUBLICATION.

The following communique is for automatic release at
7:30 P.M., E.W.T., on Wednesday, December 1, 1943.

Extraordinary precautions must be taken to hold this communication absolutely confidential and secret until the hour set
for automatic release.

No intimation can be given its contents nor shall its
contents be the subject of speculation or discussion on the part
of anybody receiving it, prior to the hour of release.

Radio commentators and news broadcasters are particularly
cautioned not to make the communication the subject of speculation
before the hour of release for publication.

　　　　　　　　　　　　　　　　STEPHEN EARLY
　　　　　　　　　　　　　　　　Secretary to the President

- -

President Roosevelt, Generalissimo Chiang Kai-Shek and
Prime Minister Churchill, together with their respective military
and diplomatic advisers, have completed a conference in North
Africa.

　　　The following general statement was issued:

　　　"The several military missions have agreed upon
future military operations against Japan. The Three
Great Allies expressed their resolve to bring unrelenting
pressure against their brutal enemies by sea, land and
air. This pressure is already rising.

　　　"The Three Great Allies are fighting this war to
restrain and punish the aggression of Japan. They covet
no gain for themselves and have no thought of territorial
expansion. It is their purpose that Japan shall be
stripped of all the islands in the Pacific which she has
seized or occupied since the beginning of the First World
War in 1914, and that all the territories Japan has stolen
from the Chinese, such as Manchuria, Formosa, and The
Pescadores, shall be restored to the Republic of China.
Japan will also be expelled from all other territories
which she has taken by violence and greed. The aforesaid
Three Great Powers, mindful of the enslavement of the
people of Korea, are determined that in due course Korea
shall become free and independent.

　　　"With these objects in view the Three Allies, in
harmony with those of the United Nations at war with
Japan, will continue to persevere in the serious and
prolonged operations necessary to procure the unconditional
surrender of Japan."

- - - - - - -

740.0011 EUROPEAN WAR 1939/32623

JAN 19 1944　FILED　PS/LH

台湾保存的《开罗宣言》影印件
"Cairo Declaration" saved Taiwan

PRESS COMMUNIQUE

PRESIDENT ROOSEVELT, GENERALISSIMO CHIANG KAI-SHEK AND PRIME MINISTER CHURCHILL, TOGETHER WITH THEIR RESPECTIVE MILITARY AND DIPLOMATIC ADVISERS, HAVE COMPLETED A CONFERENCE IN NORTH AFRICA. THE FOLLOWING GENERAL STATEMENT WAS ISSUED:

"THE SEVERAL MILITARY MISSIONS HAVE AGREED UPON FUTURE MILITARY OPERATIONS AGAINST JAPAN. THE THREE GREAT ALLIES EXPRESSED THEIR RESOLVE TO BRING UNRELENTING PRESSURE AGAINST THEIR BRUTAL ENEMIES BY SEA, LAND AND AIR. THIS PRESSURE IS ALREADY RISING.

"THE THREE GREAT ALLIES ARE FIGHTING THIS WAR TO RESTRAIN AND PUNISH THE AGGRESSION OF JAPAN. THEY COVET NO GAIN FOR THEMSELVES AND HAVE NO THOUGHT OF TERRITORIAL EXPANSION. IT IS THEIR PURPOSE THAT JAPAN SHALL BE STRIPPED OF ALL THE ISLANDS IN THE PACIFIC WHICH SHE HAS SEIZED OR OCCUPIED SINCE THE BEGINNING OF THE FIRST WORLD WAR IN 1914, AND THAT ALL THE TERRITORIES JAPAN HAS STOLEN FROM THE CHINESE, SUCH AS MANCHURIA, FORMOSA, AND THE PESCADORES, SHALL BE RESTORED TO THE REPUBLIC OF CHINA. JAPAN WILL ALSO BE EXPELLED FROM ALL OTHER TERRITORIES WHICH SHE HAS TAKEN BY VIOLENCE AND GREED. THE AFORESAID THREE GREAT POWERS, MINDFUL OF THE ENSLAVEMENT OF THE PEOPLE OF KOREA, ARE DETERMINED THAT IN DUE COURSE KOREA SHALL BECOME FREE AND INDEPENDENT.

"WITH THESE OBJECTS IN VIEW THE THREE ALLIES, IN HARMONY WITH THOSE OF THE UNITED NATIONS AT WAR WITH JAPAN, WILL CONTINUE TO PERSEVERE IN THE SERIOUS AND PROLONGED OPERATIONS NECESSARY TO PROCURE THE UNCONDITIONAL SURRENDER OF JAPAN."

秘书长 囯圣
十一月二十七日
028

中国抗日战争暨世界反法西斯战争胜利七十周年特展
An Exhibition Dedicated to 70th Anniversary of Victory of War of Resistance against
Japanese Aggression and World Anti-fascist War

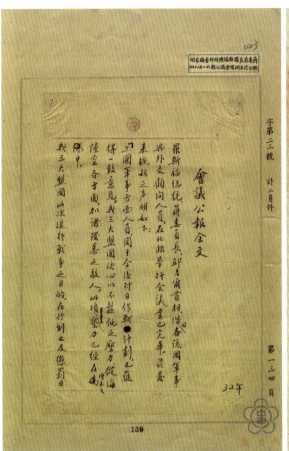

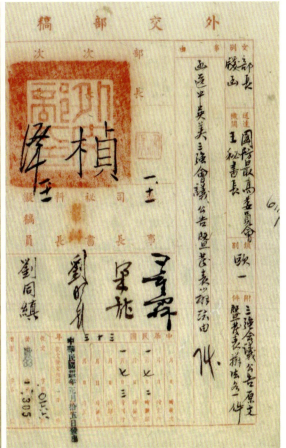

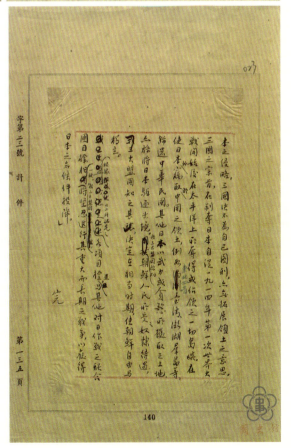

台湾保存的《开罗宣言》钞本
Chinese "Cairo Declaration" saved Taiwan

开罗会议上蒋介石夫妇、罗斯福、邱吉尔等人合影

Chiang Kai-shek and his wife Soong May-ling, Franklin D. Roosevelt, and Winston Churchill at the Cairo Conference, 1943

开罗会议后，重庆举办了介绍中、美、苏、英四强的展览会。图为市民参观展览会时的情形

Chongqing residents visit an exhibition organized after the Cairo Conference to showcase the national power of China, the United States, the Soviet Union and the United Kingdom

盟军飞机在台湾上空投掷的《开罗宣言》公报传单

Copy of the Cairo Declaration airdropped by the Allies over Taiwan

中国抗日战争暨世界反法西斯战争胜利七十周年特展
An Exhibition Dedicated to 70th Anniversary of Victory of War of Resistance against
Japanese Aggression and World Anti-fascist War

20 德黑兰会议(1943.11.28–12.1)
Teheran Conference (1943.11.28-12.1)

1943年反法西斯战争各主要战场形势发生根本转折，美、英、苏三国首脑罗斯福、丘吉尔和斯大林在伊朗首都德黑兰举行会晤，商讨加速战争进程和战后世界秩序。苏联承诺，在对德战争结束后，参加对日作战。其中使用旅顺港未经中国政府批准。

In 1943, the situation of all the major Anti-Fascist War battlefields underwent fundamental changes, the leaders of the United States, Britain, and the Soviet Union, represented by Roosevelt, Churchill and Stalin, respectively, met in Tehran, capital of Iran, to discuss the accelerating progress of war and to envisage the postwar settlement. The Soviet Union pledged to join the war against Japan after its war against Germany ended. However, Chinese government did not authorize the utilization of Lvshun Port.

德黑兰会议三巨头
The "Big Three" at the Tehran Conference

21 雅尔塔会议（1945.2.4–11）
Yalta Conference (1945.2.4-11)

雅尔塔会议，美、英、苏三国首脑罗斯福、丘吉尔、斯大林在苏联克里米亚半岛雅尔塔举行的会议。会议协调了对德日法西斯的作战行动及在二战后惩处战争罪犯、消除纳粹主义和军国主义，制定战后国际新秩序和列强利益分配方针，对战后世界格局的形成产生了深远影响。

Yalta Conference was the meeting of the leaders of the United States, Britain, and the Soviet Union, represented by Roosevelt, Churchill and Stalin, respectively, held in Yalta in Crimea of the Soviet Union. This meeting agreed upon coordinating military operations against the German and Japanese fascists, disciplining the war criminals after World War II, eliminating Nazism and militarism, establishing postwar order and the allocation policy of world powers' interest, carrying a profound impact on postwar world.

雅尔塔会议三巨头
The "Big Three" at the Yalta Conference

22 波茨坦会议（1945.7.17−8.2）
Potsdam Conference (1945.7.17-8.2)

　　1945年德国无条件投降后，为尽快结束远东对日作战，商讨对战后问题，美、英、苏三国首脑杜鲁门、丘吉尔（7月28日后改为新首相艾德礼）和斯大林在柏林近郊的波茨坦举行会议发表公告，继承开罗宣言成果要求日本无条件投降。8月14日，日本天皇宣布接受波茨坦公告。8月15日，日本正式投降。

　　After Germany's unconditional surrender in 1945, in order to end the war against Japan in the Far East as soon as possible and to discuss the postwar issues, leaders of the United States, Britain, and the Soviet Union, represented by Roosevelt, Churchill (after July 28 was the new Prime Minister Attlee) and Stalin, respectively, met in Potsdam at the outskirts of Berlin and issued a statement that followed the outcome of Cairo Declaration, and demanded Japan's unconditional surrender. On August 14, the Emperor of Japan announced the acceptance of Potsdam Proclamation, and Japan's formal surrender occurred on August 15.

1945年7月美、英、苏三国商定《波茨坦公告》现场
Representatives from the United States, the United Kingdom and the Soviet Union discuss the Potsdam Proclamation, July 1945

尤金·迦勒底（Евгений Халдей）摄，俄罗斯俄中友协提供

中国抗日战争暨世界反法西斯战争胜利七十周年特展
An Exhibition Dedicated to 70th Anniversary of Victory of War of Resistance against
Japanese Aggression and World Anti-fascist War

波次坦会议公报全文钞本

A copy of the Potsdam Proclamation

1945年

纵27、横19.5 厘米

香港翰墨轩（香江博物馆）藏

本《波茨坦公告》钞本约1949年后从国民政府立法院档案中流出。《波茨坦公告》明确剥夺日本自1914年第一次世界大战开始后在太平洋上所夺得或占领之一切岛屿；归还侵占中国的东北、台湾、澎湖列岛；日本之主权限于本州、北海道、九州、四国及盟国所决定其他小岛之内。

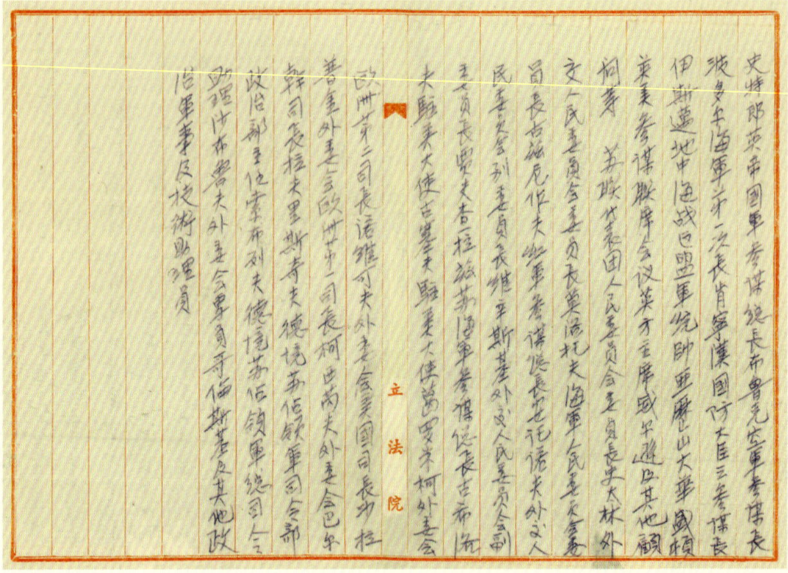

（立法院）

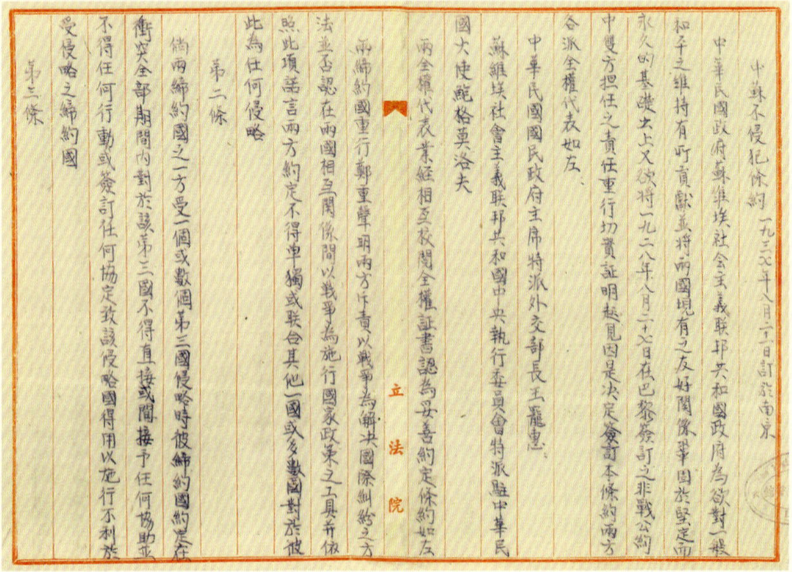

中蘇不侵犯條約　一九三七年八月二十一日訂於南京

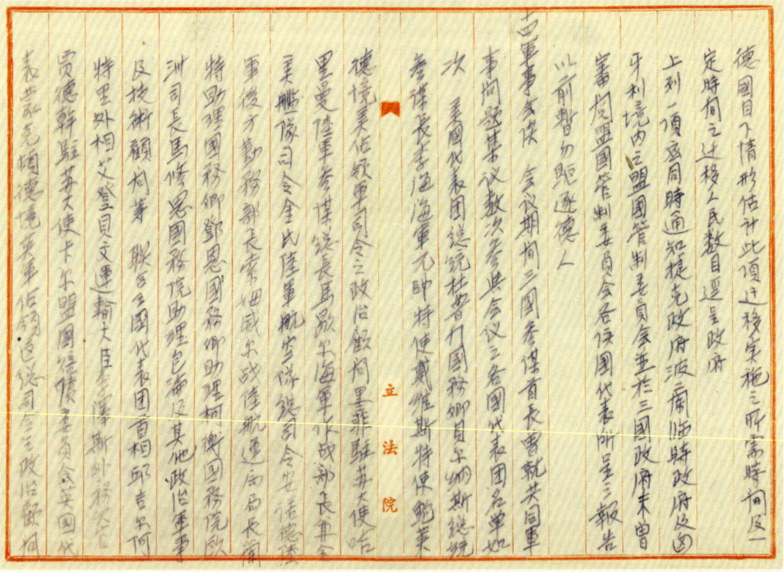

第二條

第三條

第四條

本條約用英文繕成兩份本條約於上列全權代表簽字之日發生效力其有効期間為五年……

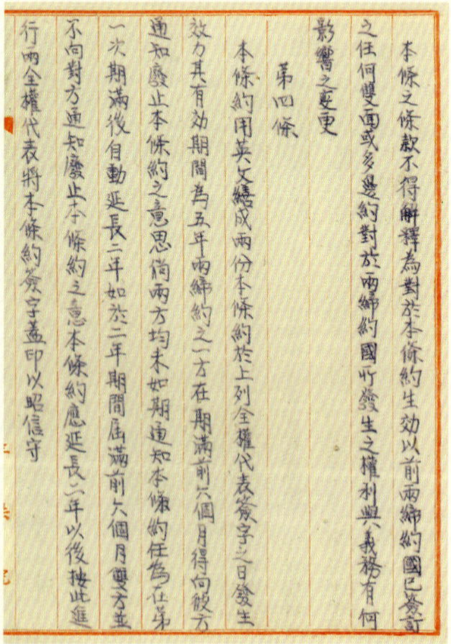

中国抗日战争暨世界反法西斯战争胜利七十周年特展
An Exhibition Dedicated to 70th Anniversary of Victory of War of Resistance against
Japanese Aggression and World Anti-fascist War

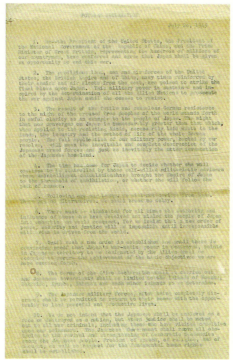

《波茨坦公告》英文版.

English "Potsdam Proclamation"

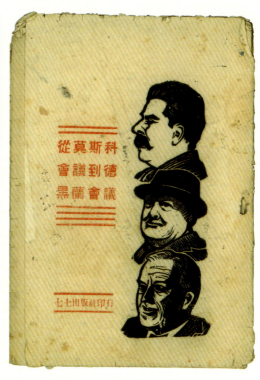

《从莫斯科会议到德奥兰会议》

From the Moscow Conference to the Tehran Conference

抗战时期
纵19.8、横14.7厘米
湖北省博物馆藏
七七出版社出版。

1945年5月1日，苏军胜利的旗帜插上柏林

The Soviet Union troops raise the "Hammer & Sickle" flag atop
the Reichstag in Berlin, May 1, 1945

维克多泰明（Виктор Темин）摄，俄罗斯俄中友协提供

23 联合国
United Nations

1942年1月1日，美国总统罗斯福在《联合国家宣言》中首次使用"联合国"名称。1943年10月30日，中、美、英、苏在莫斯科宣言中，号召尽早建立一个维护世界和平与安全的国际机构，后在德黑兰会议上予以确认。1945年4月25日，50个国家的代表在旧金山开会，6月25日通过了《联合国宪章》，以美、英、中、苏、法为安理会的常任理事国，确定解决重大问题常任理事国须一致的原则。

The term "United Nations" was first seen in the Declaration by United Nations, coined by US President Franklin D. Roosevelt on January 1, 1942. On October 30, 1943, China, the United States, Britain, and the Soviet Union called for an establishment of an international mechanism to safeguard world peace and security as soon as possible in Moscow Declaration, which was later confirmed in the Tehran Conference. On April 25, 1945, representatives from 50 countries met in San Francisco, and ratified the Charter of the United Nations on June 25, which determined five permanent members of the Security Council: the United States, Britain, China, the Soviet Union, France, as well as the principle that any solution to critical issue should have the agreement/consensus of permanent members.

董必武出席旧金山会议时穿过的衣帽
A hat and clothes worn by Dong Biwu during the San Francisco Conference

1945年4-6月
上装长73、宽68厘米，
下装长101、宽40厘米，帽子长38、宽27厘米
董必武夫人何莲芝捐赠
湖北省博物馆藏

董必武（1886-1975），湖北红安人。中共一大代表。抗战中任中共中央南方局副书记、中共重庆工委书记。1945年代表解放区参加旧金山联合国制宪会议，并在《联合国宪章》上签字。

1942年1月，26个国家的代表在华盛顿举行《联合国家宣言》签字仪式。其中，坐者左二为罗斯福，站者右十二为中国外交部长宋子文
Representatives from 26 countries at the signing ceremony of the Charter of the United Nations in Washington, January 1942, including American president Roosevelt (seated, second from left) and foreign minister of the Republic of China Soong Tse-ven (standing, twelfth from right)

中国抗日战争暨世界反法西斯战争胜利七十周年特展
An Exhibition Dedicated to 70th Anniversary of Victory of War of Resistance against
Japanese Aggression and World Anti-fascist War

1945年6月，国民政府代表顾维钧出席旧金山会议，参加《联合国宪章》起草工作。顾维钧代表中国第一个在《联合国宪章》上签字

Gu Weijun, on behalf of the KMT government, involves in the drafting of the Charter of the United Nations in the San Francisco Conference, June 1945.Dong Biwu signs the Charter of the United Nations, on behalf of the Communist Party of China

顾维钧（1888-1985），江苏定县人，中国卓越的外交家。1912年任袁世凯总统英文秘书，后任中华民国国务总理摄行大总统职，国民政府驻法、英大使，联合国首席代表、驻美大使，海牙国际法院副院长。被誉为"民国第一外交家"。1985年病逝于美国纽约。顾维钧口述的600余万字的回忆录，为研究中国近现代外交史的重要资料。

中共代表董必武代表解放区在《联合国宪章》上签字

Dong Biwu signs the Charter of the United Nations, on behalf of the Communist Party of China

金陵女大校长吴贻芳代表无党派在《联合国宪章》上签字，成为史上第一位在联合国文件上签字的女性

The president of Ginling Women's College Wu Yifang signs the Charter of the United Nations, making herself the first woman to sign on the United Nations documents

24-1 日本投降
Japan's Surrender

1945年8月15日正午，日本天皇向全国广播，接受《波茨坦公告》，无条件投降。8月21日今井武夫飞抵芷江请降。9月2日上午9时，在停泊于东京湾的美国战列舰密苏里号上举行向同盟国投降的签降仪式。日本新任外相重光葵代表日本天皇和政府、陆军参谋长梅津美治郎代表帝国大本营在投降书上签字。9月9日上午，中国战区受降仪式在中国首都南京中央军校大礼堂举行。1945年10月25日，中国政府在台湾举行受降仪式。中国抗战至此取得完全胜利。

On the noon of August 15, 1945, the Emperor of Japan announced via the radio broadcast the acceptance of the Potsdam Proclamation to surrender unconditionally. Takeo Imai arrived in Zhijiang to negotiate Japan's surrender on August 21. The signing ceremony of the Japanese Instrument of Surrender took place on the US battleship Missouri anchored in Tokyo Bay at 9:00 on September 2. Japan's new foreign minister Mamoru Shigemitsu on behalf of the Emperor of Japan and the government, together with General Yoshijiro Umezu, Chief of Army General Staff representing Imperial General Headquarters attended the ceremony to sign the instrument of surrender. The surrender ceremony for the Chinese Theater was held in the Central Military Academy's auditorium in China's capital Nanjing on the morning of September 9. The Chinese government held a ceremony of accepting surrender in Taiwan on October 25, 1945, which marked the complete victory of the China's resistance war.

24-2 1945年8月7日、9日，美军在日本广岛、长崎投下原子弹，促使日本投降
Atomic bomb mushroom clouds over Hiroshima (left) and Nagasaki (right)

1945年7月30日，美英中三国在波茨坦向日本发出最后通牒，日本拒绝接受波茨坦公告后，杜鲁门在回国途中向军方下达投掷原子弹命令。

On July 30, after the Japanese government repeatedly refused surrender demands as specifically outlined in the Potsdam Declaration and with the invasion of mainland Japan imminent, Truman authorized the atomic bombing of Japan.

原子弹在广岛（左）、长崎（右）爆炸时的蘑菇云
Atomic bomb mushroom clouds over Hiroshima (left) and Nagasaki (right)

中国抗日战争暨世界反法西斯战争胜利七十周年特展
An Exhibition Dedicated to 70th Anniversary of Victory of War of Resistance against
Japanese Aggression and World Anti-fascist War

苏联政府对日本政府声明，远东前线任务1号文件

The Soviet government statement on the Japanese government, Document No. 1 about the Far East Front Mission

俄罗斯联邦武装力量中央博物馆供图

苏联在德黑兰会议上同意战胜德国后对日本作战。斯大林在雅尔塔会议上同意欧战结束三个月内参加对日作战。苏联参战加速了日本投降。

原子弹爆炸前后的广岛

Before and after the atomic bombing of Hiroshima

《鲁中日报》号外

An extra to Luzhong Daily

1945年10月1日
纵20.6、横29.7 厘米
香港翰墨轩（香江博物馆）藏

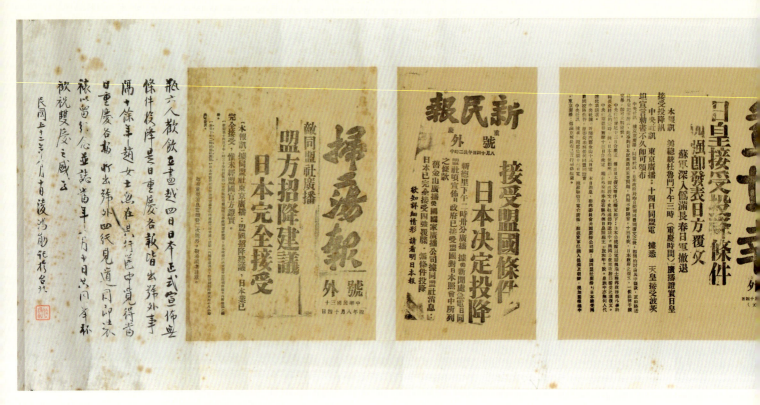

日本投降当日《波士顿先驱报》号外

An extra to The Boston Herald about the surrender of
Japan, August 15, 1945

美国康乃尔大学潘安仪教授藏，台湾美术馆提供

日本投降当日《波士顿环球报》号外

An extra to The Boston Globe about the surrender of Japan,
August 15, 1945

美国康乃尔大学潘安仪教授藏，台湾美术馆提供

中国抗日战争暨世界反法西斯战争胜利七十周年特展
An Exhibition Dedicated to 70th Anniversary of Victory of War of Resistance against
Japanese Aggression and World Anti-fascist War

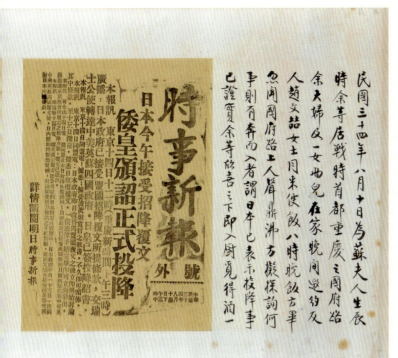

日本投降重庆报纸号外

An extra to a Chongqing newspaper about the surrender of Japan, August 10, 1945

台湾中华海峡两岸文化资产交流促进会名誉理事长王水衷藏，台湾美术馆提供

《时事新报》由1907在上海创刊的《时事报》和1908年2月29日创刊的《舆论日报》于1909年合并而成，1937年11月26日迁重庆。抗战后在上海复刊，1949年5月27日停刊。共出14785期。《益世报》1915年在天津创刊，与《大公报》、《申报》、《民国日报》并称民国四大报，1949年停刊。《新民报》1929年9月创刊于南京，1948年停刊。新中国后在上海改《新民晚报》发行。

本件为凌鸿勋（1894-1981）先生装裱。凌鸿勋，广东番禺人。抗战中主持西南铁路建造，1948年当选为中央研究院院士，后任台湾大学教授。题跋描述8月10日重庆民众获知日寇投降消息庆祝情景，历历在目。

日本投降次日《新华日报》报道

A news report of the surrender of Japan in Xinhua Daily, August 16, 1945

1945.8.16
纵21.5、横14.6厘米
湖北省博物馆藏

胜利之夜

日本投降后三日于重庆

子恺画

丰子恺 胜利之夜图

The Night of Victory, by Feng Zikai

1945年
纵64、横32 厘米
香港翰墨轩（香江博物馆）藏

丰子恺（1898-1975），浙江嘉兴人，抗战居重庆，日本投降后三日画此画。

闻道干戈战中原血战馀国人看露布岛
寇递降书八载云霄消息一朝快霸除故乡
满生意漉酒钓鲈余

倭首於卅四年八月十五日为瑛仲隆派赋此璞

罗瑛（叔重）行书抗战胜利诗

A poem celebrating the victory over Japan, running script, by Luo Ying

1945年8月15日
纵134.5、横32.5厘米
香港翰墨轩（香江博物馆）藏

罗瑛（1898-1968），广东南海人。书画、篆刻家。八一五日寇投降即赋诗一首，诗云："闻道干戈缉，中原血战余。国人看露布，岛寇递降书。八载虚消息，一朝快霸除。故乡满生意，漉酒钓鲈鱼。"

中国抗日战争暨世界反法西斯战争胜利七十周年特展
An Exhibition Dedicated to 70th Anniversary of Victory of War of Resistance against
Japanese Aggression and World Anti-fascist War

反法西斯战争胜利文献
Literatures about the victory over fascism
抗战时期
纵17.8、横12.5厘米
湖北省博物馆藏

抗战胜利国民政府主席蒋介石偕夫人莅临上海召见东南敌后工作人员
Chiang Kai-shek and Soong May-ling meeting anti-Japanese staff behind enemy lines in southeastern China, in Shanghai

1945年9月
纵12.5、横17 厘米
香港翰墨轩（香江博物馆）藏

24-3 芷江受降
Surrender at Zhijiang

1945年8月21日下午4时，侵华日军副总参谋长今井武夫来湖南芷江向国民革命军总参谋长肖毅肃洽谈正式投降事宜，正确说法是"芷江洽降"，它标志日军侵华战争结束。

At 4:00 p.m. on August 21, 1945, Takeo Imai, Deputy Chief of Staff of Japanese troops arrived at Zhijiang of Hunan to meet Xiao Yisu, the Chief of Staff of National Revolutionary Army, and to discuss the planning for formal surrender; to be more accurately, it should be referred to as "Zhijiang Negotiation on Surrender", which marked the end of the Japanese invasion of China.

签字者为中国派遣军副总参谋长今井武夫
Signer is Takeo Imai of Deputy Chief of Chinese Expeditionary Army

24-4 南京受降
Surrender at NanKing

芷江洽降后，中国在南京设立中国陆军总司令部安排中国战区在1945年9月9日举行正式受降典礼。日本投降全权代表是侵华日军最高指挥官冈村宁次，中国受降全权代表是中国陆军总司令何应钦。侵华日军128万余人向中国投降，中国抗战于此取得了最后胜利。

After negotiations with Japanese representatives in Zhijiang, Hunan province, China organized a ceremony for receiving the surrender of Japan to China Theater, at the headquarters of the Chinese army in Nanjing on September 9, 1945. He Yingqin, representative of the Chinese government, accepted the instrument of surrender submitted by Yasuji Okamura, who was General Commander of Japanese troops in China. Following the surrender of 1.28 million Japanese troops, the war of resistance against Japanese aggression ended with success.

降書

降書

一、日本帝國政府及日本帝國大本營已向聯合國最高統帥無條件投降

二、聯合國最高統帥第一號命令規定「在中華民國（東三省除外）台灣與越南北緯十六度以北地區內之日本全部陸海空軍與輔助部隊應向蔣委員長投降」

三、吾等在上述區域內之全部日本陸海空軍及輔助部隊之將領願率領所屬部隊向蔣委員長無條件投降

四、本官當立即命令所有上第二欵所述區域內之全部日本陸海空軍各級指揮官及其所屬部隊與所控制之部隊向蔣委員長特派受降代表中國戰區中國陸軍總司令何應欽上將及何應欽上將指定之各地區受降主官投降

五、投降之全部日本陸海空軍立即停止行動暫留原地待命所有武器彈藥裝具器材補給品情報資料地圖文獻檔案及其他一切資産等當時保管所有航空器及飛行場一切設備艦艇船舶車輛碼頭工廠倉庫及一切建築物以及現在上第二欵所述地區內日本陸海空軍或其控制之部隊所有或所控制之軍用或民用財産亦均保持完整全部待繳於蔣委員長及其代表何應欽上將指定之部隊長及政府機關代表接收

六、上第二欵所述區域內日本陸海空軍所停聯合國戰俘及拘留之人民立予釋放並保護送至指定地點

七、自此以後所有上第二欵所述區域內之日本陸海空軍當即服從蔣委員長之節制並接受蔣委員長及其代表何應欽上將所頒發之命令

八、本官對本降書所列各欵及蔣委員長與其代表何應欽上將以後對投降日軍所頒發之命令當立即對各級軍官及士兵轉達遵照上第二欵所述地區之所有日本軍官佐士兵均須負有完全履行此項命令之責投降之日本陸海空軍中任何人員對於本降書所列各欵及蔣委員長與其代表何應欽上將嗣後所授之命令偷有未能履行或遲延情事各級官長及違犯命令者願受懲罰

九、投降之日本帝國政府及日本帝國大本營各員及各級官長及遵照日本帝國政府及日本帝國大本營命令而簽字人中國派遣軍總司令官陸軍大將

岡村寧次（印）

昭和二十年（公曆一九四五年）九月九日午前九時

分簽字於中華民國南京

代表中華民國美利堅合衆國大不列顛聯合王國蘇維埃社會主義共和國聯邦並為對日本作戰之其他聯合國之利益接受本降書於中華民國三十四年（公曆一九四五年）九月九日午前九時分在中華民國南京

中國戰區最高統帥特級上將蔣中正特派代表中國陸軍總司令陸軍一級上將

何應欽（印）

日本降书

Japan's surrender

1945年

纵32、横24厘米

台湾国史馆藏，中正文教基金会授权世界大同文创公司复制

本件为日本向中国战区的投降书。

九.
級軍官及士兵轉達遵照上第二欵所述地區之所有
日本軍官佐士兵均須負有完全履行此類命令之責
投降之日本陸海空軍中任何人員對於本降書所列
各欵及將委員長與其代表何應欽上將嗣後所授之
命令倘有未能履行或遲延情事各級負責官長及違
犯命令者願受懲罰
奉日本帝國政府及日本帝國大本營命簽字人中
國派遣軍總司令官陸軍大將 岡村寧次
昭和二十年（公曆一九四五年）九月九日午前
九時　分簽字於中華民國南京

代表中華民國美利堅合衆國大不列顛聯合王國
蘇維埃社會主義共和國聯邦並為對日本作戰之
其他聯合國之利益接受本降書於中華民國三十
四年（公曆一九四五年）九月九日午前九時
分在中華民國南京
中國戰區最高統帥特級上將蔣中正特派代表中
國陸軍總司令陸軍一級上將
何應欽

日本在南京向中国投降，国军陆军总司
令何应钦将军在检查日本投降文件

Japanese surrender to Chinese in Nanjing, General Ho
Ying-chin Commander in chief of Chinese staff forces,
examines the surrender documents

美国国会图书馆藏
台湾世界大同文创公司供图

中国抗日战争暨世界反法西斯战争胜利七十周年特展
An Exhibition Dedicated to 70th Anniversary of Victory of War of Resistance against
Japanese Aggression and World Anti-fascist War

24-5　密苏里号战舰受降
Surrender Acceptance on Battleship Missouri

　　日本投降后，美国为同时体现陆军和海军的荣耀，安排同盟国受降仪式在美国战列舰"密苏里"号上举行。麦克阿瑟上将代表盟军，尼米兹上将代表美国，徐永昌上将代表中国，接受日方代表外相重光葵、日军代表梅津美治郎的投降。

　　Upon Japan's surrender, the United States held a ceremony for Allies to accept the surrender of Japan in the US battleship Missouri so as to honor the army and the navy at the same time. General MacArthur on behalf of the Allied Powers, Admiral Nimitz on behalf of the United States, and Xu Yongchang representing China, accepted the surrender presented by Mamoru Shigemitsu, Minister of Foreign Affairs on behalf the Japanese Government, and General Yoshijiro Umezu, Chief of Army General Staff representing Japanese army.

日本降书

Japan's surrender

1945年9月2日，在东京湾密苏里号航空母舰的甲板上，美、中、英、苏、澳、加拿大、法、荷、新西兰国代表在日本帝国投降书上签字。它标志着第二次世界大战的结束。

265

抗战胜利纪念章

A copper badge inscribed with Chinese characters for "victory"

1945年
直径2.3厘米
滇西抗战纪念馆藏

中、美、英、苏抗战胜利纪念章

Badge dedicated to the victory over Japan (China, the US, the UK and the Soviet Union)

1945年
长3.6、宽1.7厘米
滇西抗战纪念馆藏

英国发行抗战胜利银质纪念章

A silver badge dedicated to the victory over Japan (UK)

民国
章径3.6厘米
滇西抗战纪念馆藏

中国抗日战争暨世界反法西斯战争胜利七十周年特展
An Exhibition Dedicated to 70th Anniversary of Victory of War of Resistance against
Japanese Aggression and World Anti-fascist War

花鸟纹 "1945胜利" 纪念铜锁（兴顺号造）

A copper lock dedicated to the victory over Japan in 1945

民国
长6.4、宽4.5、厚1.4厘米
滇西抗战纪念馆藏

日制瓷偶

Porcelain figurine made in Japan

日本战后美军占领时期
高9、宽5.8厘米
吉星文将军之子吉民立提供

本件底款："Made in Occupied
Japan（被占领的日本制）"。

日制咖啡杯

Coffee cup made in Japan

日本战后美军占领时期
直径6、高 6.8厘米
吉星文将军之子吉民立提供

本件底款："Made in Occupied
Japan（被占领的日本制）"。

267

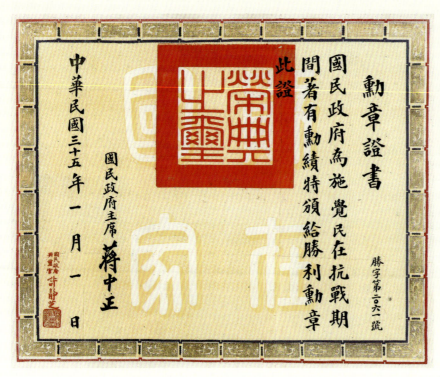

国民政府颁施觉民将军抗战胜利勋章证书

A certificate of honor for Shi Juemin, a top KMT military official

1945年
纵40.2、横51.6厘米
施觉民将军家属提供

施觉民将军(1904-1990)，浙江武义人。黄埔军校二期生。1932年任俞济时部第八十八师团长，参加一·二八淞沪战役。抗战时任陆军新编第二十师副师长、福建省第一保安纵队司令、1944年奉调军事委员会委员长侍从室侍卫组少将组长。

国民政府颁青天白日勋章

Medal of Blue Sky and White Sun granted by the Kuomintang government

1945年
章径6、厚0.25厘米
台湾董良彦先生提供

此章为抗战期间国民政府授予有功将士最高殊荣之勋章。

国民政府颁空军彤弓奖章

Medal of Vermilion Bow granted by the Kuomintang government

1945年
章径3.5、厚0.2厘米
台湾董良彦先生提供

此章为1945年6月制颁，两个月后抗战胜利，国共内战时"红日"改为"红星"，故"红日"版因颁发时间甚短、存世甚希而益显珍贵。

中国抗日战争暨世界反法西斯战争胜利七十周年特展
An Exhibition Dedicated to 70th Anniversary of Victory of War of Resistance against
Japanese Aggression and World Anti-fascist War

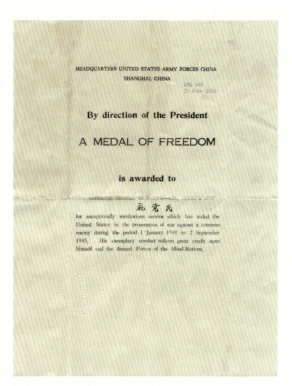

美国驻华派遣军总部颁发施觉民将军美国自由奖章证书

Medal of Freedom granted to General Shi Juemin by the headquarters of American Expeditionary Army in China

1946年
纵26.5、横20.3厘米
施觉民将军家属提供

美国驻华派遣军总部颁施觉民将军美国自由奖章

Medal of Freedom granted to General Shi Juemin by the headquarters of American Expeditionary Army in China

1945年
章径3.2、厚0.25厘米
施觉民将军家属提供

国民政府颁施觉民将军三等云麾勋章

Grade-3 Medal of the Cloud and Banner awarded by the Kuomintang government

1946年
章径8.2 厘米
施觉民将军家属提供

国民政府颁施觉民将军抗战胜利勋章

Medal awarded by the Kuomintang government for the victory of the Chinese people's War of Resistance against Japanese Aggression

1946年
章径7厘米
施觉民将军家属提供

国民政府颁施觉民将军抗战纪念章

Commemorative medal awarded by the Kuomintang government for the Chinese people's War of Resistance against Japanese Aggression

1944年
章径3.8、厚0.2厘米
施觉民将军家属提供

国民政府颁施觉民将军抗战纪念章

Commemorative medal awarded by the Kuomintang government for the Chinese people's War of Resistance against Japanese Aggression

1944年
章径3.8、厚0.2厘米
施觉民将军家属提供

国民政府颁空军洛书勋章

Order of Book of Nature granted by the Kuomintang government

1945年
章径5.5、厚0.16厘米
台湾董良彦先生提供

国民政府颁空军乾元勋章

Order of Sulime Commencement granted by the Kuomintang government

1945年
章径4.3、厚0.18厘米
台湾董良彦先生提供

中国抗日战争暨世界反法西斯战争胜利七十周年特展
An Exhibition Dedicated to 70th Anniversary of Victory of War of Resistance against
Japanese Aggression and World Anti-fascist War

国民政府颁忠贞奖章

Medal of Loyalty and Integrity granted by the
Kuomintang government

高4.2、宽3.5、厚0.15厘米
台湾董良彦先生提供

国民政府颁空军二等复兴荣誉勋章

Grade-2 Medal of Renaissance and Honour
granted by the Kuomintang government

1945年
章径7.2、厚0.3厘米
台湾董良彦先生提供

国民政府颁空军一等宣威奖章

Grade-1 Medal of Awe-Inspiring granted by
the Kuomintang government

1945年
长6.9、高3.7、厚0.1厘米
台湾董良彦先生提供

国民政府颁空军三等复兴荣誉勋章

Grade-3 Medal of Renaissance and Honour
granted by the Kuomintang government

1945年
章径 7、厚0.3厘米
台湾董良彦先生提供

国民政府颁空军二等宣威奖章

Grade-2 Medal of Awe-Inspiring granted by the
Kuomintang government

民国政府颁抗战胜利奖章
Medal of Victory of Resistance against Aggression awarded by the Kuomintang government

章径 3.6、厚0.2厘米
台湾董良彦先生提供

陆人燿抗战胜利纪念章
A badge dedicated to the victory over Japan of Mr. Lu Renyao

2005年

陆人燿（1900–1951），云南保山人。抗战时任第58军31团团长，参加武汉、长衡、滇缅等会战。1949年任保山县长随龙云起义，后被冤杀。1982年平反。2005年，官方为其颁发抗战胜利纪念章。

中国抗日战争暨世界反法西斯战争胜利七十周年特展
An Exhibition Dedicated to 70th Anniversary of Victory of War of Resistance against
Japanese Aggression and World Anti-fascist War

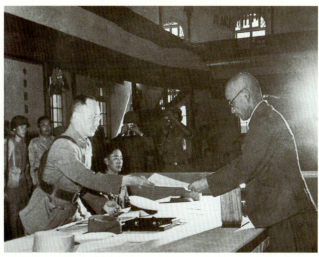

1945年9月2日，日本在东京湾密苏里号战舰上向盟国投降，中国代表徐永昌上将在日本降书上签字

General Xu Yongchang, representing China, signs the Japanese Instrument of Surrender on board USS Missouri anchored in Tokyo Bay, September 2, 1945

1945年9月9日，中国派遣军中将总参谋长小林浅三郎代表日本在南京向中国投降，何应钦将军接受降书

Lieutenant General Kobayashi Asasaburo, Chief of General Staff of the China Expeditionary Army, presented the Instrument of Surrender to He Yingqin in Nanjing, on September 9, 1945

10月25日，日本台湾总督安藤利吉大将签署投降书

Rikichi Andō, the Japanese Governor-General of Taiwan, signs the Instrument of Surrender, October 25, 1945

吉星文将军在湖北孝感受降

General Ji Xingwen accepted the Japanese at Xiaogan county, Hubei

1945年
纵15、横12.6厘米
吉星文将军之子吉民立提供

日本第六方面军司令官冈部直三郎陆军大将，在武汉、孝感向第六战区上将司令长官孙蔚如将军投降。照片右一、二、四分别为吉星文、孙蔚如、冈部直三郎。照片后有吉星文亲笔注。

273

1945年9月3日，重庆庆祝
抗战胜利
September 3, 1945, Chongqing
celebrate the victory

南京人民庆祝抗战胜利
Nanjing People celebrating victory

解放区欢庆抗战胜利
Liberated People celebrating victory

北京人民庆祝抗战胜利

Beijing People celebrating victory

东北人民庆祝抗战胜利

Northeast People celebrating victory

**1945年10月25日，台湾
人民庆祝胜利**

October 25, 1945, Taiwan people
celebrate the victory

25 纽伦堡审判
The Nuremberg Trials

世界反法西斯战争结束后，同盟国在欧洲设立国际军事法庭，于1945年11月21日至1946年10月1日在德国纽伦堡对欧洲轴心国的军事、政治和经济头目进行军事审判。审判纳粹德国的军政首领22名、团体6个。

Following the World Anti-fascist War, the Allied powers set up the International Military Tribunal in Nuremberg, Germany, to prosecute the military, political and economic leaders of the European Axis from November 21, 1945 to October 1, 1946. Twenty-two Nazi Germany's military and political leaders, and 6 groups were put to trial.

中国抗日战争暨世界反法西斯战争胜利七十周年特展
An Exhibition Dedicated to 70th Anniversary of Victory of War of Resistance against
Japanese Aggression and World Anti-fascist War

26 东京审判
Tokyo Trials

　　日本投降后，远东最高盟国统帅部根据同盟国授权，于1946年1月19日至1948年11月12日在东京成立远东国际军事法庭，由美国、中国、苏联、英国、法国等11国法官对第二次世界大战中28名日本甲级战犯进行国际审判。

　　After Japan's surrender, the Supreme Allied Commander of the Far East, with authorization of the Allies, set up the International Military Tribunals for the Far East from January 19, 1946 to November 12, 1948 in Tokyo; a panel of judges from 11 countries, including the United States, China, the Soviet Union, Britain, and France, brought international trials against 28 Japanese Class-A war criminals in World War II.

远东国际军事法庭场景
A scene of the International Military Tribunal for the Far East

1948年11月12日，日本头号战犯东条英机被远东国际军事法庭以战争罪等判处死刑
Hideki Tojo is sentenced to death for Japanese war crimes by the International Military Tribunal for the Far East, November 12, 1948

27 审判汪伪汉奸
Trying the Wang Jingwei Collaborationist Regime

　　抗日战争胜利后，国民政府成立战犯处理委员会，除参与远东军事法庭审判日本战犯外，1945年12月起，分别在南京、汉口、广州、沈阳、太原、北平、徐州、上海、济南、台北10个城市设立军事法庭及战犯拘留所以审判投敌汉奸。其中华北伪政权的殷汝耕1947年在南京被处决，王揖唐1948年在北平被处决。伪"中华民国维新政府"行政院长梁鸿志1946年在上海被枪决。汪伪政权的第二号人物陈公博1946年在江苏第三监狱被处决。周佛海1948年2月死于狱中。其他各地大小汉奸都分别受到不同程度的制裁。

　　After the victory of the Chinese people's War of Resistance against Japanese Aggression, the Kuomintang government set up the Commission on War Criminals. Besides participating in trying Japanese war criminals at the International Military Tribunal for the Far East, it also had military tribunals and war criminal prisons to try traitors in Nanjing, Hankou, Guangzhou, Shenyang, Taiyuan, Beiping, Xuzhou, Shanghai, Jinan and Taipei. Yin Rugeng from the North China Collaborationist Regime was put to death in Nanjing in 1947, so did Wang Yitang in Beiping in 1948. Liang Hongzhi, President of the Executive Yuan of the Reformed Government of the Republic of China, was executed by shooting in Shanghai in 1946. Chen Gongbo, second President of the collaborationist regime, was put to death in the 3rd Prison of Jiangsu in 1946. Zhou Fohai died in the prison in February 1948. Traitors in other places had also been punished to different degrees.

国民政府战犯处理委员会
Commission on War Criminals of the Kuomintang government

地点	军事法庭庭长	检察官
南京	石美瑜	陈光虞、李璿
武汉	唐守仁	悟俊
广州	刘贤年	蔡丽金、吴念祖
沈阳	岳成安	未详
太原	刘之瀚	胡伊
北平	余彬	伍钟堹
徐州	陈珊	未详
上海	李良	林我朋
济南	李法先	李鸿希
台北	钱国成	施文藩

中国抗日战争暨世界反法西斯战争胜利七十周年特展
An Exhibition Dedicated to 70th Anniversary of Victory of War of Resistance against
Japanese Aggression and World Anti-fascist War

 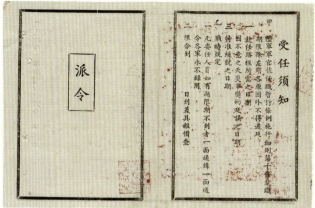

国民政府主席广州行辕派令

Dispatch Order by Beiping Field Headquarters in the Republic of China

1946年

本件为国民政府主席广州行辕委派吴念祖代理本行辕审判战犯军事法庭军法检察官命令。

 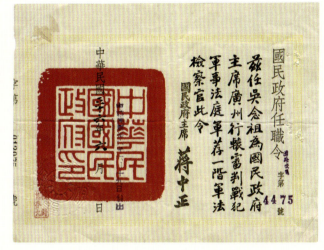

国民政府任职令

Commission by the Kuomintang government

1947年

本件为任命吴念祖为国民政府主席广州行辕审判战犯军事法庭军法检察官任职令。

吴念祖等审判法官在广州军事法庭合影

Wu Nianzu and other trial judges at Guangzhou Military Tribunal

审判战犯法庭相关公文
Related official document on trying
war criminals

1948年

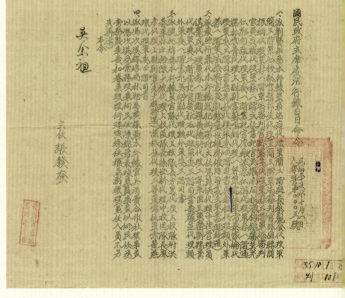

中国抗日战争暨世界反法西斯战争胜利七十周年特展
An Exhibition Dedicated to 70th Anniversary of Victory of War of Resistance against
Japanese Aggression and World Anti-fascist War

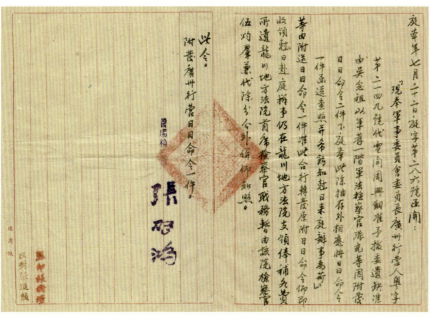

廣東高等法院檢察處訓令

事由　令為推薦該員先任軍事委員會廣州行營軍法庭軍法檢察官
　　　希令仰備領遄赴國廣州行營軍法

令代理龍川地方法院首席檢察官吳念祖

　　查　前准軍事委員會廣州行營軍法庭軍法檢察官吳念祖
　　　本年七月間奉令以前由本廳推薦之周興翔任
　　　軍法檢察官久未到差希請另行推薦檢察官一員以便
　　　轉請委派等由業經推薦該員廣查　至兹據
　　　司法行政部鑒核辦理去後茲復准廣州行營軍事法

　　　此令　附發部令乙件

主席檢察官　張忍鴻

廣東高等法院檢察處訓令

由　報由

　　奉　部令知該員准派署本院檢察官檢察官吳念祖

令署本院檢察官吳念祖

　　　司法行政部三十六年一月十七日京(卅)指人(二)字第二五五號指令善開
　　　「呈悉准派吳念祖署該院檢察官仰飭遵照赴任六級傳由
　　　郭東勤懋登記郭令隨發仰即飭領並飭將該員就職
　　　日期呈報備查。」
　　　等因附發部令一件奉此合行撥發部令仰即飭領仍將就職
　　　日期呈報備查。

　　此令　附發部令乙件

主席檢察官　張忍鴻

廣東高等法院檢察處訓令

　檢人　字第　二○九七　號

令署本院檢察官吳念祖

　　查　前准軍事委員會廣州行營軍法庭軍法檢察官吳念祖

主席檢察官　張忍鴻

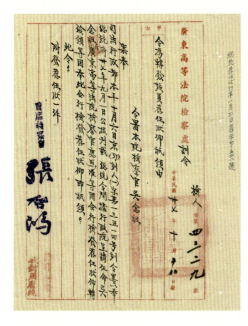

廣東高等法院檢察處訓令

　檢人　字第　四三二九　號

令署本院檢察官吳念祖

　　查奉
　　　司法行政部本年十月六日京(卅)訓人(二)字第三五二四號訓令畧奉
　　　總統府卅二年九月一日公派列載茲奉令開該行政院呈請任命吳
　　　念祖廣東高等法院檢察官應照准等因合行檢發希任命吳
　　　念祖領等由奉此令仰檢發希任狀仰即飭領。

　　此令　附發委任狀一件

主席檢察官　張忍鴻

　　期呈報備查。」
　　等因附發部令一件奉此合行撥發部令仰即飭領仍將就職
　　日期呈報備查。

此令　附發部令乙件

主席檢察官　張忍鴻

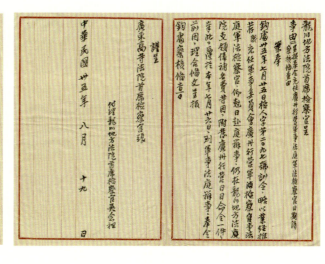

　　龍川地方法院首席檢察官呈

　　事由　為呈復遵令於本年七月十五日接任廣州行營軍法庭軍法檢察官日期恭請
　　　　　鈞察核備查由

　　竊屬呈為軍事委員會廣州行營軍法庭
　　　　軍法檢察官何起周興翔以前由本廳推薦之
　　　　院支領傳補免費
　　　　庭軍法檢察官日赴庭辦事仍在龍川地方法
　　　　院支領傳補免費等因奉此
　　　　等因理合據文呈報
　　　　前因理合將文呈報
　　　　到軍事法庭辦事一件奉令
　　　　此令　附發委任狀一件

　　謹呈
　　　廣東高等法院首席檢察官張
　　代理龍川地方法院首席檢察官吳念祖

　　現奉
　　　司法行政部本年二月六日檢人字第六一八號訓令附發
　　　察官吳念祖領廣東高等法院撥
　　　三一號令內開派吳念祖署廣東高等法院撥
　　　遵於本年二月七日就職視事。奉令前因理合將
　　　就職日期呈報
　　　察核備查。
　　謹呈
　　　廣東高等法院首席檢察官張
　　署廣東高等法院檢察官吳念祖

　　呈民國三十六年二月八日
　　中華民國廿五年八月十九日

28 德国总理勃兰特谢罪
A Kneeling of Willy Brandt, Chancellor of Germany

1970年12月7日，西德总理威利·勃兰特在拜谒华沙犹太隔离区起义纪念碑时，突然下跪为被纳粹杀害的死难者默哀。这一举动在德国和世界各国产生积极反响。勃兰特也因此获得了1971年诺贝尔和平奖。

When West German Chancellor Willy Brandt paid homage at the Memorial of Warsaw Ghetto Uprising on December 7, 1970, he suddenly fell to his knees in silence before the monument to mourn for the victims killed by the Nazis. The move generated a positive response in Germany and around the world, which won Brandt the 1971 Nobel Peace Prize.

29 村山讲话
Murayama Statement

1995年8月15日，日本无条件投降50周年之际，时任日本首相村山富市发表了著名的"村山谈话"，反省侵略战争历史，为殖民统治和侵略历史谢罪，誓言日本走和平道路，永不再战。此后历届日本政府均表示继承"村山谈话"。

On August 15, 1995, which marked the 50th anniversary of Japanese unconditional surrender, Japanese Prime Minister Tomiichi Murayama published the famous "Murayama Statement", in which he reflected on the war of aggression, apologized for a history of colonization and aggression, vowed to pursuit the path of peace and never be engaged in war. Since then "Murayama Statement" has been the official guideline recognized by successive Japanese governments.

中国抗日战争暨世界反法西斯战争胜利七十周年特展
An Exhibition Dedicated to 70th Anniversary of Victory of War of Resistance against
Japanese Aggression and World Anti-fascist War

附 录 APPENDIX

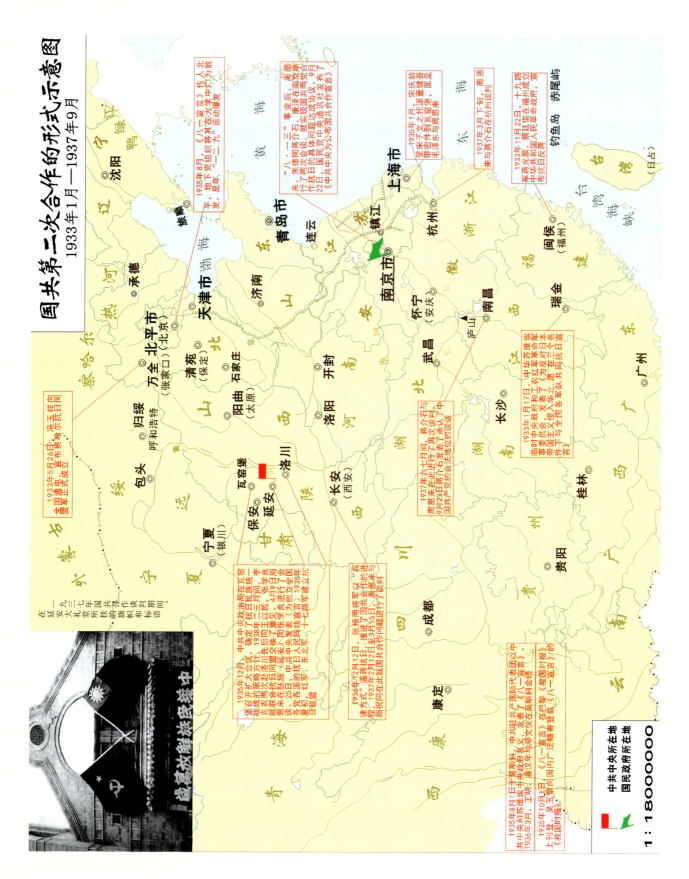

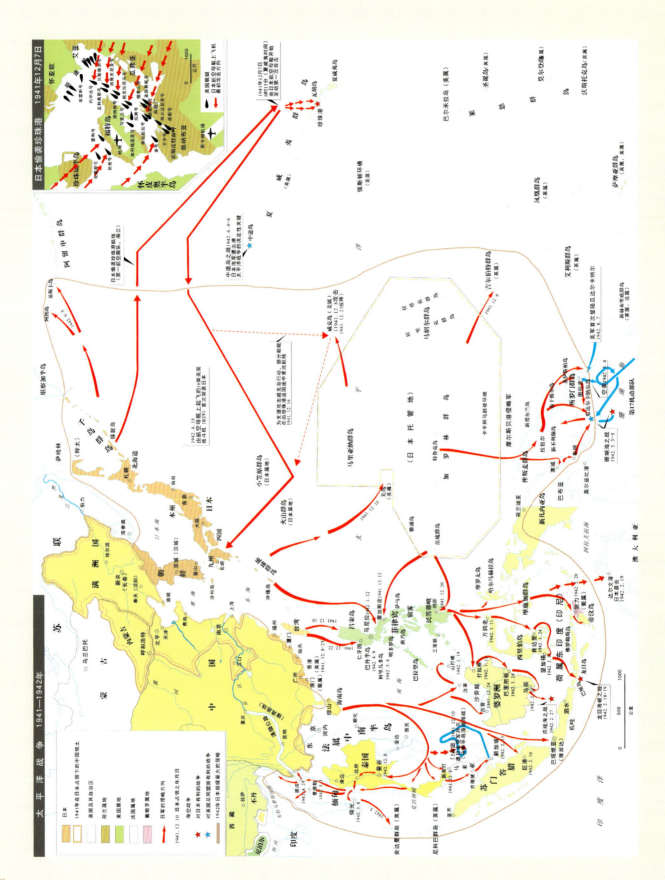

中国抗日战争暨世界反法西斯战争胜利七十周年特展
An Exhibition Dedicated to 70th Anniversary of Victory of War of Resistance against
Japanese Aggression and World Anti-fascist War

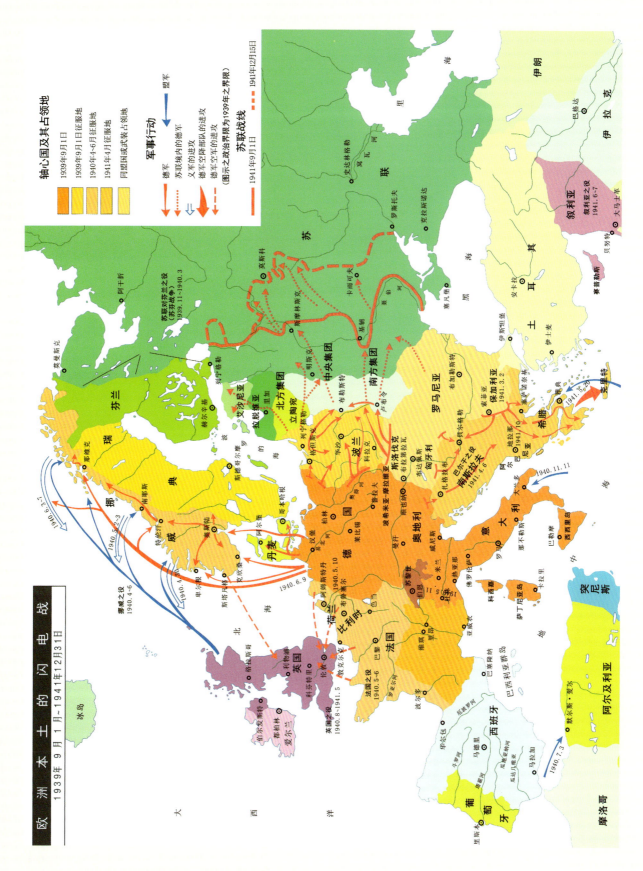

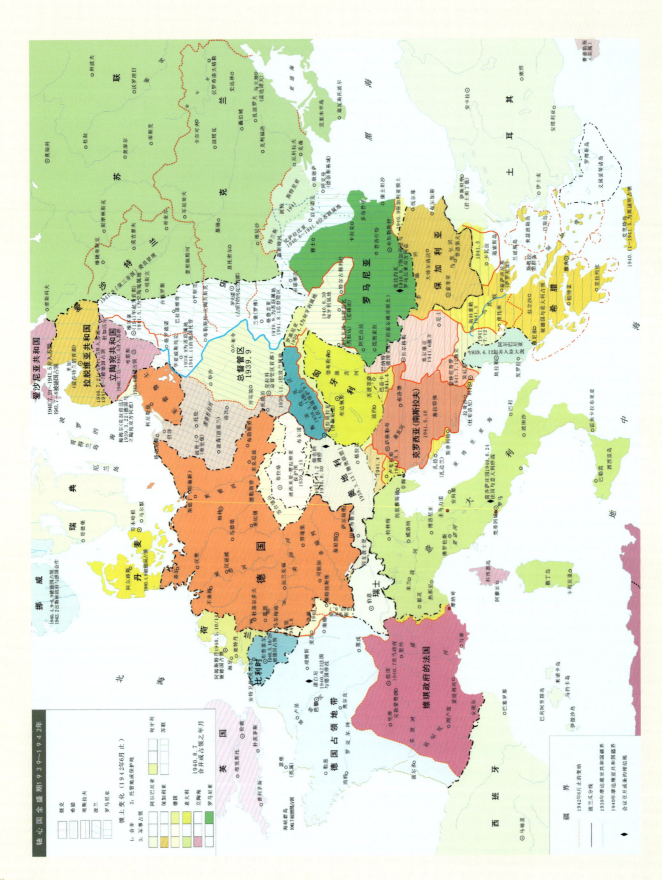

中国抗日战争暨世界反法西斯战争胜利七十周年特展
An Exhibition Dedicated to 70th Anniversary of Victory of War of Resistance against
Japanese Aggression and World Anti-fascist War

后 记 POSTSCRIPT

2014年，有关方面希望本馆与滇西抗战纪念馆合作，举办介绍有关抗战时期中国远征军的展览，以纪念中国抗日战争和世界反法西斯战争胜利七十周年。国内的抗战展已有许多，内容相似，往往图片多，实物少。当我们在滇西抗战纪念馆展厅，尤其是在滇西我远征军阵亡将士墓地前，我们仍被震撼。这些文物，和展馆外面漫山遍野埋葬的那些有名有姓的士兵墓碑，尽管是中国远征军的遗存，但它反映的是四万万人民的不屈精神。湖北作为是中国抗战的主要战场之一，武汉、随枣、枣宜、鄂西、豫西—鄂北等正面战场的重大会战都发生在湖北；中共领导的国民革命军新编第四军在武汉组建，新五师的敌后抗战也在湖北；苏联援华志愿航空队、美国飞虎队也都在湖北与日军作战。因此本馆认为仅举办反映滇西抗战的主题展览似嫌薄弱，借助滇西馆的材料做一个较全面客观反映抗战的展览更有意义。当然，策展难度也相当大。庆幸的是，中华世纪坛世界艺术中心副主任冯光生、北京华协国际文化有限公司老总汤毅嵩非常支持本馆的设想。于是我们几家一边着手策划反映抗战全貌的展览大纲，一边分头邀请昆明市博物馆、香港翰墨轩（香江博物馆）、台湾鸿禧美术馆等博物馆加盟。也因为有这些博物馆的加盟，展览大纲才得以圆满落实。

需要指出的是，由于两岸分治的历史原因，大陆博物馆有关正面战场的材料较少。香港翰墨轩的许礼平先生是香港著名近现代文物研究大家，他毫无保留地将所藏极为重要的藏品送来参展，并撰写专文，使展览为之增色。在策展和展览期间，台湾鸿禧美术馆、台湾周海圣先生、董良彦先生、施觉民将军的家属都给予了大力支持，特别是吉星文将军之子吉民立先生将吉星文将军的珍贵文物和有关七七事变宛平城的照片提交本次展览，令人十分感动。此外，台湾中国航运股份公司董事长彭荫刚先生、世界大同文创公司总经理车守同先生、经理罗荣格先生也为展览提供了十分宝贵的资料。可以说，两岸三地共同举办的抗战展览还是第一次，其意义已超出了展览本身。在筹展过程中，我们还荣幸地得到重庆中国三峡博物馆、北京鲁迅博物馆、监利县博物馆、宜昌夷陵区博物馆、四川建川博物馆、国民党党史馆、台湾世界大同文创公司、俄中友协、新加坡国立亚洲文明馆等多家单位在提供展品、历史照片等方面的协助。武汉海关、海关宁波审单分中心、华协国际珍品货运服务有限公司都为展览的成功举办作出了贡献，在此一并致谢。

编者

2015年于武昌东湖

责任印制：梁秋卉

责任编辑：王　伟

图书在版编目（ＣＩＰ）数据

　　四万万人民：中国抗日战争暨世界反法西斯战争胜

利七十周年特展／湖北省博物馆编．－－北京：文物出

版社，2015.8

　　ISBN 978−7−5010−4363−7

　　Ⅰ．①四… Ⅱ．①湖… Ⅲ．①抗日战争－史料−中国

Ⅳ．①K265.06

中国版本图书馆CIP数据核字(2015)第187871号

四万万人民——中国抗日战争暨世界反法西斯战争胜利七十周年特展

编　　者　湖北省博物馆

出版发行	文物出版社
社　　址	北京东直门内北小街2号楼
网　　址	www.wenwu.com
邮　　箱	web@wenwu.com
制　　版	北京图文天地制版印刷有限公司
印　　刷	北京图文天地制版印刷有限公司
经　　销	新华书店
开　　本	889×1194　1/16
印　　张	18
版　　次	2015年8月第1版
印　　次	2015年8月第1次印刷
书　　号	ISBN 978-7-5010-4363-7
定　　价	298.00元